CASE STUDIES ON
EDUCATIONAL ADMINISTRATION

Sixth Edition

Case Studies on Educational Administration

Theodore J. Kowalski
University of Dayton

Boston   Columbus   Indianapolis   New York   San Francisco   Upper Saddle River
Amsterdam   Cape Town   Dubai   London   Madrid   Milan   Munich   Paris   Montreal   Toronto
Delhi   Mexico City   Sao Paulo   Sydney   Hong Kong   Seoul   Singapore   Taipei   Tokyo

Vice President and Editor in Chief: Jeffery W. Johnston
Senior Acquisitions Editor: Meredith Fossel
Senior Marketing Manager: Christopher Barry
Editorial Assistant: Nancy Holstein
Vice President, Director of Marketing: Margaret Waples
Marketing Manager: Chris Barry
Senior Managing Editor: Pamela D. Bennett
Project Manager: Kerry J. Rubadue
Senior Operations Supervisor: Central Publishing
Operations Specialist: Laura Messerly

Senior Art Director: Jayne Conte
Text Designer: Central Design
Cover Designer: Suzanne Behnke
Cover Art: Shutterstock/Pokaz
Full-Service Project Management: Karpagam Jagadeesan,
    PreMediaGlobal
Composition: PreMediaGlobal
Printer/Binder: R.R. Donnelley/Harrisonburg
Cover Printer: R.R. Donnelley/Harrisonburg
Text Font: Minion

Credits and acknowledgments borrowed from other sources and reproduced, with permission, in this textbook appear on appropriate page within text.

Every effort has been made to provide accurate and current Internet information in this book. However, the Internet and information posted on it are constantly changing, so it is inevitable that some of the Internet addresses listed in this textbook will change.

Library of Congress Cataloging-in-Publication Data
Kowalski, Theodore J.
  Case studies on educational administration / Theodore J. Kowalski.—6th ed.
    p. cm.
  Includes bibliographical references and index.
  ISBN-13: 978-0-13-707130-2 (alk. paper)
  ISBN-10: 0-13-707130-2 (alk. paper)
  1. School management and organization—United States—Case studies.   I. Title.
  LB2805.K63 2011
  371.200973—dc22

                                                                                    2010042704

10 9 8

www.pearsonhighered.com

ISBN 10:   0-13-707130-2
ISBN 13: 978-0-13-707130-2

CONTENTS

PREFACE

Problem solving and decision making have always been core responsibilities for school administrators. Their importance, however, is arguably higher now than at any previous time. In part, this is true because strategic plans for school improvement are being developed at the district and school levels in an effort to tailor goals and tactics to real student needs.

At the same time that principals and superintendents are expected to be instructional leaders and change agents, they retain traditional responsibilities such as managing human and material resources. Further, they are concurrently education experts providing policy recommendations and public servants subjected to the public will and political pressures. The complexity and demanding nature of their practice is captured in the Educational Leadership Constituents Council's (ELCC) Standards. One major change in this edition of the book is connecting cases to the six ELCC Standards and their indicators (see the matrix inside the front cover).

As in previous editions, this book is intended to help prospective and practicing administrators develop problem-solving and decision-making skills. Open-ended case studies provide an excellent venue for developing these competencies. First, they inject contemporary issues into the classroom, making instruction more relevant. Second, they connect theoretical and tacit knowledge with the conditions of a changing society. By using the cases as an instructional tool, you engage in problem framing, critical thinking, decision making, and reflective practice. The overall goals are to have you learn how to (a) use information to identify and solve problems, (b) develop and evaluate alternative solutions, and (c) continuously refine your professional knowledge through critical analysis prior to, during, and after decision making.

The 24 cases cover a range of problems encountered by principals and superintendents. The cases are not taken to a conclusion purposefully so that you can assume an administrator role, frame the problem, and make related decisions.

NEW TO THIS EDITION

The following are primary changes that have been made in this edition of the book:

- *Educational Leadership Constituent Council (ELCC) Standards Matrix.* The matrix inside the front cover identifies the alignment of the cases with the Standards. Relatively recent changes in program accreditation standards require institutions to collect evidence that students have met these criteria. The cases provide an ideal process for collecting such data.
- *A new case: School Improvement through Better Grading Practices.* Case 8 injects one of the greatest contemporary challenges for administrators—developing and enforcing rules for assigning grades to high school students.
- *A new case: Let's Get Strategic.* Case 14 details the leadership challenges faced by a new principal of an underperforming urban school. She accepts the position knowing that her predecessor was dismissed for failing to carry out this responsibility and knowing that many of the teachers were displeased because of his dismissal. The case centers on the need for and barriers to strategic planning.

- *A new case: The Career Center's Revolving Door.*   Case 5 describes a career center that has had an especially high turnover rate of teachers in academic areas, most notably in English and mathematics. The principal's indifference toward assisting novice teachers leads to his dismissal. The case deals with two prevalent problems: retention of high-quality teachers in career-technical schools and the administrator responsibilities for helping novice teachers.

- *A new case: Individualizing Staff Development.*   Case 11 describes the efforts of a new principal to move a middle school away from traditional staff development. He promotes the idea of individual career plans that are integrated with teacher teams and the school's vision. Thus, the case addresses two growing concerns for administrators—providing relevant staff development and being accountable for the effects of staff development in relation to school improvement.

- *Updated Introduction.*   The Introduction provides the reader information about using cases to engage in problem solving and decision making. The content on both topics has been expanded and revised.

- *Revisions in continuing cases.*   All cases retained from the 5th edition have been revised; specifically, elements of background information, case content, questions, and suggested readings have been updated.

- *Problem framing instructions/questions at the end of each case.*   The challenges for problem framing presented at the end of each case have been revised. The new format provides readers with a consistent and more detailed approach for defining problems requiring administrative decisions.

ACKNOWLEDGEMENTS

Appreciation is expressed to those who helped me complete this edition. They include:

- Elizabeth Pearn and Colleen Wildenhaus, editorial assistants at the University of Dayton
- Michael Amakyi, former doctoral assistant at the University of Dayton and now a professor at the University of Cape Coast in Ghana
- Lesley McCue, current doctoral assistant at the University of Dayton
- District and school administrators from across the country who provided information for and comments about the cases
- Professors and graduate students from many universities who voluntarily suggested content and format changes after they had worked with the cases
- Reviewers Connie Ballard, University of Houston, Clear Lake; Hazel M. Carter, The City College of New York; and Greg Gibbs, St. Bonaventure University

INTRODUCTION

*In the varied topography of professional practice, there is a high
hard ground overlooking the swamp. On the high ground,
manageable problems lend themselves to solutions through
the application of research-based theory and technique.
In the swampy lowland, messy, confusing problems
defy technical solution.*

(DONALD SCHÖN, 1990, p. 3)

Most students enrolled in school administration courses are either preparing to be principals or they already are principals aspiring to district-level positions. They are adult learners, many in the middle stage of their careers. They appropriately expect classroom learning experiences, even those involving abstract theories, to be relevant to the real world of elementary and secondary education. Therefore, effective professional preparation, especially in applied fields such as school administration, is an intricate combination of theoretical and tacit knowledge. Curricula, clinical experiences, and internships should be designed to meet three objectives:

1. Students master theoretical knowledge that they can deploy in districts and schools. Specifically, this knowledge helps them to describe, explain, or predict behavior that influences institutional effectiveness.
2. Students master the process of reflection and demonstrate their ability to apply it. Specifically, they learn to critique their behavior and outcomes in relation to existing professional knowledge.
3. Students use reflective practice to produce tacit knowledge. Specifically, they interface theory and experience by analyzing their decisions in relation to contextual variables in schools (Björk, Kowalski, & Ferrigno-Brown, 2005).

Donald Schön (1983) observed that practitioners in all professions are baffled when the theory and technical skills they acquired during academic preparation prove to be ineffective when they are applied to real problems. Their bewilderment usually stems from a misunderstanding of theory and limited insights about the effects of contextual variables on the consistency of theoretical applications. Context is an intricate mix of people, resources, societal expectations, and organizational conditions. For example, disciplining a student in the context of one middle school may be considerably different from disciplining a student in the context of another middle school—even if the two middle schools are in the same school district. Contextual dissimilarities largely explain why administrators and students preparing to be administrators perceive a problem in different ways, even when given identical information (Kowalski, 1998).

Sergiovanni (2005) categorizes principals into three groups based on their views toward knowledge and decision making. He calls members of the first group *mystics*. These principals view school administration as a non-science. Therefore, they have little interest in learning or applying theory; instead, they rely on tacit knowledge and intuition to make important decisions.

He calls members of the second group *neats*. These principals view administration as an applied science. Therefore, they rely heavily on theoretical knowledge to make important decisions. He calls members of the third group *scruffies*. These principals view school administration as a "craftlike science characterized by interacting reflection and action episodes" (p. 73). They see theoretical knowledge as only one segment of their knowledge base and they apply it to inform rather than to prescribe important decisions. Unlike their peers, they continuously develop tacit knowledge by interfacing experience with theoretical knowledge. Most scholars believe that highly effective administrators are in the last category. Over time, they develop artistry permitting them to deal with problems that defy textbook solutions.

Consider motivation theories and their application to school administration. Theoretically, praising a teacher is supposed to be motivating; however, principals occasionally encounter employees who do not respond as expected. The challenge is to determine why the application of a theory was occasionally unproductive. Analysis (reflection) leads the administrator to consider the possible influence of contextual variables (e.g., the teacher's health, the relationship between the principal and teacher, the teacher's prior experiences) on the unexpected outcome.

PROBLEM SOLVING AND DECISION MAKING

Problem solving is often characterized as a five-stage, six-step process as depicted in Figure I.1. Kowalski, Lasley, and Mahoney (2008) summarized the elements of this paradigm.

Stage 1: Understanding

The first level of problem solving requires you to understand what you are trying to do. There are two steps in this stage: *framing the problem* and *analyzing the problem.*

Cognitive psychologists generally agree that a problem has three dimensions: (a) a current state, (b) a desired state, and (c) the lack of a direct, obvious way to eliminate the gap between the current state and the desired state (Mayer, 1983). Sometimes administrators fail to frame a problem correctly because they lack requisite knowledge concerning the first two dimensions. Assume you are principal of a high school in which 10th grade students are not performing at an acceptable level on the proficiency test in mathematics. The superintendent asks you to define the problem for him and the school board. In order to comply, you must first determine the extent to which the current and desired states are known. According to Reitman (1965), your knowledge exists at one of the following four levels:

1. *A poorly defined current state and a poorly defined goal.*   At this level, you do not have accurate data concerning the school's test scores and the state benchmarks are either unknown or vague.
2. *A poorly defined current state and a well-defined goal.*   At this level, you do not have accurate data for the school's test scores and the state benchmarks are known and specific.
3. *A well-defined current state and a poorly defined desired state.*   At this level, you have accurate data for the school's test scores and the state benchmarks are unknown or vague.
4. *A well-defined current state and a well-defined desired state.*   At this level, you have accurate data for the school's test scores and the state benchmarks are known and specific.

If your knowledge is below the fourth level, you would need to acquire additional information before moving forward to actually frame the problem. So further assume that the state has set the benchmark for acceptable school performance as follows: to achieve acceptable school performance, 90% of the students must score at or above the 70th percentile. Official

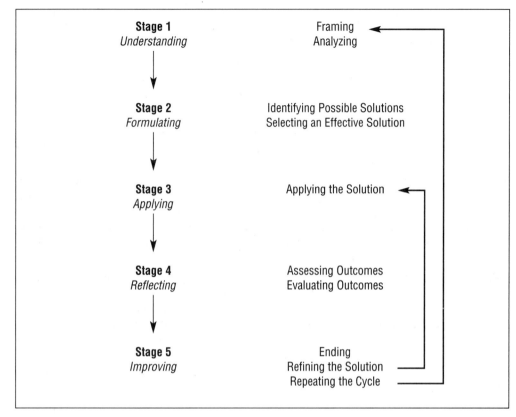

Stage 1 *Understanding*	Framing Analyzing
Stage 2 *Formulating*	Identifying Possible Solutions Selecting an Effective Solution
Stage 3 *Applying*	Applying the Solution
Stage 4 *Reflecting*	Assessing Outcomes Evaluating Outcomes
Stage 5 *Improving*	Ending Refining the Solution Repeating the Cycle

FIGURE I.1   Problem Solving as a Five-Stage Process

data sent to you (the principal) indicates that only 76% of the students scored at or above the 70th percentile. Thus, you have information that satisfies the first two dimensions—that is, you are at the fourth knowledge level. At this point, many administrators are inclined to define the deficiency (the gap between the current state and desired state) as the problem, thus ignoring the third dimension (the lack of a direct obvious way to eliminate the gap between the current state and the desired state). In most cases, the problem principals face in such a situation is not knowing how to eradicate the 14 percentage-point deficiency (Reys, Lindquist, Lambdin, Smith, & Suydam, 2003).

Once a problem has been correctly framed, an administrator must analyze it. This step entails asking and answering pertinent questions such as these:

- *How serious is the problem?*   The attention an administrator gives to a problem often depends on perceived consequences. Serious problems require more and immediate attention.
- *What causes the problem?*   Administrators often confuse causes and problems. Problems are products and causes are the variables responsible for the product. Not knowing how to eradicate the gap between current achievement scores and the state benchmark may be caused by factors such as a negative school culture, incompetent leadership, ineffective teaching, a lack of employee learning opportunities (staff development), inappropriate instructional materials, or the principal's lack of knowledge.

- *Can the problem be divided into manageable components?* By dividing a problem into parts, the search for a solution may be more efficient and effective. For example, increasing the number of students scoring at the 70th percentile by 14 percentage points is usually a daunting task. If addressed over a 5-year period, however, the principal can establish yearly goals that incrementally move the school toward eliminating the problem.

Stage 2: Formulating

This stage also has two elements: identifying possible solutions and selecting a preferred solution. Because information and time are common constraints, administrators and teachers usually identify only the most obvious solutions rather than all possible solutions and they pursue a satisfactory solution rather than conducting a protracted search for the best solution (Hanson, 2003). Although this behavior usually is not disadvantageous for minor decisions, it often is detrimental for major decisions.

Consider an example of a superintendent faced with insufficient instructional space in the district's middle school. Rather than considering all the possible solutions, he focused solely on the option of constructing a modest addition to the school. Architects assured him that the space included in this option would alleviate the current problem. Further, it was inexpensive compared to other options such as building a new middle school or constructing a major addition. By not being more thorough, however, the superintendent ignored population projections. Just 6 years after the addition was completed, the middle school's enrollment had increased by 5%. As a result, the school had another space deficiency. When the superintendent proposed constructing second addition to the middle school, he and the school board were criticized for not being more thorough before building the previous addition.

Stage 3: Applying

At this stage, the preferred solution is applied in an effort to solve the problem. A solution's effectiveness is determined by a mix of its potentiality, the quality of application, and the context in which it is applied. The best solutions fail when they are applied incorrectly or inappropriately. Even if the superintendent in the previous example had opted for a much larger addition to the middle school, his preferred solution could have been ineffective if the new spaces were designed improperly. When considering possible solutions, application is as important as potential.

Stage 4: Reflecting

The effects of the preferred solution should be assessed objectively and then evaluated. Assessment involves measuring. Assume that a principal adopts a new approach for teaching language arts in an elementary school. Assessing effectiveness entails measuring student performance, such as scores on achievement tests. Evaluation entails judgments about assessments; for example, determining if test score gains are sufficient and comparable to those reported for other schools using the same instructional approach. An evaluation of a decision can be summative (e.g., determining the extent to which a decision solved or alleviated a problem) or formative (e.g., determining what could be done to improve the solution if the problem has not been resolved sufficiently).

Stage 5: Improving

At the improvement stage, one of three choices is made: (a) the problem is deemed to be resolved so no further improvement is warranted; (b) the preferred solution is adjusted and the application stage is repeated; (c) the solution is deemed to be ineffective and the problem cycle is repeated by returning to the understanding stage.

Problem solving actually entails a series of decisions and the effectiveness of a decision is often determined by its value to problem solving. Basically, a decision has three components: *a goal, options for attaining the goal,* and *the selection of the preferred option* (Welch, 2002). In making decisions, school administrators have two important challenges. First, they must separate consequential from inconsequential decisions. Consequential decisions are those that influence serious problems. Second, they must approach consequential decisions differently than they do inconsequential decisions. For example, deciding whether to invest in a staff development program that has the potential to improve student-achievement test scores is far more consequential than determining what to have for lunch. Inconsequential decisions require little forethought and analysis because they are relatively unimportant.

Basically, decisions can be guided by several forces. The most evident include:

- Rationality—a dependence on evidence and objective analysis of facts
- Emotion—feelings and sentiments
- Philosophy—values and beliefs
- Politics—self-interests or the interests of powerful groups
- School culture—basic assumptions shared by individuals and used to guide behavior

Often, these forces interact so that any given decision may reflect a combination of them. The passage of the No Child Left Behind Act in 2001 heightened expectations that educators make data-based decisions, especially in relation to problems that affect students, schools, and society. Advocacy for rational decision making also has been elevated by the realities of an information-based society. Specifically, the quantity and quality of information available to educators is much greater now than it was just 25 years ago (Popham, 2006). Moreover, principals are being encouraged to build learning communities in schools—a condition in which teachers and principals work collaboratively to identify and solve problems (Kowalski, 2010). Consequently, decision-making skills have become increasingly important for all educators.

REFLECTION

Schön (1990) differentiated between "knowing-in-action" and "reflection-in-action." The former is embedded in the socially and institutionally structured context shared by members of a given profession. In school administration, for example, graduate students preparing to be principals are expected to possess basic knowledge related to their practice (e.g., curriculum theory and school law). Reflection in-action represents a form of artistry that is critical when conditions are less than rational. As an example, effective school administrators develop skills and techniques that help them deal with problems that defy textbook solutions. If human behavior was entirely predictable, knowing-in-action would suffice. But in districts and schools, people are not always rational and their behavior can be unpredictable. Under these conditions, your ability to engage in reflection-in-action is quite important. The process of reflection was described earlier.

DEFINING CASE STUDIES

A case is a description of a situation, commonly involving a decision or problem (Erskine, Leenders, & Mauffette-Leenders, 1981). The terms *case study* and *case method* have different definitions. A case study is the general description of a situation that can be deployed for research or teaching. Case method is a term used to describe an instructional approach relying on case studies.

There is no universal definition of or style for a case study; some case studies may be only a few paragraphs, others are hundreds of pages (Immegart, 1971). As Lincoln and Guba (1985) wrote, "while the literature is replete with references to case studies and with examples of case study reports, there seems to be little agreement about what a case is" (p. 360). Variance in case length and style is often related to their intended purpose.

With respect to the manner in which they are written, cases commonly are divided into three categories:

1. *True cases.* These are factual case studies and names, dates, or other information have not been altered.
2. *Disguised cases.* These are factual case studies but names, dates, or other information have been altered.
3. *Fictitious cases.* These are hypothetical case studies written to illustrate a principle, concept, or specific set of conditions (Matejka & Cosse, 1981).

THE CASE METHOD

The case method first gained acceptance in professional preparation programs for business administration, law, and medicine. The best-known successes belong to Harvard University's Business School, where instructors use case studies to sharpen student skills with regard to problem solving, formulating and weighing alternative decisions, and assessing leadership behaviors (Christensen, 1987).

Some instructors use the case method to teach new information, concepts, and theories. For example, a professor may use a case study of a grievance in a high school to teach students the meaning of organizational conflict. When cases are used to teach new knowledge, the student learns inductively. That is, the case study is used to demonstrate associations between variables that reveal the nature of the concept being taught. Cases used to teach new knowledge are usually fact-driven and complete, including describing outcomes (Herreid, 1997).

Cases also can be deployed for skill development. For example, a professor may use cases to encourage moral reasoning, critical thinking, decision making, and problem solving. Cases used to develop and improve skills are typically open-ended; that is, they purposely are not taken to their conclusion so that learners can become actively involved as a decision maker (Kowalski, 1998). Open-ended cases are often called Type B cases.

There are two universal characteristics of teaching with cases. One is the Socratic method. This is a dialectical approach in which the instructor asks questions and encourages the critical analysis of multiple propositions. The other is the presentation of *situational knowledge.* This knowledge includes information about contextual variables such as individuals, school culture, or the local community.

As you undoubtedly will discover, students do not define problems uniformly after reading open-ended case studies, largely because of information processing or *abstraction.* When engaging in abstraction, students filter situational knowledge through personal values, beliefs, experiences, biases, and previously acquired knowledge. They not only have unique filters, their ability to process differs. Consequently, abstraction does not produce uniformity in problem framing, decision making, and administrative behavior. Studying teacher decision making, Shavelson and Stern (1981) observed:

> people selectively perceive and interpret portions of available information with respect to their goals, and construct a simplified model of reality. Using certain heuristics, attributions and other psychological mechanisms, people then make judgments and decisions that carry them out on the basis of their psychological model of reality (p. 461).

Advocacy for using case studies in school administration dates back more than 60 years. Several case-study texts were published as early as the mid-1950s (e.g., Hamburg, 1955; Sargent & Belisle, 1955) and by the early 1960s, leading scholars (e.g., Culbertson & Coffield, 1960; Griffiths, 1963) were promoting cases to bridge theory and practice. Nevertheless, their widespread use in principal preparation did not occur until the late 1980s (Kowalski, 1998).

SIMULATION AND CASE STUDIES

Simulations provide vicarious experiences for students—an approximation of the practitioner's challenges, problems, opportunities, and so forth. They can be used at all stages of professional preparation. There are two general approaches to simulations. In the first, students are provided complete data about a given situation and then asked to solve a problem. This approach is commonly called an *in-basket simulation* and requires students to spend considerable time studying data. As an example, a student may be given complete financial records for a school district and then asked to determine where an accounting error occurred.

In the second approach, students are provided only essential information. It is far less time consuming and is employed when general problem-solving skills are the instructional objective. Cunningham (1971) referred to this alternative as a *nonmaterial-based approach.* After studying the use of this approach with graduate students in school administration at the University of Chicago in the mid-1960s, he concluded that the technique was more efficient than and as successful as the in-basket approach. The research caused Cunningham to change his own views about the necessity of providing students with detailed information for simulations.

Using open-ended cases to conduct simulations can be highly effective, especially in terms of demonstrating how theoretical knowledge can be integrated with tacit knowledge. Further, case-based simulations can be used to develop critical thinking, moral reasoning, and decision-making skills.

USING THEORY TO GUIDE PRACTICE

Theory often is incorrectly characterized as supposition, speculation or philosophy (Kowalski, 2010). In reality, theories synthesize, organize, and classify facts that emerge from observations and data collections in varying situations (e.g., research studies). Hoy and Miskel (2005) characterize administrative theories as interrelated concepts, assumptions, and generalizations that systematically describe and explain regularities in behavior.

When confronted with circumstances demanding action, superintendents, principals, and other administrators may choose one of several behaviors (Kowalski, 2006):

1. They can ignore the situation, hoping that the problem will disappear or solve itself.
2. They can act instinctively or intuitively, relying on "common sense."
3. They can delegate the decision to a subordinate, hoping that such action frees them of responsibility and risk.
4. They can look for a precedent; that is, they identify an administrator who faced the same problem and then duplicate that person's decision.
5. They can use their professional knowledge to formulate decisions based on the contextual variables surrounding a given problem.

Any of the first four alternatives may be effective occasionally, but more commonly they are ineffective for major problems.

Among the numerous decision-making models used in administration, the best known and most widely used is probably the *rational-analytical model*. This paradigm consists of four steps:

1. Defining the problem
2. Diagnosing the problem
3. Searching for alternative solutions
4. Evaluating alternative solutions (Romm & Mahler, 1986)

The paradigm captures the early stages of the problem-solving model discussed previously. This model also is congruent with mandates for data-based decision making in NCLB.

Cases in this book include contextual variables—such as the nature of the school district, the community, and individual personalities—that can affect choices you make. Community size, school district, diversity and individual personalities are examples. When you employ theoretical constructs and technical skills to analyze these variables in relation to the challenge presented, you are using a scientific approach to decision making. Accordingly, you should become increasingly skillful in applying general problem-solving abilities to specific situations. When using cases, however, you should recognize that emotion and bias temper rationality. That is, decision makers often reject, modify, or selectively accept evidence based on their dispositions toward a problem or challenge.

The evolution of literature on decision making exhibits that the study of school administration has evolved from training to education. In training, a person learns to apply predetermined solutions to a problem; in education, a person learns to treat each problem as potentially unique, thus requiring diagnostics and prescriptive measures. Noting that knowledge of decision making exposed the myth of simple solutions, Estler (1988) wrote:

> we might replace recipes with skills in analysis of organizational dynamics and con-
> texts. Though the ambiguities of educational decision making cannot be eliminated,
> they can be made more understandable and less threatening. By understanding a va-
> riety of approaches to decision making and the range of organizational conditions
> under which they may be applicable, the administrator can be better prepared to re-
> spond to, and even enjoy, organizational ambiguity and complexity (p. 316).

EFFECTIVELY PARTICIPATING IN THE CASE METHOD

The objective in working with open-ended cases is not to arrive at "one right answer." Romm and Mahler (1986) noted that this is particularly true if a rational-analytical model is applied to address the perceived problem:

> Basing the analysis of the case on the rational-analytical decision-making model, im-
> plicitly carries the message that there are no "right" or "wrong" solutions to the case.
> By applying the model to cases, students realize that a case always has many prob-
> lems, and the definition of one of these problems as the "main" problem is often sub-
> jective and arbitrary. They also realize that once a problem has been defined, it can
> have different reasons and be solved in different ways, depending on whose interests
> are being served or being given priority (p. 695).

Cases provide an open invitation to generalize (Biddle & Anderson, 1986), and consequently, you are apt to observe a range of behaviors as your peers react to them. Remember, rationality is tempered by bias, beliefs, emotions, and political considerations.

One other dimension of the case method is commonly undervalued. Your work with cases occurs in a social context (the classroom, chat rooms, or other discussion formats). The presence of others approximates the real world of practice because superintendents and principals rarely make decisions in isolation. Their behavior is continuously influenced and evaluated by others.

CONTENT OF THIS BOOK

This edition contains 24 cases selected to exemplify the diversity of challenges in contemporary school administration. The narrative formats are not uniform. Some cases are divided into sections with information about the community, school district, school, and the incident presented under subheadings. Other cases contain a great deal of dialogue. Information in the real world of practice is neither predictable nor uniform. Variance in the way information is presented in the cases reflects the unevenness of communication that exists in districts and schools. Each case, however, is preceded by an introduction identifying key concepts and areas for reflection and followed by these three components:

1. Problem framing. This component directs you to define the problem you will address.
2. Questions and suggested activities.
3. Suggested readings and references.

FINAL WORDS OF ADVICE

Your experiences working with cases will be more fruitful and enjoyable if you follow several recommendations. First, the process is active, dialectical, and a form of cooperative learning; to achieve maximum benefits, be an active participant. Second, be candid and do not fear stating your convictions; you want to learn how you and others make decisions. Third, respect dissimilar viewpoints and try to understand their origins. Last, focus on the extent to which professional variables (e.g., knowledge and skills) and personal variables (e.g., needs and motivations) influence choices you and your classmates make.

References

Biddle, B., & Anderson, D. (1986). Theory, methods, knowledge, and research on teaching. In M. Wittrock (Ed.), *Handbook of research on teaching* (3rd ed., pp. 230–252). New York: Macmillan.

Björk, L. G., Kowalski, T. J., & Ferrigno-Brown, T. (2005). Learning theory and research: A framework for changing superintendent preparation and development. In L. G. Björk & T. J. Kowalski (Eds.), *The contemporary superintendent: Preparation, practice, and development*, (pp. 71–106). Thousand Oaks, CA: Sage.

Christensen, C. (1987). *Teaching and the case method.* Boston: Harvard Business School Press.

Culbertson, J., & Coffield, W. (Eds.). (1960). *Simulation in administration training.* Columbus, OH: University Council for Educational Administration.

Cunningham, L. (1971). A powerful but underdeveloped educational tool. In D. Bolton (Ed.), *The use of simulation in educational administration* (pp. 1–29). Columbus, OH: Charles E. Merrill.

Erskine, J., Leenders, M., & Mauffette-Leenders, L. (1981). *Teaching with cases.* London, Ontario: School of Business Administration, University of Western Ontario.

Estler, S. (1988). Decision making. In N. Boyan (Ed.), *Handbook of research on educational administration* (pp. 305–350). New York: Longman.

Griffiths, D. (1963). The case method of teaching educational administration. *Journal of Educational Administration, 2,* 81–82.

Hamburg, M. (1955). *Case studies in elementary school administration.* New York: Bureau of Publications, Teachers College, Columbia University.

Hanson, E. M. (2003). *Educational administration and organizational behavior* (5th ed.). Boston: Allyn and Bacon.

Herreid, C. F. (1997). What is a case? *Journal of College Science Teaching, 27*(2), 92–94.

Hoy, W., & Miskel, C. (2005). *Educational administration: Theory, research and practice* (7th ed.). New York: McGraw-Hill.

Immegart, G. (1971). The use of cases. In D. Bolton (Ed.), *The use of simulation in educational administration* (pp. 30–64). Columbus, OH: Charles E. Merrill.

Kowalski, T. J. (1998). Using case studies in school administration. In M. Sudzina (Ed.), *Case study applications for teacher education* (pp. 201–217). Boston: Allyn and Bacon.

Kowalski, T. J. (2006). *The school superintendent: Theory, practice, and cases* (2nd ed.). Thousand Oaks, CA: Sage.

Kowalski, T. J. (2010). *The school principal: Visionary leadership and competent management.* New York: Routledge.

Kowalski, T. J., Lasley, T. J., & Mahoney, J. (2008). *Data-driven decisions and school leadership: Best practices for school improvement.* Boston: Allyn and Bacon.

Lincoln, Y., & Guba, E. (1985). *Naturalistic inquiry.* Newbury Park, CA: Sage.

Matejka, J., & Cosse, T. (1981). *The business case method: An introduction.* Richmond, VA: Robert F. Dame.

Mayer, R. E. (1983). *Thinking, problem solving, cognition.* New York: W. H. Freeman and Company.

Popham, W. J. (2006). *Assessment for educational leaders.* Boston: Allyn and Bacon.

Reitman, W. R. (1965). *Cognition and thought: An information processing approach.* New York: Wiley.

Reys, R., Lindquist, M., Lambdin, D., Smith, N., & Suydam, M. (2003). *Helping children learn mathematics* (6th ed.). New York: John Wiley and Sons.

Romm, T., & Mahler, S. (1986). A three-dimensional model for using case studies in the academic classroom. *Higher Education, 15*(6), 677–696.

Sargent, C., & Belisle, E. (1955). *Educational administration: Cases and concepts.* Boston: Houghton Mifflin.

Schön, D. (1983). *The reflective practitioner.* New York: Basic Books.

Schön, D. (1990). *Educating the reflective practitioner.* San Francisco: Jossey-Bass.

Sergiovanni, T. J. (2005). *The principalship: A reflective practice Perspective* (5th ed.). Boston: Allyn and Bacon.

Shavelson, R., & Stern, P. (1981). Research on teachers' pedagogical thoughts, judgments, decisions, and behavior. *Review of Educational Research, 51*(4), 455–498.

Welch, D. A. (2002). *Decisions, decisions: The art of effective decision making.* Amherst, NY: Prometheus Books.

1 WHO NEEDS LESSON PLANS?

BACKGROUND INFORMATION

Federal mandates imposed on elementary and secondary schools are often viewed negatively by local administrators and teachers for at least two reasons. First, the directives almost always are inadequately funded; second, they are considered contraventions of local control. The No Child Left Behind Act (NCLB), an extension of the Elementary and Secondary Education Act of 1965 that was signed into law in January 2002, is a quintessential example. Proponents argue, however, that the legislation actually emphasizes local control, provides flexibility for local officials, and promotes parental involvement.

The intent of NCLB is to raise the educational performance of all students by setting higher standards, requiring annual testing, using test data analysis to ensure progress, and imposing rewards and penalties for outcomes (Kowalski, Lasley, & Mahoney, 2008). Students in grades 3 through 8 must be tested each year in reading, mathematics, and science, and schools must demonstrate adequate yearly progress. All special student groups (e.g., by ethnicity, socioeconomic status) must report progress separately. At least 95% of each of these groups must be tested, and if one subgroup fails to make yearly progress, the school as a whole fails. In addition, NCLB requires administrators and teachers to (a) collect assessment data, (b) disaggregate those data by student groups, and (c) develop explicit plans for meeting the needs of students, especially those exhibiting low achievement (Protheroe, Shellard, & Turner, 2003).

This case is about a principal who assumed the leadership role in a troubled school. She quickly discovered that the teachers had little interest in pursuing change, and they were bitter because the previous principal was dismissed. As you read this case, pay particular attention to evidence that reveals the nature of the school's culture.

Culture constitutes the symbolic dimension of a school's climate. Climate is a characteristic that causes us to feel the way we do about an institution; in this vein, it is analogous to an individual's personality (Hanson, 2003). Culture consists of shared values and beliefs; it provides an invisible framework of guiding standards intended to influence employee behavior—especially in relation to solving common problems. The guiding standards are nested in assumptions about what people in the organization hold to be true, sensible, and possible (Hoy & Miskel, 2005). Although school cultures are not easily changed, scholars (e.g., Fullan, 2005; Sarason, 1996) have concluded that improvement in low-performing schools will not occur without such transitions.

One reason why culture is so difficult to change is that underlying beliefs creating internal conflict for educators are often suppressed mentally but expressed behaviorally. This is particularly true when assumptions are known to be incongruent with the profession's knowledge base or with a community's prevailing philosophy. Even when not suppressed, educators are usually unwilling to admit that they abide by such assumptions (Kowalski, 2003). When all or most teachers share the same assumptions, the culture is said to be "strong." When all or most of the assumptions shared are congruent with the profession's knowledge base, the culture is said to be "positive" (Kowalski, 2006).

Key Areas for Reflection

1. Federal involvement in public elementary and secondary education in general, and NCLB specifically
2. School culture
3. Lesson planning
4. Change in school leadership
5. Changing unproductive values and beliefs about students

THE CASE

After she became principal of Buchanan Elementary School 2 years ago, Maureen Hulbert knew she had assumed a difficult assignment. The school is in an economically depressed school district, the Harper City Community Schools. As she sat in her silent office on a cold, rainy November day, she reflected on her brief tenure in the troubled school.

Harper City

The population in Harper City has declined by more than 20% over the last 25 years. The largest outmigration of residents occurred in the early 1980s after a steel company closed its plant there. At its peak level of operation in 1972, the plant had slightly over 1,800 employees. After it closed, many who lost their jobs left the community. Today, Harper City is a collage of ethnic neighborhoods. The only newer homes are near the hospital in a small neighborhood. In all other sections of the city, the homes are more than 45 years old. Most of the single-family dwellings are prefabricated low-cost structures that were built between 1952 and 1960. Four government housing projects are in the city limits. The unemployment rate in Harper City is 21% higher than the national average.

The School District

The Harper City School District serves 6,885 students. In addition to a high school, the district operates two middle schools and six elementary schools. Last year, the dropout rate for the high school was 28%, and only 18% of the graduating seniors enrolled in a 4-year or 2-year college.

Nearly 70% of the students in the school system are classified as "disadvantaged" by virtue of qualifying for free or reduced-price lunches. Among these disadvantaged students, 38% are African American and 22% are Hispanic.

Since the enactment of No Child Left Behind (NCLB), both the composition of the school board and the district's administrative staff have changed substantially. The five-member school board continues to represent the community's diversity; however, only one member who was in office when NCLB took effect is still on the board. The superintendent, Dr. Mark Simon, has been in his position for 5 years. He is an energetic leader committed to improving the school district's academic performance and is supported by the school board and Harper City's mayor.

Since Dr. Simon arrived in Harper City, over two-thirds of the administrative staff, including school principals, has changed. Turnover in these positions resulted from a combination of retirements, dismissals, and reassignments. Three years ago, Superintendent Simon transformed one of the district-level administrative vacancies into a new position: director of technology and research. The director was given the assignment of constructing an infrastructure to facilitate data-based decision making, and, a substantial investment was made in the new department. Most notably, computer networking was upgraded and staff development sessions were added to prepare principals and teachers to generate, access, and apply data.

Buchanan Elementary School

Buchanan Elementary School is just one block from Main Street in the heart of the city's business district. The two-story brick structure, built originally as a junior high school in 1947, was renovated in 1983 when it was converted to an elementary school. Two of the government housing projects in the district are within a half mile of the school, and children living in them attend Buchanan.

Buchanan has an enrollment of 390; approximately 90% are students of color (58% are African American and 31% are Hispanic). The percentage of disadvantaged students is above the district's average (82% compared to 69%). The school also has the highest percentage of students in the district failing to score at or above the state proficiency level on achievement tests. In the aftermath of NCLB, the number of student retentions in first grade increased significantly. The principal and the first-grade teachers said publicly that they were "pushed" to retain more students as a result of higher standards.

The average age of Buchanan teachers is 53, and only 6 of 17 teachers had ever taught in a school other than Buchanan. The previous principal, Walter Sampson, was popular with the staff but was seen as a liability by Superintendent Simon. Two years ago, Principal Sampson was placed on probation and required to meet specific performance goals in order to retain his administrative position. After conducting an evaluation and determining that the conditions had not been met, the superintendent and assistant superintendent for instruction concurred that he should be dismissed. Their recommendation to that effect was approved by the school board. After being informed that he would be reassigned to a teaching position the following school year, Mr. Sampson opted to retire. Angered by his removal, all the Buchanan employees signed and sent a letter to the school board expressing displeasure with the way Mr. Sampson had been treated by Superintendent Simon.

Principal Hulbert Arrives

Why did Maureen Hulbert accept the daunting challenge of being the principal at Buchanan Elementary School? When asked that question by a friend, her response was quick and direct: "Because the school district has a dynamic superintendent, Dr. Mark Simon, who is committed to turning this school system in a positive direction."

Before coming to Buchanan, Principal Hulbert had not met a single staff member in the school. Only the superintendent and two other district-level administrators were present at her employment interview. During that meeting, Superintendent Simon explicitly told her that Buchanan was a under-performing school staffed by teachers strongly opposed to new ideas. He also made it clear that the school had to improve and he would provide whatever support he could to achieve that goal.

After beginning her assignment at Buchanan, Principal Hulbert made a concerted effort to develop positive relationships with faculty and staff. She met with employees individually and made two pledges: She would not be biased by the past and she would work actively and closely with teachers to improve student learning. Most employees were unimpressed with her promises; they viewed Principal Hulbert as naive and unrealistic. In their eyes, they could do relatively little to help students overcome the social, psychological, and economic problems they faced outside of school.

A fourth-grade teacher summarized the attitude shared by most school employees: "Over the past few years, we have been unfairly criticized. After NCLB, we were also threatened. We were told that the school might be closed if more students were unable to meet state standards. Morale, which wasn't very good in the first place, got worse. The bureaucrats responsible for NCLB intend to destroy local public schools by setting unattainable goals. Neither Superintendent Simon nor a new principal can perform miracles."

This and similar comments disappointed Principal Hulbert. Attitudes being expressed suggested the faculty and support staff were pessimistic about school improvement, generally, and her ability to be a change agent, specifically. She decided to look at records for the past 5 years to determine what, if any, changes had been made by her predecessor, Mr. Sampson. She identified three that related to instruction.

1. The previous principal had discouraged social promotions from first to second grade, believing that the lowest-performing students would benefit from being retained.
2. The quantity of staff development provided for teachers increased slightly, but only because of the sessions required for data-based decision making.
3. Responding to one of his probationary conditions, he issued a directive requiring teachers to develop unit lesson plans.

There was no evidence indicating that any of these efforts improved student learning. In fact, after the retention rate in first grade increased achievement tests declined. Despite the workshops, many teachers did not rely on data to make important decisions. And, after examining the teacher lesson plans, Principal Hulbert concluded that they were generic and written for grade levels, not individual teachers. Not one word in any of the lesson plans had changed since they were first written 3 years ago, and no mention of the lesson plans was found in any of the teacher performance evaluations completed during that same period.

After speaking with several teachers about the lesson plans, Principal Hulbert learned that the requirement for developing and using them was actually a mock rule—that is, the rule had not been followed by teachers nor enforced by the principal. In fact, Principal Sampson told teachers he thought the rule was an infringement on their professional status. He added that he would not have adopted it if the superintendent had not forced him to do so.

Lessons Learned from the Lesson Plans

Instead of devising their own plans, as intended by the superintendent, the teachers at each grade level collectively produced one set of unit plans that they all would supposedly apply. The following lesson plan for a unit on teaching fractions to second-grade students was typical.

Principal Hulbert also noticed that the lesson plans were entirely teacher-centered; that is, they only addressed teacher objectives. Thus, the lesson plans were void of learning targets, continuous assessments, and the use of data to determine student progress. Perhaps most troubling, the lesson plans made no mention of instructional alignment with prevailing standards.

After examining the lesson plans, Principal Hulbert expressed her concerns about them at a faculty meeting. She emphasized that the documents focused largely, if not exclusively, on what the teachers were to do rather than on what the students were to learn. She said that the plans would have to be revised so that they were more explicit about learning expectations, evaluation, and alignment with state standards. She also was emphatic that lesson plans had to include guidelines for recording information about student learning so that information would be available for future instructional decisions.

　　Some teachers were visibly upset. Several pointed out that the previous principal had never criticized the lesson plans. Bill Osborne, a fifth-grade teacher and often the spokesperson for the employees, was the most vocal.

　　"Ms. Hulbert," he began, "we might as well put all the cards on the table even though we haven't gotten to know each other very well. It's no secret why they put you in this job—and it's no secret that we opposed Mr. Sampson's dismissal. Every teacher in this room has been here for at least 5 years. We know these kids, we know their problems, and we know how to teach. Federal mandates, administrative dictates, and lesson plans aren't going to change reality. Many of our students aren't going to meet the state proficiency standard, and there is nothing you or we can do about that. The government can set lofty expectations and require us to use statistics, but the fact is these kids are not going to do well in school. Here's another fact. Motivated students learn and unmotivated students rarely learn. Poor teaching is not the reason why many Buchanan students fail to meet state standards. The real reasons are outside these four walls. They include things like poverty, abuse, and emotional instability—things we can't control. You're the boss and you can force us to revise the lesson plans. Just tell us what you want in the lesson plans, we'll copy it, and we can go on to more important issues. After we go through all of your hoops, ask yourself how much difference these plans will make behind closed classroom doors."

Problem Framing

1. Assume you are Principal Hulbert. First determine the main issue (problem) in this case. Then describe the current state and the desired state of this issue. (The section on problem framing in the Introduction section of this book defines the problem framing process.)

2. Based on evidence provided in the case, describe the difficulty associated with eliminating the gap between the present state and desired state.

Questions and Suggested Activities

1. Share and critique the problem statements prepared by students in your class.
2. Describe the nature of the school culture at Buchanan Elementary School.
3. Why do Mr. Osborne and presumably the other Buchanan teachers have such a negative attitude about NCLB?
4. Evaluate Principal Hulbert's decision to have the teachers rewrite the lesson plans.
5. Mr. Osborne implies that experienced teachers do not need lesson plans. Do you agree? Why or why not?
6. Mr. Osborne believes that many of the Buchanan students will not succeed academically because of the negative social and economic conditions they face outside of school. Do you agree? Why or why not?
7. Buchanan employees indicate that they supported the previous principal, Mr. Sampson, and they criticized the decision to remove him from the school. Is this fact relevant to shaping a plan to improve student learning? Why or why not?
8. How have teachers and principals across all districts and schools responded to NCLB? What evidence do you have to support your response?
9. No Child Left Behind requires administrators and teachers to collect assessment data, disaggregate those data by student groups, and develop explicit plans for meeting the needs of students, especially those exhibiting low achievement. Is this a realistic expectation for an elementary school teacher who has 20 or more pupils in class? Is it a realistic expectation for secondary school teachers who have over 100 pupils in their classes?
10. What actions could Principal Hulbert take to improve employee morale at Buchanan?
11. To what extent does the school's culture affect teacher behavior?

Suggested Readings

Calabrese, R. L. (2003). The ethical imperative to lead change: Overcoming the resistance to change. *International Journal of Educational Management, 17*(1), 7–13.

Colantonio, J. N. (2005). On target: Combined instructional supervision and staff development. *Principal Leadership, 5*(9), 30–34.

DuFour, R. (2002). The learning-centered principal. *Educational Leadership, 59*(8), 12–15.

Garcia, J. (Ed.). (2002). No Child Left Behind: Meeting challenges, seizing opportunities, improving achievement. *Achieve Policy Brief, 5.*

Hardy, L. (2002). Half full or half empty? Scrutinizing the effects of NCLB. *American School Board Journal, 193*(5), 4–6.

Hoy, W. K., Gage, C. Q., & Tarter, C. J. (2006). School mindfulness and faculty trust: Necessary conditions for each other? *Educational Administration Quarterly, 42*(2), 236–255.

Kowalski, T. J., Lasley, T. J., & Mahoney, J. (2008). *Data-driven decisions and school leadership: Best practices for school improvement.* Boston: Allyn and Bacon (Chapters 9 and 11).

Lewis, A. C. (2002). A horse called NCLB. *Phi Delta Kappan, 84*(3), 179–180.

Lewis, A. C. (2006). A muddle of NCLB. *Education Digest, 71*(9), 44–46.

Lewis, A. C. (2006). NCLB's murky mess. *Education Digest, 71*(5), 67–68.

McBride, B. (2004). Data-driven instructional methods: "One strategy fits all" doesn't work in real classrooms. *T.H.E. Journal, 31*(11), 38–39.

McCaslin, M. (2006). Student motivational dynamics in the era of school reform. *Elementary School Journal, 106*(5), 479–490.

Neill, M. (2003). High stakes, high risk: The dangerous consequences of high-stakes testing. *American School Board Journal, 190*(2), 18–21.

Paige, R., & Ferrandino, V. (2003). No principal left behind. *Principal, 82*(4), 52–55.

Porter-Magee, K. (2004). Teacher quality, controversy, and NCLB. *Clearing House, 78*(1), 26–29.

Rose, L. C. (2003). No child left behind: Promise or rhetoric? *Phi Delta Kappan, 84*(5), 338.

Thomas, M. D., & Bainbridge, W. L. (2002). No Child Left Behind: Facts and fallacies. *Phi Delta Kappan, 83*(10), 781–782.

Thompson, S. (2006, March 1). The importance of "reculturing." *Education Week, 25*(25), 44, 30–31.

Torff, B., & Sessions, D. N. (2005). Principals' perceptions of the causes of teacher ineffectiveness. *Journal of Educational Psychology, 97*(4), 530–537.

References

Fullan, M., (2005). *Leadership and sustainability: System thinkers in action.* Thousand Oaks, CA: Corwin Press.

Hanson, E. M. (2003). *Educational administration and organizational behavior* (5th ed.). Boston: Allyn and Bacon.

Hoy, W. K., & Miskel, C. G. (2005). *Educational administration: Theory, research, and practice* (7th ed.). New York: McGraw Hill.

Kowalski, T. J. (2003). *Contemporary school administration: An introduction* (2nd ed.). Boston: Allyn and Bacon.

Kowalski, T. J. (2006). *The school superintendent: Theory, practice, and cases* (2nd ed.). Thousand Oaks, CA: Sage.

Kowalski, T. J., Lasley, T. J., & Mahoney, J. (2008). *Data-driven decisions and school leadership: Best practices for school improvement.* Boston: Allyn and Bacon.

Protheroe, N., Shellard, E., & Turner, J. (2003). *A practical guide to school improvement: Meeting the challenges of NCLB.* Arlington, VA: Educational Research Service.

Sarason, S. B. (1996). *Revisiting the culture of the school and the problem of change.* New York: Teachers College Press.

2 | WHO SHOULD CREATE THE SCHOOL'S VISION?

BACKGROUND INFORMATION

Recognizing that effective schools adjust to societal change, policymakers in most states now require public schools to develop strategic plans. Their intent is to ensure that these institutions identify and respond to changing social conditions and education needs.

Vision statements are probably the most essential facet of strategic planning because these declarations describe what schools will look like in meeting their missions at some designated point in the future (Kowalski, 2011). The visioning process, however, often has been attenuated for two reasons: the nature of the task often has been misinterpreted and the development process is difficult (Kowalski, Petersen, & Fusarelli, 2007). With regard to the former issue, school officials fail to differentiate among three essential documents: *mission*, *philosophy*, and *vision*.

- A mission statement describes a school purpose; that is, it essentially details what a school is supposed to accomplish. It is written in present tense.
- A philosophy statement describes espoused values and beliefs; that is, it identifies guiding principles that influence curriculum, instruction, discipline, and other core functions. It, too, is written in present tense.
- A vision statement describes a desired future state—most notably, what a school should look like in meeting its mission and pursuing its philosophy at some designated point in the future. It is written in future tense (Kowalski, 2010).

With respect to process difficulty, visioning has been hampered by the following three variables:

1. *Uncertainty.* Visioning requires administrators and others to make important decisions in the context of uncertainty. Decision uncertainty stems from an inability to predict the future accurately, either because of not having critical information or because the types of information needed are indeterminable (Nutt, 1989). To diminish uncertainty, decision makers must identify future conditions, accurately describe their effects on schools, and formulate responses to these effects (Milliken, 1987).
2. *Risk.* In simple terms, risk is the possibility that a decision will be detrimental to either an institution (e.g., school) or decision maker (e.g., a principal). The level of risk involved in visioning is determined by the level of uncertainty surrounding the decisions that must be made (Kowalski, Lasley, & Mahoney, 2008).
3. *Conflict.* Scholars agree that visioning, especially for public institutions, should be an inclusive process. Inclusiveness means that a broad range of stakeholders should participate in making decisions democratically. Shared decision making in public education, however, almost always magnifies fundamental philosophical differences among primary stakeholders—disagreements about foundational issues such as the purposes of education, pedagogy, and standards (Cooper, Fusarelli, & Randall, 2004).

Some school boards and superintendents have approached strategic planning by employing "visionary" administrators, believing that such individuals can predict the future accurately. Further, they assume that these leaders can and will forge effective school vision statements independently and quickly. This line of reasoning, though, is flawed. Even if some administrators are capable of developing relevant vision statements alone, there is a high probability that their product will be rejected by one or more stakeholder groups (Wirt & Kirst, 2009). Recognizing this fact, scholars, such as Fullan (2003), posit that vision statements should be developed collaboratively by those who have vested interest in public schools.

This case takes place in a rural community where school officials are preparing to open a new middle school. The founding principal, employed from outside the district, attempts to create a broad-based committee to develop a vision statement. Her efforts are opposed by several influential teachers who believe that the principal, a recognized expert on middle school education, should produce the vision independently. As you read this case, try to identify factors that contribute to philosophical dissonance between the principal and the teachers and to identify possible reasons why a principal-developed vision might be ineffective.

Key Areas for Reflection

1. Visioning
2. School culture
3. Principal leadership style
4. Professionalism versus democracy
5. Principal role expectations

THE CASE

Community and School District

The Lightville Community School District serves two predominately rural townships and just over 60% of its residents live on farms. The system has two schools: an elementary facility housing Grades K–6 and a junior-senior high facility housing Grades 7–12. Both are located on a 65-acre site two miles from the town of Lightville. The elementary school opened 22 years ago and the secondary school was constructed 11 years later.

Despite its rural location, the school district's population is increasing. Twenty-five years ago, the district official enrollment was 758; now, it is just over 1,200 and increasing at a rate of about 2% per year. Population growth is attributable to the district's demography and land values. Located within 10 miles of a major city in an adjoining county, the district's rural environment, low land costs, and relatively new schools have attracted new residents.

When the junior-senior high school facility opened, most residents believed that no additional construction would be needed for at least 40 years. Unanticipated in-migration, however, altered that conviction. The influx of new families, most with school-age children, changed the social and political environment in the district. Two of the five school board members were relatively new residents with children enrolled in the district, and they vigorously promoted the idea of building a new middle school to alleviate space problems at the two existing schools.

Middle School and the New Principal

The idea of building a separate middle school quickly became controversial. In an effort to manage the conflict, Superintendent Joe Rawlings recommended that the board retain an architectural firm to study the inadequate space problems. The firm, working in conjunction with an education planner, identified three possible solutions:

1. Build an addition to the junior-senior high school and move the sixth grade from the elementary facility to the junior-senior high school facility
2. Build additions to both existing schools
3. Build a new middle school, housing Grades 6-8, thus removing the sixth grade from the elementary school and the seventh and eighth grades from the secondary school

After evaluating these alternatives, the architects and planner recommended the third option. Their rationale was that even though it was the most expensive, it provided the most favorable and long-term education solution. Shortly after receiving the report, Superintendent Rawlings announced that he concurred with the recommendation and urged the school board to adopt it.

After the superintendent announced his recommendation but before the board acted on it, the community divided into three factions. The first included primarily large landowners opposed to any additional construction for at least the next 10 years. Although they did not dispute the need for additional space, they argued that no new debt obligations for construction should be incurred until current debt obligations were retired in approximately 9 years. The second group included residents who favored either the first or second options presented by the architects and planner. They contended that either of these options was less expensive—and hence, required a lower tax increase. The third faction, primarily new residents with school-age children, supported the superintendent's recommendation and campaigned for it. After 4 months of public debate, the school board finally voted 4 to 1 to conduct a referendum to build the new middle school. The initiative was approved by the voters with a margin of 53% to 47%.

The new middle school was to be built on the same site with the existing two schools and would be designed to accommodate up to 450 pupils. The construction was to be completed in approximately 18 months and the superintendent recommended and the board approved that a new principal be employed at least 12 months prior to the new school opening. This action would allow the principal to have input into staffing and designing the curriculum. Mr. Rawlings received 22 applications for the new position, and four of the candidates were interviewed by the selection committee, the superintendent, and the school board. The selection committee consisted of four teachers, the elementary school principal, the secondary school principal, and four parents. Susan Potter, an experienced teacher and currently a middle school assistant principal in a suburban school district, emerged as the preferred candidate and was offered the position. Although she was apprehensive about moving to a predominately rural community, the challenge of shaping a new middle school outweighed her reservations.

Susan Potter's employment with Lightville started officially on August 1—approximately 12 months before the new school would become operational. Superintendent Rawlings identified the following objectives that she was to complete in her initial year of employment:

- Make staffing decisions. This task included determining the size of the staff, staff recruitment, and staff selection.
- Organize the school's programs. This task primarily included determining the scope of the curriculum, extra-curricular programs, and instructional approaches.
- Collaborate with architects and construction managers. This task primarily included attending progress meetings and involvement in equipment and furniture acquisitions.

Staffing proved to be the easiest of the assignments. Many teachers already employed in the district applied for vacancies at the new school. After making selections from this group, Ms. Potter had to hire only four other teachers. Because so many faculty were already employed in the district, she involved them in making organizational decisions.

The Advisory Committee

With input from Superintendent Rawlings and the school board members, Principal Potter appointed four teachers (each from a different subject area) and four parents to serve on the advisory committee, a group she called the "visioning and planning committee." At the group's first meeting, Principal Potter pointed out that she would be a committee member but preferred not to be the chair. She also presented the following guidelines:

- The committee would operate democratically; that is, each member would have a vote in making decisions.
- Consensus should be the preferred method for making decisions. Although each member had a vote, the ideal should be to make decisions that all found to be acceptable.
- The committee's first task would be to develop a vision statement providing parameters for planning program scope and implementation.
- The vision statement would reflect the collective values and beliefs of the committee members and hopefully of the community at-large.
- All stakeholders would be given an opportunity to suggest elements of the vision and to react to elements proposed by others.

The committee members agreed with the guidelines but disagreed with Ms. Potter's contention that she should not chair the committee because they felt she was the most qualified person for this key role. Principal Potter pointed out that she wanted to share leadership responsibilities with teachers, and therefore, the decision to not chair the committee was symbolically important. The others agreed to honor her request, and they selected another member to be chair. Helen Burke, an English and social studies teacher, was selected. She also is the sister of one of the school board members. Her brother, a farmer, was influential in the decision to build a new school because he was the only farmer on the board to support the project. Helen actively campaigned for the referendum to build the new middle school.

Conflict

Helen had agreed to be the committee's chair only after Susan agreed to help her perform the role. So, the two met after the first meeting to construct the agenda for the next meeting. During their conversation, Helen said, "Susan, I want you to know that I will do what I can to help you develop a quality school. We are thrilled you are here. We believe you can provide the leadership we need to establish a first-class middle school. So don't hesitate to call upon me or the other teachers for support, even for issues that are beyond the committee's scope."

"Thank you, Helen," Susan responded. "The committee has a great deal of work to do in the next few months, and therefore we need to keep everyone focused and involved."

The committee's first task was to construct a vision statement. Susan explained the nature of a vision statement and pointed out how it interfaced with a school's mission. But since the school was a new facility, the committee also had to oversee the development of mission and philosophy statements.

Helen agreed about the need for the documents but was not convinced that the process Susan was proposing for developing them was the best. She told the principal, "My brother (the school board member) says you are a visionary leader. He thinks you should design our middle school philosophy and draft our mission and vision statements. This community respects administrators and relies on them to make important decisions. I speak for our entire planning committee in telling you that we are comfortable having you shape these documents. We believe we can help you to get them approved."

Susan interpreted Helen's comments to mean that the planning committee would first "rubber stamp" whatever the principal proposed and then become involved politically to ensure school board approval.

"Helen, I really appreciate your support and confidence. However, I don't think having me develop the philosophy, mission, and vision alone is appropriate. A vision statement should reflect the collective thinking of stakeholders. Committee members and subsequently others should have opportunities to promote their beliefs and hopes. I'm new here, and even if I fully understood the community, I would feel uncomfortable making these important decisions by myself."

"But Susan," Helen said, "you're the expert—the person the school board employed to lead us and to manage our new school. Why should we pretend that we know as much as you do about middle school education?"

"I will share my philosophy and facilitate decisions, but I don't want to be an autocrat. Nor do I want to be put in a position where everyone blindly accepts what I propose."

Helen thought for a moment and then said, "I don't think we need to worry about us being mindless robots. I can assure you that I and other committee members will let you know if we disagree with your ideas. We are not bashful. If we begin our planning having each committee member state his or her personal values and a vision for the middle school, we may never make decisions. And as we know, our time is limited."

Sensing that she was not going to convince Helen to change her mind, Susan suggested that the issue they were discussing be addressed by the entire committee at the next meeting. Helen agreed but commented that the others would express the same feelings she already had articulated.

At the next planning committee meeting, Helen recounted her discussion with Susan including detailing her disposition on the matter. After she finished, Susan spoke to the group.

"I can give you boilerplate philosophy and vision statements. But aspects of these documents may not be appropriate for or acceptable to the community. For example, should sixth-grade students be allowed to attend school dances? Should sixth-graders be integrated academically with seventh- and eighth-grade students? Often, community values and beliefs influence the answers to such questions. This is why it is important to identify what the community wants and needs before shaping a vision."

Dan Kelby, a physical education teacher, was the first committee member to speak after Susan. "I have several thoughts about the new school, especially related to athletic programs. But if we all start sharing our dreams, we may end up arguing endlessly. I think we should follow Helen's suggestion. We should start by having you give us a vision statement. We can then determine whether we agree with it. If certain aspects are unacceptable to me, I'll say so."

Two other committee members, both parents, quickly agreed with Mr. Kelby. Ms. Potter, however, was not ready to surrender. She said, "Several days ago I met with Helen and shared my apprehension about doing what Dan just suggested. The new middle school is not mine; it is ours. Therefore, we all have a duty to shape its future."

Helen asked Susan, "Would you tell us specifically how you prefer to move forward?"

"Certainly. Ideally, we would begin by creating a philosophy statement. Each member would share his or her values and beliefs about a middle school. These individual philosophies would then be discussed and hopefully we could arrive at consensus. Once we do that, the philosophy statement would be presented to the superintendent and school board for approval. Once approved, the philosophy statement serves as a guide for creating a vision statement. Again, we would begin by having each member state his or her mental image of what the school should look like in 5 or 10 years. These images are debated and hopefully we arrive at consensus. Ideally, the board and superintendent would solicit community input prior to approving both the philosophy and vision."

Helen asked whether any of the committee members supported Principal Potter's views. Only one parent member said she was comfortable following her suggested process. The others were silent. Helen reiterated her preference that Susan draft a philosophy statement and present it to the committee for approval. The same procedure would recur for the vision statement. At that point, a motion was made to formalize Helen's preference. Seven members voted to support the motion, one abstained, and one (Susan) voted against the motion.

After the meeting ended and the others left, Helen commented to Susan, "I hope you don't feel discouraged by what just happened. Our community expects you to lead. Trust me on this matter. When the committee is finished, we will have a philosophy and a vision statement embraced by all our stakeholders."

After Helen left, Susan sat in her room alone and thought about what she could and should do before next week's committee meeting.

Problem Framing

1. Assume you are Susan. First determine the main issue (problem) in this case. Then describe the current state and the desired state of this issue. (The section on problem framing in the Introduction section of this book defines the problem framing process.)

2. Based on evidence provided in the case, describe the difficulty associated with eliminating the gap between the present state and desired state.

Questions and Suggested Activities

1. Share and critique the problem statements prepared by students in your class.
2. What is your definition of a visionary leader? What is the basis of your definition?
3. Why is it important to develop a philosophy statement prior to shaping a vision statement?
4. If you were the principal, would you honor the committee's vote about procedures? Why or why not?
5. Do you believe that too much emphasis is being placed on the development of a vision statement prior to the school opening? Why or why not?
6. According to the case, the committee has considered two proposals for developing a vision statement: the

one proposed by Helen and the one proposed by Susan. Are there other alternatives? If so, what are they?

7. At several points in the case, Helen alludes to the community's expectations of administrators. Are these expectations typical of those found in most school systems?
8. To what extent is the outcome of the referendum to build the new middle school relevant to the disagreement between the new principal and planning committee?
9. What should be the relationship between a mission statement and a vision statement?
10. What are the advantages and disadvantages of the new principal following the wishes of the committee regarding procedures?

Suggested Readings

Brouillette, L. (1997). Who defines "democratic leadership"? Three high school principals respond to site-based reforms. *Journal of School Leadership, 7*(6), 569–591.

Chance, P. L., & Björk, L. G. (2004). The social dimensions of public relations. In T. J. Kowalski (Ed.), *Public relations in schools* (3rd ed., pp. 125–148). Upper Saddle River, NJ: Merrill, Prentice Hall.

Fullan, M. (2003). *Change forces with a vengeance.* Philadelphia: Taylor and Francis.

Fullan, M., & Hargreaves, A. (1997). 'Tis the season. *Learning, 26*(1), 27–29.

Hallinger, P., & Heck, R. H. (1999). Exploring the principal's contribution to school effectiveness: 1980–1995. *School Effectiveness and School Improvement, 9*(2), 157–191.

Keedy, J. L., & Finch, A. M. (1994). Examining teacher-principal empowerment: An analysis of power. *Journal of Research and Development in Education, 27*(3), 162–175.

Krajewski, B., & Matkin, M. (1996). Community empowerment: Building a shared vision. *Principal, 76*(2), 5–6, 8.

Rideout, G. W., McKay, L. M., & Morton, L. L. (2004). The framework and measure of effective school visioning strategy (MCP-FIV). *Alberta Journal of Educational Research, 50*(1), 68–86.

Smith, S. C., & Stolp, S. (1995). Transforming a school's culture through shared vision. *OSSC Report, 35*(3), 1–6.

Starratt, R. J. (1995). *Leaders with vision: The quest for school renewal.* Thousand Oaks, CA: Corwin.

Williamson, R., & Blackburn, B. R. (2009). Personal and shared vision: A commitment to increase rigor. *Principal Leadership, 10*(3), 56–58.

Yearout, S., Miles, G., & Koonce, R. H. (2001). Multi-level visioning. *Training & Development, 55*(3) 7, 30.

References

Cooper, B. S., Fusarelli, L. D., & Randall, E. V. (2004). *Better policies, better schools: Theories and applications.* Boston: Allyn and Bacon.

Fullan, M. (2003). *Change forces with a vengeance.* Philadelphia: Taylor and Francis.

Kowalski, T. J. (2010). *The school principal: Visionary leadership and competent management.* New York: Routledge.

Kowalski, T. J. (2011). *Public relations in schools* (5th ed.). Boston: Allyn and Bacon.

Kowalski, T. J., Lasley, T. J., & Mahoney, J. (2008). *Data-driven decisions and school leadership: Best practices for school improvement.* Boston: Allyn and Bacon.

Kowalski, T. J., Petersen, G. J., & Fusarelli, L. D. (2007). *Effective communication for school administrators: An imperative in an information age.* Lanham, MD: Rowman and Littlefield Education.

Milliken, F. J. (1987). Three types of perceived uncertainty about the environment: State, effect, and response. *Academy of Management Review, 12*(1), 133–143.

Nutt, P. C. (1989). *Making tough decisions: Tactics for improving managerial decision making.* San Francisco: Jossey-Bass.

Wirt, F. M., & Kirst, M. W. (2009). *The political dynamics of American education* (4th ed.). Berkeley, CA: McCutchan.

3 | A BULLY'S THREAT

BACKGROUND INFORMATION

Not all administrators recognize the difference between *safety* and *security*. The former addresses issues such as accident prevention, air quality, and fire or storm damage. Security, on the other hand, is concerned with preventing and responding to criminal acts and severe misbehavior (Trump, 1998). Highly publicized criminal acts committed in schools provide clear evidence that educational environments are not immune from society's ills. The potential for violence generates three critical questions for school administrators:

1. How can behaviors that threaten a school's security be prevented?
2. What measures should be taken when threats of violence are made?
3. What measures should be taken when violence occurs?

When violence is threatened in schools, principals have a responsibility to collect the facts in order to determine the seriousness of the situation (Brunner, Emmendorfer, & Lewis, 2009). But in the heat of the moment, this is not always the case. Security experts, such as Kenneth Trump, warn that schools are especially vulnerable to crises generally and to violent acts specifically (Kowalski, 2005). The following are primary reasons for this exposure:

- Administrators are often unprepared to deal with violence, either because they have not been sufficiently educated or because they lack relevant experience dealing with this type of crisis.
- School or district crisis plans have often been perfunctory documents receiving little or no attention from school personnel. In the past, some administrators feared that such documents would be interpreted as an admission that serious security problems already existed (Moriarity, Maeyama, & Fitzgerald, 1993).
- Chaos often occurs during a crisis situation because implementation of the district's or school's plan has not been coordinated with community agencies (e.g., police and fire departments; Kowalski, 2011).
- The content of crisis plans may have been influenced by political conditions such as demands that principals reduce expulsions and out-of-school suspensions. Such pressures can dissuade principals from integrating best practices in school safety plans (Trump, 1998). As a result, offenders who should have been excluded from school for violent acts received punishment that allowed them to remain active students.

This case occurs in an urban high school. A student who has a reputation as a bully threatens the life of another student. The threat is brought to the attention of the principal, and he must decide how to deal with the situation. He enlists the counsel of three of the high school's staff members. As you read the case, try to identify conditions that may have influenced the student's behavior and principal's reaction to that behavior.

Key Areas for Reflection

1. Dealing with threats of violent behavior
2. Political influences on crisis management
3. Racial tensions in schools
4. Principal leadership style
5. Multicultural school environments

THE CASE

Community

Like most urban areas in the United States, Central City has changed considerably in the past 30 years. The total population has declined from 325,000 in 1960 to its current level of 258,000. The property-tax base has been eroded by the flight of businesses and middle-class families to the suburbs. The current mayor, serving a second 4-year term, has been slightly more successful than his predecessors in curbing population erosion and tax-revenue declines. Nevertheless, other statistics have been less positive. Crime and poverty rates continue to move upward. Nearly 40% of the city's school-age children live in poverty-level families; an estimated 20% are being reared in dysfunctional families; an estimated 15% have been victims of physical or emotional abuse.

The following demographic profile extracted from the most recent national census reveals the level of racial diversity among the district's residents:

- 48% identified themselves as African American.
- 18% identified themselves as Hispanic.
- 5% identified themselves as Asian American.
- 28% identified themselves as white (non-Hispanic).
- 1% identified themselves as "other."
- White residents are heavily concentrated in two sections of the city: Memorial Park (where virtually all of the Asian American families also reside) and Kensington.

The School District

The Central City School District (CCSD) remains the state's largest district; however, its enrollment has declined about 25% in the past 3 decades. Two high schools, two middle schools, and six elementary schools have been closed during that period. Most of the remaining school buildings are more than 50 years old and should be completely renovated or replaced.

The district is governed by a seven-member school board. Five members are elected by voters in designated geographic regions; the remaining two are elected at-large. The following data profile the present board:

Member	Board position	District	Occupation	Race
Venus Bronson	President	3	Lawyer	African American
Walter Sully	Vice President	At-large	Plumber	Caucasian
Emily Drovak	Secretary	5	Housewife	Caucasian
Alexander Adams	Member	1	Minister	African American
James Chin	Member	4	Engineer	Asian American
Rose Hildago	Member	2	Social worker	Caucasian
Maynard Truax	Member	At-large	Dentist	African American

Districts 1, 2, and 3 are in the city's core area; each has high concentrations of African American residents, with District 2 being almost evenly divided between African American and Hispanic populations. District 4, known as the Memorial Park area, is at the southern perimeter of the city. Nearly all of the district's residents are either white or Asian American. District 5, known as Kensington, is in the northern perimeter of the city; the population here is about 60% white with the remainder being predominately African American.

Dr. Ruth Perkett is the district's first female and first African American superintendent. A long-time employee of CCSD, she has been the school system's top administrator for only 2 years. Prior to assuming this position, she was an elementary school principal, director of federal programs, and associate superintendent for elementary education in the district. Over her long tenure in CCSD, she has established close ties with many government officials, including Central City's current mayor.

Memorial Park High School

Forty years ago, Memorial Park High School was considered an outstanding academic institution. Though that is no longer true, it remains the most effective academic school in the district (as measured by state achievement tests, graduation rates, and enrollment of graduates in higher education). Memorial Park now enrolls approximately 1,350 students in Grades 9 to 12. Only one-third of these students, however, reside in the Memorial Park neighborhood; the others are bused to the high school from other neighborhoods in compliance with the district's desegregation plan, a document that became effective 13 years ago.

Joseph Milhoviak has been the principal at Memorial Park High School for 14 years. He grew up in the Memorial Park neighborhood and graduated from the school. After college, he was employed as a teacher and coach. During his entire 28-year career as an educator, he has never worked in another school.

Prior to the desegregation plan, Memorial Park High School enrolled just a handful of African American and Hispanic students. The present demographic profile provides evidence of the depth of change that has occurred in the student body since then:

- African American: 40%
- Hispanic: 10%
- Asian American: 16%
- Caucasian: 34%

Despite the student body's diversity, approximately two-thirds of the teachers and adminis-trators remain Caucasian.

Principal Milhoviak has always resided in the Memorial Park neighborhood, where he is viewed positively as an education and community leader. Friends have often encouraged him to run for elected office, but he has declined, preferring instead to remain a high school principal. He has played an active part in political campaigns, however; for example, two of his closest friends are on the city council.

Mr. Milhoviak has a reputation as a "tough" principal—a disciplinarian not afraid to act decisively and harshly when punishing disruptive students. Though his demeanor is applauded by most parents and other stakeholders residing in the Memorial Park area, other parents and the superintendent have been less inclined to praise him. In her most recent performance evaluation of him, Superintendent Perkett cited three criticisms:

1. The total number of expulsions and suspensions has increased approximately 2% in each of the last two school terms.
2. Although Principal Milhoviak is popular with parents residing in the Memorial Park neighborhood, parents who live elsewhere often complain-that he does little to make them feel welcome at the school.
3. Discipline data show that students being bused from neighborhoods outside of Memorial Park are excluded from school more frequently than other students.

Based on these concerns, Dr. Perkett recommended that Mr. Milhoviak focus on building rela-tionships with parents outside of Memorial Park and on deploying alternatives for disciplining stu-dents that would reduce the number of student exclusions—options such as in-school suspension and group counseling. The performance evaluation had little effect on Principal Milhoviak, largely because he felt his political relationships with school board members provided job security.

The Incident

His face flushed and breathing heavily, Brian Isaacs entered the principal's office between the third and fourth periods. He told the receptionist, "I need to see Mr. Milhoviak right now. It's an emergency!"

"What's wrong?" the receptionist inquired.

He answered, "I need to talk with the principal. I don't think I should discuss the problem with any other person."

Convinced the student was experiencing a crisis, the receptionist asked the student to iden-tify himself and then she interrupted Mr. Milhoviak, who was in his office meeting with a parent. The principal knew the student. A sophomore, Brian was an above-average student academically and generally well behaved. Mr. Milhoviak quickly concluded the meeting with the parent and brought Brian into his office.

The principal could see that Brian was visibly shaken. He asked the student to sit down and calm himself. Brian took a deep breath and then said, "Carl Turner told me that he is going to blow my brains out. Mr. Milhoviak, he is crazy. He'll do it."

"Why is Carl threatening you?" the principal asked.

"This whole thing really isn't about me. Carl had a couple of dates with my sister, Angie, and now she doesn't want to see him anymore. He's blaming my parents and me. He said we are prevent-ing her from dating him. He told me he is in love with Angie. He called my parents and me racists."

Mr. Milhoviak was very familiar with Carl Turner, a senior who resided outside the Memorial Park area. Though he had played varsity football for 2 years, he had been dismissed from the team prior to the start of the current school year for pushing an assistant coach during a locker room argument. Carl had an extensive discipline record, including two 5-day suspensions during the school year for fighting. The faculty and students generally regarded him as a bully.

Brian's sister, Angie, also is a senior. Somewhat introverted, she is a good student but not very involved in extracurricular activities. Mr. Milhoviak was surprised to learn that Angie had dated Carl, primarily because the two students had dissimilar personalities and interests.

Refocusing his attention to the student in his office, the principal asked, "Tell me exactly everything Carl said to you."

"He said he loved Angie, and he wasn't going to let my family destroy his relationship with her. He said he had a gun and wasn't afraid to use it. He said unless we stopped pressuring Angie not to see him, he would settle the score with me and my parents."

The principal then inquired, "Is it true that your family has told Angie not to date him? What has Angie told you about the relationship?"

"I have never heard anyone in my family talk about Angie dating Carl. I was surprised to learn that they had gone out on several dates. My parents probably don't know about this, either. To answer your second question, Angie has never mentioned Carl to me."

"Brian, I am going to inform the school security officer about this threat. He will keep an eye on Carl. If he threatens you again, even away from school, you let me know immediately. In the meantime, I'll decide how to handle this. Stay away from Carl. Don't speak to him, and if he tries to talk to you again, just walk away."

I'm still worried, Mr. Milhoviak," Brian said as he started to leave the principal's office. As he opened the door, he turned to face the principal again and added, "Carl said he was tired of being treated like dirt. Do you think he's crazy enough to shoot someone?"

Mr. Milhoviak said that Carl would not shoot anyone and again told Brian to return to class. As soon as Brian departed, the principal asked the receptionist to get Angie Isaacs and bring her to his office. When she arrived, Mr. Milhoviak told her about the conversation he had with Brian minutes earlier. She was visibly stunned.

"I went out with Carl twice, and no one in my family knew about it. He had asked me to go out with him at least six times before I eventually said yes. On the first date, we went to a movie. I met him at the theater. The second time, we went to a rock concert. My parents thought I was at a girlfriend's house both times. After the second date, I just decided that I didn't want to go out with him again. He was nice to me, but I didn't think we had a future. Two days ago after he asked me to go on another date with him, I told him that I did not think we had a future other than as friends. He got really mad and said I could change my mind if we spent more time together."

"Did he threaten you in any way?" asked the principal.

"No. But he scares me. He can be very nice one minute and very hostile the next. On our second date, for example, he threatened to beat up the guy sitting in front of him because that person kept standing and blocking his vision."

Mr. Milhoviak instructed Angie as he had Brian to return to class and to avoid contact with Carl. He also said that he would try to reach her parents by phone and alert them of the alleged threat made against Brian and them. After Angie left his office, he tried to reach her father at work and her mother at home; neither of them answered the phone.

The principal then asked the school's security officer, Carl Turner's counselor, and the assistant principal in charge of student discipline to meet with him. He briefed them on the matter. The four school officials agreed that Carl should be brought to the office immediately. They wanted to hear his side of the story. The principal contacted the teacher in Carl's fourth-period class via the intercom and was told that Carl was not in class. Checking the attendance records, the principal learned that Carl had attended classes in the preceding three periods.

Carl's counselor, Mrs. Breslin, urged Principal Milhoviak to call the police immediately and report the incident. Though she doubted that Carl even had a gun, she feared he might attack Brian physically. The assistant principal, Mr. Tyler, disagreed with her suggestion; he wanted to find Carl and get his side of the story before calling the police.

"What if we call the police and then discover that Brian is lying? Dr. Perkett will be livid and accuse us of jumping to conclusions. Let's search the building and if we don't find Carl, then call the police."

Jamel Atkins, the school's security guard and a retired deputy sheriff, offered a third alternative. He urged the principal to locate Mr. and Mrs. Isaacs before doing anything else. "After being briefed, they may want to file a complaint with the police on behalf of their son. I'll take responsibility for protecting Brian and Angie for the remainder of the school day."

Each school in the CCSD was required to have a crisis plan. The one for Memorial Park provided suggestions for handling threatened violence, but it did not require a specific course of action. Among the suggested actions were:

- Notifying the police if the incident was considered sufficiently serious
- Notifying the parents of all students involved
- Notifying the teachers of all students involved
- Suspending the student from school pending a full investigation if the incident was considered sufficiently serious

After considering the suggestions made by the three staff members and after reviewing the crisis plan, the principal decided to delay notifying the police. The administrators and the security guard started searching the building for Carl, and staff in the principal's office continued their efforts to reach Mr. and Mrs. Isaacs by phone. Neither endeavor was fruitful. Two hours before the school day would end, the same four school officials reassembled in the principal's office to determine what they would do next.

Problem Framing

1. Assume you are the principal. First determine the main issue (problem) in this case. Then describe the current state and the desired state of this issue. (The section on problem framing in the Introduction section of this book defines the problem framing process.)

2. Based on evidence provided in the case, describe the difficulty associated with eliminating the gap between the present state and desired state.

Questions and Suggested Activities

1. Share and critique the problem statements prepared by students in your class.
2. What racial, social, and economic characteristics of the community and school district are relevant to the problem described in the case?
3. Identify and discuss factors that appear to affect the course of action being pursued by the principal and his support personnel.
4. Is Carl Turner's discipline record an issue the principal should consider in deciding to call the police? Why or why not?
5. Based on policy and the crisis plan in your district or school, what should the principal have done after learning about the threat?
6. If you were the principal, how would you interpret Carl Turner's unexcused absence in his fourth-period class?

7. Should the principal have instructed Brian and Angie Isaacs to return to their classes? Why or why not?
8. List and then evaluate alternatives the principal could have considered in dealing with the situation.
9. Imagine that Principal Malhoviak ordered a lockdown immediately after learning of the threat.

Would this have been a prudent decision? Why or why not?

10. To what extent is Principal Malhoviak's most recent performance evaluation relevant to this case?

Suggested Readings

Baker, J. A. (1998). Are we missing the forest for the trees? Considering the social context of school violence. *Journal of School Psychology, 36*(1), 29–44.

Barton, R. (2008). Keeping schools safe through threat assessment. *The Education Digest, 74*(1), 20–25.

Brunner, J., Emmendorfer, B., & Lewis, D. (2009). Assessing student threats. *Principal Leadership, 9*(5), 40–45.

Canter, A. S. (2005). Bullying at school: Strategies for intervention. *Principal, 85*(2), 42–45.

Christie, K. (2005). Chasing the bullies away. *Phi Delta Kappan, 86*(10), 725–726.

Crothers, L. M., & Levinson, E. M. (2004). Assessment of bullying: A review of methods and instruments. *Journal of Counseling and Development, 82*(4), 496–503.

Edmonson, H. M., & Bullock, L. M. (1998). Youth with aggressive and violent behaviors: Pieces of a puzzle. *Preventing School Failure, 42*(3), 135–141.

Elinoff, M., Chafouleas, S. M., & Sassu, K. A. (2004). Bullying: Considerations for defining and intervening in school settings. *Psychology in the Schools, 41*(8), 887–897.

Furlong, M. J., Felix, E. D., & Sharkey, J. D. (2005). Preventing school violence: A plan for safe and engaging schools. *Principal Leadership (High School Ed.), 6*(1), 11–15.

Hamarus, P., & Kaikkonen, P. (2008). School bullying as a creator of pupil peer pressure. *Educational Research, 50*(4), 333–345.

Haynes, R. M., & Chalker, D. M. (1999). A nation of violence. *American School Board Journal, 186*(3), 22–25.

Johns, B. H. (1998). What the new Individuals with Disabilities Act (IDEA) means for students who exhibit aggressive or violent behavior. *Preventing School Failure, 42*(3), 102–105.

Jones, R. (1997). Absolute zero. *American School Board Journal, 184*(10), 29–31.

Levin, J. (1998). Violence goes to school. *Mid-Western Educational Researcher, 11*(1), 2–7.

Lodge, J., & Frydenberg, E. (2005). The role of peer bystanders in school bullying: Positive steps toward promoting peaceful schools. *Theory into Practice, 44*(4), 329–336.

Myles, B. S., & Simpson, R. L. (1998). Aggression and violence by school-age children and youth: Understanding the aggression cycle and prevention/intervention strategies. *Intervention in School and Clinic, 33*(5), 259–264.

Orpinas, P., Horne, A. M., & Staniszewski, D. (2003). School bullying: Changing the problem by changing the school. *School Psychology Review, 32*(3), 431–444.

Rasicot, J. (1999). The threat of harm. *American School Board Journal, 186*(3), 14–18.

Ruder, R. (2005). A customized campaign against bullying. *Principal Leadership (Middle School Ed.), 6*(1), 36–38.

Smokowski, P. R., & Kopasz, K. H. (2005). Bullying in school: An overview of types, effects, family characteristics, and intervention strategies. *Children & Schools, 27*(2), 101–110.

Stephens, R. D. (1998). Ten steps to safer schools. *American School Board Journal, 185*(3), 30–33.

Trump, K. S. (2001). Assessing and managing student threats. *School Administrator, 58*(9), 50.

Vail, K. (2009). From words to action. *The American School Board Journal, 196*(9), 40–45.

Valois, R. F., & McKewon, R. E. (1998). Frequency and correlates of fighting and carrying weapons among public school adolescents. *American Journal of Health Behavior, 22*(1), 8–17.

Will, J., & Neufeld, P. J. (2002). Taking appropriate action. *Principal Leadership, 3*(4), 51–54.

Will, J. D., & Neufeld, P. J. (2003). Keep bullying from growing into greater violence. *Education Digest, 68*(6), 32–36.

Zirkel, P. A. (2002). Written and verbal threats of violence. *Principal, 81*(5), 63–65.

References

Brunner, J., Emmendorfer, B., & Lewis, D. (2009). Assessing student threats. *Principal Leadership, 9*(5), 40–45.

Kowalski, T. J. (2005). Revisiting communication during a crisis: Insights from Kenneth Trump. *Journal of School Public Relations, 26*(1), 47–55.

Kowalski, T. J. (2011). *School public relations* (5th ed.). Boston, MA: Allyn and Bacon.

Moriarity, A., Maeyama, R. G., & Fitzgerald, P. J. (1993). A clear plan for school crisis management. *NASSP Bulletin, 77*(552), 17–22.

Trump, K. S. (1998). *Practical school safety: Basic guidelines for safe and secure schools.* Thousand Oaks, CA: Corwin Press.

4 | LOUNGE TALK

BACKGROUND INFORMATION

Role conflict occurs when you face two or more incompatible expectations regarding your behavior as an administrator. This problem is common in organizations including districts and schools. In the case of principals, for example, teachers, students, and parents have dissimilar preferences regarding administrative behavior. Some want principals to be relationship oriented—that is, friendly and caring administrators who value and respond to individual needs, interests, and goals. Others want principals to be task oriented—that is, firm and decisive administrators who value and respond to institutional needs, interests, and goals.

Role conflict has always been a concern for administrators, because public schools operate at a point where individual rights and societal rights (Levin, 1999) and professionalism and democracy (Kowalski, 1995) intersect. On the one hand, superintendents and principals are expected to be competent, professional leaders making critical recommendations that determine what should be done to improve schools. On the other hand, they are expected to be efficient managers subservient to the will of the people (Wirt & Kirst, 2001). In fact, consequential policy is rarely established by one individual; rather, it is promulgated in political arenas in which individuals and groups seek to advance or protect their interests. In the realm of school reform, dissimilar philosophies and political dispositions virtually ensure that every proposed change to policy or programs will be opposed by one or more stakeholder groups (Kowalski, 2006).

Studies of role conflict and leadership styles have contributed to theory building in the areas of *transformational* and *charismatic* leadership. As Yukl noted (1989), these two terms:

> . . . refer to the process of influencing major changes in the attitudes and assumptions of organization members and building commitment for the organization's mission and objectives. Transformational leadership is usually defined more broadly than charismatic leadership, but there is considerable overlap between the two conceptions. (p. 204)

The seminal work of Burns (1978) described two contrasting administrative styles: *transactional* and *transformational leadership*. Transactional leaders tend to believe that people are primarily motivated by self-interests, and accordingly, they attempt to control behavior in others by offering rewards or threatening punishments (Yukl, 2006). Transformational leaders, by comparison, make others more aware of their responsibilities, induce them to transcend self-interests by behaving professionally, and emphasize higher-order needs, such as self-esteem and self-actualization (Bass, 1985). Though these two styles are distinct, they are not mutually exclusive; that is, administrators have used both depending on problems, issues, and contextual variables. Even so, the transactional style has been more prevalent historically in all types of organizations (Bennis & Nanus, 1985).

Over the past 3 decades, transformational leadership has been promoted as a normative standard for school administrators (Kowalski, 2010; Kowalski, Petersen, & Fusarelli, 2007). Advocacy stems from the conviction that organizational change most often occurs in situations where administrators believe in and trust people around them (Bennis, 1984). In the case of schools, for example, transformational principals are more likely than transactional principals to facilitate the development of shared school visions and acceptable strategic plans. Other characteristics of a transformational principal are likely to include:

- Being concerned that teachers and other school employees grow professionally and achieve self-efficacy.
- Treating teachers as peer professionals and not subordinates.
- Treating schools as learning communities in which important decisions are made democratically, individuals care about each other, and every student is treated as if he or she were a family member.

In this case, four high school teachers discuss their perceptions of the school's new principal. Three of them disapprove of her leadership style. In subtle ways, they question whether gender, age, and administrative inexperience affect her behavior. As you read this case, determine the extent to which role conflict is evident and reflect on the concepts of transactional and transformational leadership as sources of conflict. Also, imagine that you are a teacher in the school so that you can develop a personal perspective as to whether you would support this principal.

Key Areas for Reflection

1. Transformational and transactional leadership styles
2. Principal succession
3. Role conflict
4. Teacher expectations of principal behavior
5. Leadership style and change in schools

THE CASE

After Peter Weller entered the teachers' lounge, the room fell silent. Three colleagues—Debra Lowler, Linda Mays, and Jake Brumwell—were seated at one of the four small, round tables scattered randomly across the room. No one else was present. Having a common preparation period, the four teachers often spent 10 to 15 minutes a day discussing various issues while enjoying a cup of coffee.

Peter nodded as he sat down in the remaining chair at the table, but the silence continued. After a few seconds he asked, "OK, why did everyone quit talking? You look like my students after I catch them doing something wrong."

"Peter," Linda answered, "We were just discussing your favorite principal. Maybe she has a hidden listening device in this room and, after hearing our comments, sent you here to defend her!" After a brief pause, she added, "Just a joke, Peter, so don't get hostile."

Peter said, "Don't you have more important topics to discuss? I know you have a penchant for critiquing administrators and your colleagues, but your obsession with Dr. Werner is unhealthy. Ease up."

Colleen Werner had been appointed principal of Drewerton South High School, one of two high schools in the district, less than a year before. She is only the second principal in the school's 14-year history. With an enrollment of just over 1,000 students, South High School serves the most affluent neighborhoods in an upscale suburban community.

George Calbo, South High School's first and only other principal, retired at the end of the previous year. He was well liked by most of the faculty and support staff. Prior to becoming principal, he had taught social studies, coached basketball, and served as an assistant principal at Drewerton High School, then the only high school in the district. As the founding principal at South High School, he was able to personally select the school's new employees. Many of them were his friends and long-time colleagues.

The announcement that Dr. Colleen Werner would succeed Principal Calbo surprised a great many stakeholders, including faculty and staff at South High School. The superintendent had received more than 50 applications for the position, including nine from current district employees. Among the final five candidates, Dr. Werner was the only one not currently employed in the Drewerton district and the only female. Most observers concluded that she was merely the "token female candidate," especially since she was considerably younger (32 years old at the time of her appointment), less experienced, and less politically connected than the others.

The fact that Dr. Werner and her predecessor were opposites was evident almost immediately— even to most students. Mr. Calbo had devoted much of his time to managing people and material resources; Dr. Werner relegated these responsibilities to her two assistants. She devoted much of her time to visiting classrooms, working on curriculum projects, and building relationships with parents and students. Mr. Calbo spent nearly 2 hours every day in the teachers' lounge, listening to concerns and complaints, discussing politics, and seeking the latest gossip. Dr. Werner, on the other hand, rarely went to the teachers' lounge, and when she did, she usually stayed only long enough to pour a cup of coffee.

Peter Weller was one of only five or six South High School teachers who thought that Dr. Werner was more effective than her predecessor. He stated this conviction openly, especially when his colleagues questioned Principal Werner's competence. His disposition toward the new principal baffled his colleagues because Peter had always spoken positively of Principal Calbo. When challenged on this point, Peter explained that he admired Mr. Calbo's good intentions, most notably, his concern for teachers and students and his willingness to help them when needed. He added, however, that he thought Mr. Calbo was more of a politician than an educator. He saw Dr. Werner in a different light. In his eyes, she, too, cared deeply about others but her behavior was professional rather than political.

After a minute of silence, Peter spoke again. "I think I know why you became silent when I entered. You were skewering Dr. Werner again, weren't you? What did she do now?"

Jake responded, "We have to talk about somebody, and it might as well be Colleen-the-Great."

"Lately, she's the only one you talk about. You seem to be obsessed with her," Peter noted.

Debra Lowler, usually the least expressive member of the group, spoke next. "I'll tell you what bothers me about Colleen. It's her repeated comments about how we should behave professionally. She uses 'professional' as a code word that means 'do extra work without additional compensation.' Instead of looking out for us, she promotes the idea that we should assume additional responsibilities without being compensated. George [Calbo], on the other hand, fought for us. He knows what it is like to be a teacher. If the superintendent or the school board wants us to do extra jobs, let them pay us accordingly."

"Agreed," Linda chimed in, "George defended us. He even advised us, privately of course, not to do more without additional compensation. He knew how to manipulate the superintendent and school board. He never let them walk all over us."

"You really believe that Colleen doesn't care about teachers?" Peter asked. "She was and still is a teacher at heart. She knows what the public expects of us. Did you ever consider that she wants everyone, including students, to be treated fairly? Just because she doesn't praise you every minute of the day and just because she isn't dangling 'carrots' in front of you constantly doesn't mean she's indifferent or disrespectful."

Jake Brumwell, a mathematics teacher and track coach, was Mr. Calbo's closest friend and biggest defender in the group. He spoke next.

"Peter, Colleen is not ready for this job. She still has a lot to learn, especially about working with teachers. Just last week, for example, she asked if I would chaperone a weekend camping trip with a group of students in June. The trip is part of a dropout prevention program, so you know the type of kids who will be involved. Two other teachers already have agreed to be chaperones, but she wants me to go too because she thinks I can connect personally with several of the students. When I asked her how much I would get paid for playing nursemaid in the woods, she looked at me like I was an extortionist. That condescending look made me mad. I told her I was too busy to go camping. Now, I presume, she has labeled me as being unprofessional. If George was handling the camping trip, he would have secured necessary resources to pay the chaperones or he would have canceled the event."

Peter then said, "Well, Jake, I'm one of the volunteer chaperones. Did you know that Colleen is the other? And I know for a fact that she asked you to participate because several students involved think highly of you."

Debra came to Jake's defense. "Sure, Colleen is going. But she has a 12-month contract. So technically she's being paid for going on the trip."

"Wrong again," Peter shot back. "To my knowledge, she does not get additional compensation for going on a camping trip that starts on Friday afternoon and ends Saturday evening."

Linda entered the conversation again. "Look, it's more than just asking us to give up our time. Colleen's whole approach toward being principal is different. She doesn't do things George's way. You say Colleen cares about us. I disagree. She only cares about students—and she cares too much about the wrong students. Maybe her empathy for at-risk students is self-serving. Maybe she thinks the school board will reward her for being kind and considerate. Since you're her apologist, you should teach her an important lesson—teachers, not students, are going to determine if she succeeds at South High School."

"I agree totally with Linda. Colleen needs to know that principals don't do well in this district without teacher support," Jake noted. "Personally, I think she would be better off paying more attention to our best students. Maybe the high achievers should be the ones who go on camping trips and receive other favors from the principal. If you ask me, Colleen is sending the wrong message to students—and she certainly has not sent any positive messages to us."

Peter was frustrated. "Do you realize that I'm not the only one in the school who supports Colleen?" he asked rhetorically. "Why don't you give her credit for things she's accomplished in a short time? What about the way she helped Deloris Hutchins? Prior to Dr. Werner's working with her, she was an ineffective teacher. Colleen helped her improve her planning skills and classroom management. All George ever did was conceal her deficiencies. Deloris has become a more competent teacher, and she openly admits that Colleen is primarily responsible. Based on this evidence, tell me who is the better principal—the one who made excuses for poor teaching or the one who did something about it? I'll tell you how Deloris answers that question. She thinks Dr. Werner is the best administrator she has known. To casually charge that Colleen doesn't care about teachers is irresponsible."

Jake responded, "See, that's what I was trying to say a minute ago. No matter if she is dealing with teachers or students, she cares a lot more about low performers than she does about high performers. Where is the recognition for teachers who always have done a good job? Instead of praise and rewards, I get invited to spend a weekend with at-risk students in the woods! And because I said no, she probably thinks I'm insensitive. Listen, Peter, I don't like the way Werner operates. She's never going to be effective unless she wises up and develops political savvy."

Peter just shook his head in disbelief. He recognized that converting his colleagues to his way of thinking was probably impossible. There had been at least a dozen previous conversations similar to this one and each had ended with the four teachers refusing to yield their convictions. Yet the disagreements never affected their personal relationships. Peter and the others had conveniently decided to agree to disagree.

"Well, colleagues," Peter said as he stood up, "time to get back to work. But before I leave, I tell you again that you are wrong about Colleen. I hope you're teaching your students to be more objective than you are. Dr. Werner is a bright, energetic leader. She's not perfect, but who is?"

"Wipe that smile off your face," Linda said. "Don't you recognize that you have lost another argument? Just to show you that I'm open-minded, I'll concede that Colleen has good intentions— just as you conceded that George had good intentions. Regrettably, she is terribly misguided about everything else."

Jake added sarcastically, "Yeah, I'll give her a 'B' for effort and a 'D' for achievement!"

The group always had a way of ending their discussions with a little humor, perhaps to ease the tension. The four teachers scattered down different hallways to their next classes and their thoughts quickly shifted to other matters.

Problem Framing

1. Assume you are Dr. Werner. First determine the main issue (problem) in this case. Then describe the current state and the desired state of this issue. (The section on problem framing in the Introduction section of this book defines the problem framing process.)

2. Based on evidence provided in the case, describe the difficulty associated with eliminating the gap between the present state and desired state.

Questions and Suggested Activities

1. Share and critique the problem statements prepared by students in your class.
2. Do you agree with the teachers who are critical of Dr. Werner? Why or why not?
3. As principal, would you be concerned if teachers had vastly different expectations of your leadership style? Why or why not?
4. Do you think that Dr. Werner should spend more time in the teachers' lounge? Why or why not?
5. Describe and then compare the leadership styles of the previous principal, Mr. Calbo, and the current principal, Dr. Werner. Discuss the strengths and weaknesses of each style.
6. What evidence would you use to determine if a principal was transactional or transformational?
7. What do you view as the strengths and weaknesses of a transformational principal?
8. Assume that Peter Weller has never informed Dr. Werner of the criticisms being voiced about her. Should he do so?
9. What, if anything, should Dr. Werner do to establish improved relations with the faculty and staff?
10. Do you believe that the four teachers in this case have behaved professionally by critiquing the principal? Why or why not?
11. One of the teachers, Jake Brumwell, suggests that Dr. Werner should pay more attention to good students. Do you agree with him? Why or why not?

Suggested Readings

Bogler, R. (2001). The influence of leadership style on teacher job satisfaction. *Educational Administration Quarterly, 37*(5), 662–683.

Donaldson, G., Marnik, G., Mackenzie, S., & Ackerman, R. (2009). What makes or breaks a principal. *Educational Leadership, 67*(2), 8–14.

Duncan, P. K., & Seguin, C. A. (2002). The perfect match: A case study of a first-year woman principal. *Journal of School Leadership, 12*(6), 608–639.

Eden, D. (1998). The paradox of school leadership. *Journal of Educational Administration, 36*(3–4), 249–261.

Hallinger, P. (1992). The evolving role of the American principals: From managerial to instructional to transformational leaders. *Journal of Educational Administration, 3*(3), 35–48.

Hart, A. (1991). Leader succession and socialization: A synthesis. *Review of Educational Research, 61*, 451–474.

Hart, A. (1993). *Principal succession: Establishing leadership in schools.* Albany: State University of New York Press.

Kochan, F. K., Spencer, W. A., & Mathews, J. G. (2000). Gender-based perceptions of the challenges, changes, and essential skills of the principalship. *Journal of School Leadership, 10*(4), 290–310.

Kowalski, T. J. (2003). *Contemporary school administration: An introduction* (2nd ed.). Boston: Allyn and Bacon (see Chapters 9 and 15).

Leithwood, K. (1992). The move toward transformational leadership. *Educational Leadership, 49*(5), 8–12.

Marks, H. M., & Printy, S. M. (2003). Principal leadership and school performance: An integration of transformational and instructional leadership. *Educational Administration Quarterly, 39*(3), 370–397.

Meadows, B. (1992). Nurturing cooperation and responsibility in a school environment. *Phi Delta Kappan, 73*(6), 480–481.

Ogawa, R. (1991). Enchantment, disenchantment, and accommodation: How a faculty made sense of the succession of its principal. *Educational Administration Quarterly, 27*(1), 30–60.

Pepper, K., & Thomas, L. H. (2002). Making a change: The effects of the leadership role on school. *Learning Environments Research, 5*(2), 155–166.

Peterson, K., & Kelley, C. (2001). Transforming school leadership. *Leadership, 30*(3), 8–11.

Roesner, C. (1987). Principals' leadership behavior: Do you see yourself as your subordinates see you? *NASSP Bulletin, 71*(502), 68–71.

Rossmiller, R. (1992). The secondary school principal and teachers' quality of work life. *Educational Management and Administration, 20*(3), 132–146.

Tschannen-Moran, M. (2009). Fostering teacher professionalism in schools: The role of leadership orientation and trust. *Educational Administration Quarterly, 45*(2), 217–247.

Valentine, J., & Bowman, M. (1991). Effective principal, effective school: Does research support the assumption? *NASSP Bulletin, 75*(539), 1–7.

Wallace, D. D., & Colbert, E. (2002). Not just idle talk. *Principal Leadership (High School Ed.), 2*(7), 42–44.

Wells, D. (1985). The perfect principal: A teacher's fantasy. *Principal, 65*(1), 27.

References

Bass, B. M. (1985). *Leadership and performance beyond expectations.* New York: Free Press.

Bennis, W. B. (1984). The four competencies of leadership. *Training and Development Journal, 38*(8), 14–19.

Bennis, W. B., & Nanus, B. (1985). *Leaders: The strategies for taking charge.* New York: Harper & Row.

Burns, J. (1978). *Leadership.* New York: Harper and Row.

Kowalski, T. J. (1995). Preparing teachers to be leaders: Barriers in the workplace. In M. O'Hair & S. Odell (Eds.), *Educating teachers for leadership and change: Teacher education yearbook III* (pp. 243–256). Thousand Oaks, CA: Corwin.

Kowalski, T. J. (2006). *The school superintendent: Theory, practice, and cases* (2nd ed.). Thousand Oaks, CA: Sage.

Kowalski, T. J. (2010). *The school principal: Visionary leadership and competent management.* New York: Routledge.

Kowalski, T. J., Petersen, G. J., & Fusarelli, L. D. (2007). *Effective communication for school administrators: An imperative in an information age.* Lanham, MD: Rowman and Littlefield Education.

Levin, H. M. (1999). The public-private nexus in education. *American Behavioral Scientist, 43*(1), 124–137.

Wirt, F., & Kirst, M. (2001). *The political dynamics of American education.* Berkeley, CA: McCutchan.

Yukl, G. (1989). *Leadership in organizations* (2nd ed.). Englewood Cliffs, NJ: Prentice-Hall.

Yukl, G. (2006). *Leadership in organizations* (6th ed.). Upper Saddle River, NJ: Pearson, Prentice Hall.

5 | THE CAREER CENTER'S REVOLVING DOOR

BACKGROUND INFORMATION

Career and Technical Education (CTE) evolved from vocational education and has the mission of providing students knowledge and skills in occupations. CTE programs are supposed to enhance students' employability after high school and prepare them for postsecondary education opportunities related to specific occupations, especially those entailing technical skills (Association for Career and Technical Education, N.D.). In many states, students are provided CTE in career-technical centers, autonomous institutions serving students from districts that are part of a joint-services agreement or confederation of school systems.

Historically, vocational schools, and now career-technical centers, enrolled a considerable number of students for the wrong reasons. Specifically, they became a depository for troubled students who were not succeeding in traditional schools for various reasons—such as having academic deficiencies, lacking motivation, or having behavior-related problems. Consequently, teaching in a CTE institution can be especially stressful for teachers who are unprepared to deal with special-needs students.

The No Child Left Behind Act (NCLB) magnified tensions faced by many teachers in CTE schools. The federal law requires 11th-grade students to take state proficiency tests in reading and mathematics and career-technical centers are not excluded. Under NCLB regulations, all schools must make adequate yearly progress resulting in 100% of the students scoring proficient or above by the year 2014. In addition, schools are to achieve a 95% graduation rate, meet the needs of limited-English proficient students, and employ highly qualified teachers (Shibley, 2005).

Across all types of schools, teachers are most likely to leave the profession at some point during the first 3 years of employment (Ingersol, 2001). Although there are multiple reasons why they exit, stress and a lack of confidence are two of the more pervasive causes. Therefore, many forward-thinking administrators have devised induction programs intended to help novice teachers make positive adjustments (Kowalski, 2010). The need for such assistance is especially high in the realm of CTE schools because the likelihood of working with troubled students is typically greater than in traditional high schools (Backes & Burns, 2008).

This case study describes a career center that has had an especially high turnover rate of teachers in academic areas, most notably in English and mathematics. The center's principal shows little interest in trying to provide assistance to novice teachers and his inattention to the issue leads to his dismissal. As you read this case, pretend that you have just been employed as the center's new principal. Therefore, your ability to diagnose problems and to manage them are important to the center's success and your career.

Key Areas for Reflection
1. Challenges of CTE
2. Problems faced by teachers in CTE schools
3. Helping novice teachers
4. Principal's responsibility to support novice teachers

THE CASE

The Cramer Valley Career Center (CVCC) is operated by a confederation of 16 school districts collectively operating 31 traditional high schools. Located on a 22-acre campus, the CVCC facility was constructed in 1993 and provides 44 technical programs to approximately 730 students in Grades 11 and 12. The center also offers adult education and continuing education programs during evening hours.

Under state law, the CVCC operates as an independent entity with its own school board. The board has 16 members, one each from the school districts making up the confederation. Each confederation school district determines how its representative is appointed. Four of the CVCC board members are also school district board members and the remaining 12 members are administrators (district superintendents, assistant superintendents, or high school principals). The chief executive officer is employed by the CVCC board and holds the title of superintendent. Another administrator is designated as the center's principal. The principal functions as the center's instructional leader and reports directly to the superintendent.

Linda Black, a former superintendent in one of the confederation's school districts, became the CVCC superintendent 2 years ago. The principal, Max Branton, has been employed at the center for 28 years and in his present role for 13 years. The center also employs two additional administrators, a business manager/treasurer and an assistant principal, and 46 full-time and 12 part-time instructors.

Because students attend CVCC full time, the institution employs teachers for academic subjects, such as English, science, and mathematics. Since the passage of NCLB, these teachers in particular have been pressured to elevate student performance on state achievement tests. The strain has been apparent. As an example, the longest-serving math teacher has only been at the school for 2 years, and the two most recently employed math teachers have left after only 1 year.

Discussing concerns about meeting NCLB standards, Superintendent Black has told the board members that the school has been experiencing difficulty employing and retaining math teachers. She says that the problem is twofold. First, meeting NCLB standards is extremely difficult given the number of special-needs students attending the school. Second, employing competent math teachers is difficult even in high-performing traditional high schools. Both she and Principal Branton have taken the position that the federal law is unrealistic and is likely to be rescinded after policymakers realize that some of its goals are unattainable. Although some board members accepted this explanation, others thought that the superintendent and principal were not doing enough to deal with the rapid turnover of math teachers.

Though Principal Branton was the school's designated instructional leader, his behavior did not comply with that responsibility. Popular with employees, he only visited classrooms to complete mandatory observations required by policy. And during his tenure as principal, he has never recommended the dismissal of a teacher for incompetence, neglect of duty, or any other reason. Instead of trying to improve instructional quality, the principal argued that NCLB was responsible for setting unattainable standards for career centers.

After both novice math teachers submitted their resignations, the CVCC board president appointed a five-member committee to investigate why the school was unable to retain these teachers. The committee, chaired by an assistant superintendent for instruction in one of the confederation districts, issued a report criticizing the center's superintendent and principal. The document indicated that neither administrator had made an effort to help novice teachers adjust to their profession and to their specific roles in the CVCC. After interviewing the two math teachers who had recently resigned, the committee learned that the superintendent had never visited either of them and the principal had only entered their classrooms once each semester—the minimum required for conducting observations. Yet, the teachers received excellent ratings and were told to keep up the good work.

One of the two math teachers had sent 11 emails to the principal over the course of her employment asking him to provide her with assistance or at least guidance regarding disruptive students. The principal only answered two of the emails, and both responses advised the novice teacher to seek advice from an experienced teacher. The other novice math teacher who had resigned had twice told the principal he was actively seeking other employment because he was dissatisfied with conditions at the CVCC. The principal simply reacted by saying that he hoped the teacher would remain at the center.

After the committee's report was issued, the CVCC board met privately with Superintendent Black. She said that she had been unaware of the limited contact that had occurred between the principal and the two novice math teachers because she did not interfere in instructional issues. Most board members were stunned by her response. Several criticized her passive attitude openly by blaming her for allowing the principal to neglect his responsibility as the center's instructional leader.

The candidness caught Superintendent Black off guard and she was unsure how to respond. Many of the board members were personal friends and in light of the comments, she felt she was being treated unfairly. Before the meeting concluded, the board directed her to meet with Principal Branton and to prepare a response to the report.

After Black shared the committee's report and board's reaction to it with Branton, he became furious. Rather than discussing the issues rationally, he reacted emotionally and criticized the board members. He claimed that most of the board members knew little or nothing about CTE and that their only interest as board members was to ensure that their regular high schools had a place to send problem students. After witnessing his reactions, Black began to think that the board's criticisms might be warranted. She expressed her disappointment in his knee-jerk reaction to a serious problem and told him to develop induction and orientation programs to address the concerns. He responded by saying, "I'll think about it."

Rather than doing what the superintendent had requested, Principal Branton sought political support from his many faculty allies. He provided them with his interpretation of the board's criticisms and implied that the board was intending to make major changes at the school, including the possibility of demanding more from teachers. He also described Superintendent Black as being intimidated and incapable of defending the school and its employees.

Over the next 5 weeks, three additional things occurred that reflected negatively on the principal.

1. His negative comments became known to Black and several of the CVCC board members.
2. He confronted the two math teachers who had resigned and berated them for having put him in a difficult position.
3. Rather than developing induction and orientation programs, he informed the superintendent that he does not make policy; he carries out policy.

Prior to the next board meeting, Superintendent Black met with Principal Branton and told him, "Your behavior over the last several weeks is totally unacceptable. I have decided that you cannot remain principal. You have 2 weeks to give me a letter of resignation; otherwise, I will recommend to the board that you be dismissed."

Branton responded, "I'm not resigning. If you want to jeopardize your job by trying to fire me, you're not very smart."

Two weeks later, Superintendent Black, as promised, recommended that Mr. Branton not be retained as principal. Since he had tenure, he could remain at the center as a teacher if he opted to do so. Although the board approved her recommendation, the members told her privately that unless she retained a competent principal and addressed the problems that were contributing to staffing instability, she, too, would be dismissed.

Problem Framing

1. Assume you are the principal Superintendent Black employs to replace Mr. Branton. First determine the main issue (problem) in this case. Then describe the current state and the desired state of this issue. (The section on problem framing in the Introduction section of this book defines the problem framing process.)

2. Based on evidence provided in the case, describe the difficulty associated with eliminating the gap between the present state and desired state.

Questions and Suggested Activities

1. Share and critique the problem statements prepared by students in your class.
2. What is the difference between an induction program and an orientation program? Are both really necessary? Why or why not?
3. Based on your experience and knowledge, do you believe that CTE schools are a depository for troubled students?
4. To what extent is the board accurate in criticizing Superintendent Black for not intervening to address staffing instability?
5. Evaluate the principal's personal relationships with many of the teachers at the school. As the new principal, do you consider this issue to be relevant? Why or why not?
6. As the new principal, you must develop an induction program for novice teachers. What would you include in this program?
7. Do teachers in career-technical centers really have to deal with more difficult students? What evidence do you have to support your response?
8. When confronted with the committee's report, the superintendent responds that she does not interfere in instructional issues since the principal, by virtue of board policy, is the center's instructional leader. If you were a board member, would you accept this explanation? Why or why not?
9. As the new principal, describe what you want in terms of a working relationship with the superintendent?

Suggested Readings

Calabrese, R., & Tucker-Ladd, P. (1991). The principal and assistant principal: A mentoring relationship. *NASSP Bulletin, 75*(533), 67–74.

Duke, D. (1992). Concepts of administrative effectiveness and the evaluation of school administrators. *Journal of Personnel Evaluation in Education, 6*(2), 103–121.

Gerke, W. (2004). More than a disciplinarian. *Principal Leadership, 5*(3), 39–41.

Goodson, C. P. (2000). Assisting the assistant principal. *Principal, 79*(4), 56–57.

Johnson, C. M. (2004). Reflections on the vice principalship. *Leadership, 34*(1), 32–34.

Johnston, D. L. (1999). The seven no-no's of performance evaluation. *School Administrator, 56*(11), 47–48.

Lang, R. (1986). The hidden dress code dilemma. *Clearing House, 59*(6), 277–279.

Manatt, R. P. (2000). Feedback at 360 degrees. *School Administrator, 57*(9), 10–11.

Marshall, C. (1992). *The assistant principal: Leadership chores and challenges.* Newbury Park, CA: Corwin.

Marshall, C., & Greenfield, W. (1985). The socialization of the assistant principal: Implications for school leadership. *Education and Urban Society, 18*(1), 3–8.

Michel, G. J. (1996). *Socialization and career orientation of the assistant principal.* (ERIC Document Reproduction Service No. ED395 381)

Norton, M. S., & Kriekard, J. (1987). Real and ideal competencies for the assistant principal. *NASSP Bulletin, 71*(501), 23–30.

Richard, A. (2000, April 12). Toughest job in education? *Education Week, 19*(31), 44–48.

Russo, A. (2004). Evaluating administrators with portfolios. *School Administrator, 61*(9), 34–38.

Weller, L. D., & Weller, S. J. (2002). *The assistant principal: Essentials for effective school leadership.* Thousand Oaks, CA: Corwin Press.

References

Association for Career-Technical Education (N.D.). *CTE information and research.* Retrieved from http://www.acteonline.org/cteresearch.aspx.

Backes, C., & Burns, J. Z. (2008). New career-technical teachers: What gets them, and why is it important to know? *Journal of Industrial Teacher Education, 45*(1), 100–112.

Ingersol, R. M. (2001). Teacher turnover and teacher shortages: An organizational analysis. *American Education Research Journal, 38*(3), 499–534.

Kowalski, T. J. (2010). *The school principal: Visionary leadership and competent management.* New York: Routledge.

Shibley, I. A. (2005). One school's approach to No Child Left Behind. *Techniques, 80*(4), 50–53.

6 | LET THE COMMITTEE DECIDE

BACKGROUND INFORMATION

During the typical work day, administrators make dozens of decisions. Most are simple and non-threatening, such as deciding what to wear to work or what to eat for lunch. Others, however, have relatively high levels of uncertainty—that is, the outcomes of known choices are largely unknown and potentially detrimental (Kowalski, Lasley, & Mahoney, 2008). Consider a high school principal who adopts block scheduling without knowing the extent to which parents support the idea. If they oppose the concept after it is adopted, the principal and the school may become embroiled in conflict.

Basically, a decision has three components: a goal (what the administrator wants to accomplish by making a decision), options for attaining the goal (known alternatives), and the selection of the preferred option (Welch, 2002). The manner in which an administrator actually makes decisions is determined by an intricate mix of personal and contextual factors. On a personal level, behavior is shaped by the decision maker's philosophical dispositions (personal values and beliefs), biases, and leadership style (Kowalski, 2006). Contextually, it is affected by demands and constraints generated by society or by the employing district or school (Sergiovanni, 2005). When making consequential decisions, administrators are urged to consider both normative and descriptive paradigms; the former prescribe an approach for decision making and the latter explain how decisions often have been made. Four decision models have been especially prevalent in the literature on school administration (Estler, 1988).

1. *Rational-bureaucratic*: A normative paradigm emphasizing problem analysis, data collection, alternative choices, and the objective selection of the ideal decision.
2. *Participatory*: A normative paradigm nested in beliefs that participation increases productivity, morale, and the quality of information.
3. *Political*: A descriptive paradigm that shows that difficult decisions are often made through compromise.
4. *Organized anarchy*: A descriptive paradigm revealing that many decisions are made through a mix of changing participants, opportunities for change, and predetermined preferences.

Studying various models used by district and school officials, Tarter and Hoy (1998) concluded that none was universally superior. Nevertheless, these paradigms facilitate an understanding of decision-making behavior, especially in relation to answering two essential questions about process: Were essential decision-making activities completed? What processes were used to complete the activities?

Scholars have long recognized that personal, social, and political variables lead to behavioral inconsistencies in decision making. For example, the extent to which a problem has political implications may influence both a principal's decision process and the actual decision (Kowalski et al., 2008). In the realm of professions, decisions based largely on emotion, politics, or bias are viewed negatively because they elevate uncertainty—and uncertainty elevates risk (Kowalski, 2009a, 2009b). Risk refers to the possibility that a decision will have detrimental effects for the school, the administrator, or both. Decision-making models are intended to control individualism, political influence, and errors either by prescribing a process or by describing effective and ineffective processes. In seeking to guide administrator decision making, Drucker (1974) reduced the process to five steps:

1. Defining the problem
2. Analyzing the problem
3. Developing alternative solutions
4. Selecting a best solution
5. Taking action

Rational decision making is rooted in classical theories that prompt administrators to make important decisions alone. Researchers studying district and school administrators (e.g., Crowson, 1989; Konold & Kauffman, 2009; Walker, 1994), however, have found that rational models, such as Drucker's proposed paradigm, either have not been deployed consistently or have not been deployed as intended. Deviations reflect the fact that educational institutions are sociopolitical systems in which power and authority are distributed among individuals and groups. Consequently, efforts to make objective choices (i.e., decisions based primarily on data or other forms of evidence) often are influenced by subjective pressures exerted by individuals and groups with competing interests.

Participatory decision making increasingly has been advocated as the normative process for school improvement (Anderson, 1998; Guthrie & Schuermann, 2009). Involving others, and especially teachers, is deemed appropriate for at least three reasons:

1. In a democratic society, employees, parents, and others have a right to be involved in critical matters.
2. The quality of decisions is enhanced by a broader knowledge base and a variety of viewpoints.
3. Participation increases employee morale and productivity (Kowalski, 2003).

Shared decision making, however, is neither simple nor problem-free. For example, the process frequently is inefficient (Clark, Clark, & Irvin, 1997), produces decisions based on social unity rather than on evidence (a condition referred to as "groupthink;" Janis, 1982), and increases the probability of bias and error (Carroll & Johnson, 1990). Moreover, administrators involved in participatory decision making may be criticized for relegating important decisions to committees (Kowalski et al., 2008).

This case describes a new superintendent's decision to address a controversial issue by appointing a special committee having representatives of various stakeholder groups. The conflict (over whether principals should have autonomous activity funds) and the superintendent's preference for a participatory approach to resolving the conflict spawn additional tensions among the administrators. When a decision is made by the committee, several key figures criticize the superintendent's leadership style.

Key Areas for Reflection

1. Decision making
2. Conflict and conflict resolution
3. Use of committees
4. Subordinate expectations of a new superintendent
5. Leadership style

THE CASE

Fullmer, a city of 45,000 residents, is the seat of government for Oxford County (population 78,000). Located in the western part of a mid-Atlantic state, it is known for its scenic beauty. In recent years, the population has increased about 1% every 2 years, almost entirely due to the development of retirement properties (e.g., condominiums and apartments).

Over the past 20 years, most other counties in the state have benefitted financially from economic and industrial development. For example, school districts in two neighboring counties have actually lowered property tax rates as a result of growing assessed valuations. Residents of Oxford County, however, have opposed industrial development, fearing that manufacturing companies would be detrimental to the community's character and pristine environment. In the absence of commercial development, Oxford County's property tax rates have increased modestly but steadily during the same period.

In addition to its natural beauty, Oxford County has attracted retirees for three other reasons. First, real estate costs remain modest, especially when compared to states in the Northeast and Midwest; second, the climate is mild but residents can enjoy all four seasons; third, a new hospital, costing just over $90 million, has attracted additional health care providers.

The School District

The Oxford County School District (OCSD), the only public school system in the county, enrolls slightly less than 20,000 students in two high schools, four middle schools, 13 elementary schools, and a career-technical center. The district's total enrollment has essentially remained constant for the past decade.

The district's top three administrators are Rudy Quillen, the superintendent, Bob Andrevet, assistant superintendent for curriculum, and Pamela Davis, assistant superintendent for business management. The two assistants have been in their current positions for 14 and 10 years, respectively. Dr. Quillen recently replaced a superintendent who had occupied the position for 11 years.

The Incident

Dr. Quillen arrived in Oxford County in mid-July. For the previous 3 years, he had been superintendent in a much smaller district (enrollment 2,400) in a neighboring state. While making a presentation at a national conference, he attracted the attention of two OCSD board members who were in the audience. Impressed with his performance, they had encouraged him to apply for the superintendent vacancy in their district. Though only 38 years old, Rudy Quillen already had 12 years of administrative experience.

Soon after he began his new position, Dr. Quillen faced his first controversy. District schools had autonomous activity funds; that is, the funds were managed independently by principals. This arrangement had existed for as long as anyone could remember. Two years earlier, however, the previous superintendent received a written recommendation from Dr. Davis, the assistant superintendent for business, to place the activity funds under district controls. Doing so would give her fiduciary responsibility for the funds. When principals found out, most strongly opposed the recommendation and as a result, the superintendent rejected the recommendation. He defended his decision by saying that there were too many unanswered questions about centralized control of the funds.

Dr. Davis formerly served as a principal in the district, so she was well aware of how activity funds could and were being managed. Even after the former superintendent rejected her recommendation, she continued to tell school board members that the potential for misusing the funds, legally and ethically, was extensive. In light of the superintendent's excuse for not presenting her recommendation to the school board, she developed a formal plan framed by three notable changes:

1. At present, all activity fund expenditures were approved solely by a principal. She proposed that activity fund expenditures would require three signatures—that of the principal, the assistant superintendent for instruction, and the assistant superintendent for business management.

2. At present, activity fund accounting procedures were determined by principals. She proposed that all accounting activities would be completed by district personnel and would be in compliance with standard accounting procedures.

3. At present, the activity funds were audited only every other year as part of the state's audit of the entire school system (the state required that all public agencies, including schools, had to undergo a state audit every 24 months). She proposed that the activity funds be audited annually, with the district business office conducting the audit during the year in which there was no state audit.

After completing the plan, Dr. Davis again approached the previous superintendent, with a recommendation to change procedures of school activity funds. The superintendent again refused to take the matter to the school board, stating that because of his impending retirement the matter should be addressed by his successor. Although the school board members were aware of the position Dr. Davis had taken on the activity funds, they were unwilling to consider the matter formally without the superintendent taking a definitive position on the proposed plan.

Shortly after Dr. Quillen became superintendent, Dr. Davis presented him with her plan and explained why tighter controls over the activity funds would be advantageous. Although the issue of activity funds had not been raised during his employment interviews, he was aware that autonomous school activity funds were controversial. After listening politely, he agreed to read the plan and to respond in a timely manner. In weighing the plan's merits, Dr. Quillen talked with the school system's attorney and subsequently with one of the attorneys from the state school boards' association. The lawyers affirmed that autonomous school activity funds were legally permissible but, they cautioned that autonomous funds presented substantial risk of mismanagement and illegalities (e.g., embezzlement).

Next, Dr. Quillen shared the recommendation and plan developed by Dr. Davis with the principals and other district administrators at a monthly administrative council meeting. He asked them to read the plan and to provide comments before next month's meeting. During the next 4 weeks, the superintendent received feedback from only seven administrators—all were principals and all were opposed to the proposed change.

At the November administrative staff meeting, Dr. Quillen shared information he previously had received from the two attorneys and indicated that he had not yet decided whether to pursue the matter formally with the school board. He then asked for additional comments. Only a few principals elected to share their opinions and all opposed the plan. Their statements were characterized by two recurring themes: they objected to a loss of principal autonomy and authority, and they objected because there had been no known problems with the current arrangement.

Dr. Quillen spoke again. "The changes Dr. Davis is recommending provide a safety valve, for principals and for the school system. Although we may not have had problems in this school district, there have been incidents in other districts in which principals have gotten into legal or ethical difficulties because of the way they managed these funds."

One of the high school principals immediately responded. "It appears to me that we will be penalized for having managed the funds responsibly. That doesn't make sense."

At that point, Dr. Quillen asked each principal to state his or her position on the proposed change. Seventeen of the 19 principals opposed the plan; the remaining two were undecided. Dr. Davis was disappointed and surprised by the extent of the opposition to her recommendation. She told the group, "Just because I appear to be alone in supporting change does not mean that I am wrong. For example, both attorneys contacted by Dr. Quillen agree with me that the current arrangement is risky. Rather than just dismissing this matter, I suggest that persons able to be objective evaluate my recommendation."

Needing to move onto other agenda items, Dr. Quillen said, "I want to make it clear that I have not made a decision on whether to recommend the proposed changes to the school board. Nor am I prepared to decide whether to have others evaluate the plan independendently.

As pledged, Dr. Quillen revisited the activity fund controversy at the next administrators' meeting. By now, the conflict had acquired symbolic importance, and the administrators anxiously awaited the superintendent first controversial decision.

Everyone listened attentively as the superintendent began to speak.

"Most of you have shared your feelings on the activity fund proposal. Although three views have been expressed, it is clear that a majority opposes the recommended change. Some, however, believe the plan should be adopted as presented and some have urged me to accept only one part of the plan—conducting the annual audit. After weighing your input, I have decided to appoint an ad hoc committee to study this issue, evaluate the proposed change, and then make a recommendation on whether the proposed change should be presented to the school board. I am appointing the following persons to the committee: Regina Steckler, an elementary school teacher; Jackson Wells, a high school teacher; Bennett Wyler, a parent and accountant; Agnes Dupree, a parent and attorney; and Ann Major, the district's director of federal programs. Ann will chair the committee. Both assistant superintendents, Bob Andrevet and Pamela Davis, will be nonvoting advisors to the committee."

After exchanging glances with others in the room, one of the principals asked, "Why are no principals on the committee? We're the ones most directly affected."

Dr. Quillen answered. "I want the process to be as objective as possible. Most if not all of you have already made up your minds. I appointed Ann Major because she had told me she is neutral on this issue."

Immediately after the meeting, Pamela Davis met with the superintendent and expressed displeasure with the appointments to the committee. She contended that most members, especially teachers, would be influenced by principals. Likewise, Mr. Andrevet was displeased. He argued that probably 80% of the administrative staff opposed the recommendation, and by ignoring their feelings, Dr. Quillen was setting a dangerous precedent.

Problem Framing

1. Assume you are the superintendent. First determine the main issue (problem) in this case. Then describe the current state and the desired state of this issue. (The section on problem framing in the Introduction section of this book defines the problem framing process.)

2. Based on evidence provided in the case, describe the difficulty associated with eliminating the gap between the present state and desired state.

Questions and Suggested Activities

1. Share and critique the problem statements prepared by students in your class.
2. By appointing the ad hoc committee, has the superintendent undermined the authority of the assistant superintendent for business? Why or why not?
3. The assistant superintendent for business management contends that the decision on her plan should be made rationally rather than politically. What does she mean? Do you agree with her?
4. Because the superintendent is new to the district and relatively unknown to the other administrators, they believe his decision to appoint a committee is symbolically important. What does this mean?
5. Should the superintendent have appointed at least one principal to the ad hoc committee? Why or why not?
6. The strategy of appointing a committee to make a recommendation on a controversial issue is rather common in schools. What are the advantages and disadvantages of this strategy?
7. One reason principals oppose the plan is that there have not been any problems with autonomous activity funds. Do you agree that is a valid reason to leave things as they are? Why or why not?
8. The previous superintendent opted to not deal with proposed change; the current superintendent appointed a committee to study the issue. If you were the superintendent, what other options could you identify?
9. What policies exist for activity funds in your district or school?

Suggested Readings

Brost, P. (2000). Shared decision making for better schools. *Principal Leadership (Middle School Ed.) 1*(3), 58–63.

Cangelosi, B. J. (2009). Shared leadership: Lessons learned. *Principal, 88*(4), 18–21.

Conway, J. (1984). The myth, mystery and mastery of participative decision making in education. *Educational Administration Quarterly, 20*(3), 11–40.

Cuzzetto, C. E. (2000). Student activity funds: Procedures and controls. *School Business Affairs, 66*(11), 22–25.

Feld, M. (1988). The bureaucracy, the superintendent, and change. *Education and Urban Society, 47*(8), 417–444.

Jackson, J. L. (2001). Politically competent decision making. *Principal Leadership (High School Ed.), 2*(4), 25–28.

Kessler, R. (1992). Shared decision making works! *Educational Leadership, 50*(1), 36–38.

Kowalski, T. J., Lasley, T. J., & Mahoney, J. (2008). *Data-driven decisions and school leadership: Best practices for school improvement.* Boston: Allyn and Bacon (see Chapter 4).

Lakowski, G. (1987). Values and decision making in educational administration. *Educational Administration Quarterly, 23*(4), 70–82.

Meadows, B. (1990). The rewards and risks of shared leadership. *Phi Delta Kappan, 71*(7), 545–548.

Meadows, B. J., & Saltzman, M. (2002). Shared decision making: An uneasy collaboration. *Principal, 81*(4), 41–48.

Mutter, D. W., & Parker, P. J. (2004). *School money matters: A handbook for principals.* Arlington, VA: Association for Supervision and Curriculum Development.

Negroni, P. J. (1999). The right badge of courage. *School Administrator, 56*(2), 14–16.

Rshaid, G. (2009). The spirit of leadership. *Educational Leadership, 67*(2), 74–77.

Rieger, B. J. (1995). Boundary realignment in the eye of the storm. *School Administrator, 52*(2), 24–26.

Tarter, C. J., & Hoy, W. K. (1998). Toward a contingency theory of decision making. *Journal of Educational Administration, 36*(3–4), 212–228.

Turnbull, B. (2003). Research note: Shared decision making—rhetoric versus reality. *Journal of School Leadership, 13*(5), 569–579.

References

Anderson, G. L. (1998). Toward authentic participation: Deconstructing the discourses of participatory reforms in education. *American Educational Research Journal, 35*(4), 571–603.

Carroll, J. S., & Johnson, E. J. (1990). *Decision research: A field guide.* Newbury Park, CA: Sage.

Clark, S. N., Clark, D. C., & Irvin, J. L (1997). Collaborative decision making. *Middle School Journal, 28*(5), 54–56.

Crowson, R. L. (1989). Managerial ethics in educational administration: The rational choice approach. *Urban Education, 23*(4), 412–435.

Drucker, P. (1974). *Management: Tasks, responsibilities, practices.* New York: Harper and Row.

Estler, S. (1988). Decision making. In N. Boyan (Ed.), *Handbook of research on educational administration* (pp. 305–320). New York: Longman.

Guthrie, J. W., & Schuermann, P. J. (2009). *Successful school leadership: Planning, politics, performance, and power.* Boston: Allyn and Bacon.

Janis, I. L. (1982). *Groupthink* (2nd ed.). Boston: Houghton Mifflin.

Konold, T. R., & Kauffman, J. M. (2009). The No Child Left Behind Act: Making decisions without data or other reality checks. In T. J. Kowalski & T. J. Lasley (eds.), *Handbook of data-based decision making in education* (pp. 72–86). New York: Routledge.

Kowalski, T. J. (2003). *Contemporary school administration: An introduction* (2nd ed.). Boston: Allyn and Bacon.

Kowalski, T. J. (2006). *The school superintendent: Theory, practice, and cases* (2nd ed.). Thousand Oaks, CA: Sage.

Kowalski, T. J. (2009a). Evidence and decision making in professions. In T. J. Kowalski & T. J. Lasley (Eds.), *Handbook of data-based decision making in education* (pp. 3–19). New York: Routledge.

Kowalski, T. J. (2009b). Need to address evidence-based practice in educational administration. *Educational Administration Quarterly, 45,* 375–423.

Kowalski, T. J., Lasley, T. J., & Mahoney, J. (2008). *Data-driven decisions and school leadership: Best practices for school improvement.* Boston: Allyn and Bacon.

Sergiovanni, T. J. (2005). *The principalship: A reflective practice approach* (5th ed.). Boston: Allyn and Bacon.

Tarter, C. J., & Hoy, W. K. (1998). Toward a contingency theory of decision making. *Journal of Educational Administration, 36*(3–4), 212–228.

Walker, K. D. (1994). Notions of "ethical" among senior educational leaders. *Alberta Journal of Educational Research, 40*(1), 21–34.

Welch, D. A. (2002). *Decisions, decisions: The art of effective decision making.* Amherst, NY: Prometheus Books.

7 | OLD SCHOOL CULTURE AND A NEW PRINCIPAL

BACKGROUND INFORMATION

Research indicates that productive schools have principals who construct and maintain strong, positive school cultures conducive to organizational learning (e.g., Kowalski, Petersen, & Fusarelli, 2007; Sergiovanni, 2004) and to implementing reforms (e.g., Datnow & Castellano, 2001). Commonly, a strong culture is defined as a uniform set of values and beliefs, especially concerning the manner in which educators deal with problems of practice. A positive culture is one in which the shared values and beliefs are congruent with empirical evidence and other elements of the professional knowledge base (Kowalski, 2003).

Reviewing research spanning 15 years, Hallinger and Heck (1998) concluded that principals also influenced school effectiveness and student achievement in measurable but indirect ways. For example, their influence was often most discernible in school improvement documents, such as collaborative vision statements and specific planning goals.

Principals are given multiple roles, and in assuming them, they experience dissimilar and often competing stakeholder expectations (Langer & Boris-Schacter, 2003). Thus, one principal may be viewed as being successful because she is a forceful manager; another may be viewed as successful because she is an inspiring instructional leader; and a third may be viewed as being successful because she balances managerial and leadership responsibilities. In the realm of school improvement, however, scholars such as Fullan (2002) emphasize that regardless of their traditional duties, principals must be instructional leaders and change agents.

Leadership style often is shaped by an administrator's traits and skills (Hoy & Miskel, 2005). When these are the sole determinants, however, an administrator ignores contextual variables (i.e., the characteristics surrounding a situation) and behaves as if all problems and decisions were basically the same (Kowalski, 2010). For instance, a principal who believes most employees are unmotivated and uninformed makes important choices autocratically even when it is clear that political acceptance of a decision is critically important.

Shared organizational values (institutional culture) also can affect leadership style (Goldman, 1998). If an autocratic principal, for example, is employed in a school that has an institutional culture promoting and celebrating democratic decision making, he or she will be pressured to conform. Contingency models of leadership posit that the effectiveness of behavior is determined by a combination of the leader's traits and skills and contextual variables (Hoy & Miskel, 2005).

When a new principal enters a school with a leadership style incongruent with the prevailing culture, conflict almost certainly ensues. Those protective of the school's culture will seek to socialize the new principal—that is, to get him to adopt their shared values, beliefs, and assumptions. If the principal resists socialization, he will either seek to change the school's culture or to bypass it (Kowalski, 2010). As demonstrated in this case, value-based conflict between a new but highly experienced principal and teachers appears to diminish school effectiveness and prospects for school improvement.

Key Areas for Reflection
1. Principal as change agent
2. Values and beliefs as a determinant of leadership style
3. Social and political dimensions of schools
4. School culture and its effect on change initiatives
5. Resistance to change

THE CASE

Oliver Wendell Holmes Elementary School is housed in the third-oldest facility in this large California school district. Located in a deteriorating urban neighborhood, the drab brick building with its rectangular shape exemplifies the unimaginative school designs that were common prior to the 1960s. The aesthetic value of the building is also diminished by the condition of the site; as examples, the sidewalks are cracked, graffiti is visible on some exterior walls and on the playground equipment, and the lawn surrounding the school is full of weeds and litter.

John Lattimore became principal of Holmes Elementary School 3 years ago. Having previously served as principal of two of the district's other elementary schools, he has 31 years of experience as an educator with 22 of them in the role of principal. At the time he applied to be transferred to Holmes, Mr. Lattimore was principal of McKinley Elementary School, one of the best elementary schools in the district—and he was the only sitting principal in the district who expressed interest in the job. His fellow principals were baffled by his transfer request. Why would he leave a school where he was admired and respected to go to a school that has had six principals in the last 15 years?

The superintendent, Dr. Ernest Gray, and the assistant superintendent for elementary education, Dr. Roberta Danton, also were surprised by Lattimore's transfer request. At first, they thought honoring it would be a mistake. Knowing that McKinley and Holmes were very different elementary schools, the two administrators thought that the risk involved in changing his assignment outweighed possible benefits. Lattimore was highly successful at McKinley, and in the aftermath of his departure, his successor might not be able to sustain the current level of school effectiveness. On the other hand, Lattimore's leadership style might not work at Holmes. Their reservations, however, were eventually trumped by the reality of an unattractive applicant pool; among the five other applicants, none had previous experience as a principal.

During the first year at Holmes, Lattimore met with parents, got acquainted with students, and tried to develop a positive working relationship with staff. He has a pleasant personality and most everyone liked him. After that year, he began pursuing change by trying to alter rules and practices for out-of-school suspensions and for first-grade retentions. Among the district's 36 elementary schools, Holmes had the highest rates in both categories. Although the teachers were aware of this data and although many of them had come to like Principal Lattimore, they remained opposed to adopting new approaches. Frustrated by their inflexibility, he eventually decided to act unilaterally.

Two weeks after the regular school term ended, Lattimore sent a letter to teachers and support staff announcing that changes regarding suspensions and grade retentions would be made in the student handbook. School student handbooks were routinely revised in June, submitted to the superintendent in July, and presented to the school board for approval at the first board meeting in August. His letter to the teachers and support staff identified these specific changes:

- Out-of-school suspensions would be restricted to violations requiring such action by school district policy (the only mandate for such suspensions related to the possession of weapons or illegal drugs). Otherwise, students would be placed in a newly developed in-school suspension program.
- In order for a student to be retained in a grade level, the teacher making the recommendation would be required to produce data demonstrating that remedial instruction had been provided and the reasons it failed. Moreover, the teacher would be required to inform the student's parents or guardian about the potential negative effects of grade retention as articulated in a preponderance of research on this topic. A parent would be required to sign a document attesting to two provisions: he or she received the required information from the teacher and he or she granted approval for the retention.

Prior to this letter, opposition to rule changes had been largely covert; in fact, by the end of his 2nd year at Holmes, most teachers assumed that Lattimore had retreated from pursuing them because he had little support. After the letter, however, teachers overtly criticized the proposed changes and they began to attack Lattimore personally for promoting them.

Recognizing that the revisions would be given to the superintendent shortly, many of the teachers and a few teacher aides began meeting to plot a strategy to derail Lattimore's proposed changes. The opposition leader was a first-grade teacher who conducted the group's meetings at her residence. At the first session, she told the others, "Just because he's a nice guy and supposedly cares about students doesn't mean that he knows what he is doing. We've had bleeding-heart principals before and they only made things worse. I've talked to John about failing students and about suspensions, but he is closed minded. I thought he would grasp reality after spending 2 years with us, but unfortunately, he's just another terrible principal."

In mid-July, the opposition group sent a letter to the superintendent and school board members asking them not to approve the proposed changes. It was signed by all but six of the school's 22 teachers and teacher aides. Without responding to the letter, the superintendent recommended approval of the changes to the school board and the motion to approve passed by a vote of five to two.

After the next regular school term started, dissatisfaction among staff was pervasive. Their anger had become malevolent and they took their case to parents and school board members whenever possible. In early November, the same staff members who had signed the previous letter to the superintendent and school board signed a petition to remove Principal Lattimore. The petition, unlike the previous letter, also was signed by 42 parents and was addressed to Dr. Danton, the assistant superintendent, with copies sent to school board members, the superintendent, and the teachers' union president.

Dear Dr. Danton:

Over the past several years, the teachers at Oliver Wendell Holmes Elementary School have observed the leadership style of John Lattimore. While he appears friendly, caring, and intelligent, his behavior reveals the fact that he is an autocratic administrator. He has basically ignored the wisdom of the faculty and has attempted to implement changes that will only make things worse. Nearly 90% of our students are being raised in poverty. Many receive little or no discipline outside of school. Truthfully, most parents and guardians recognize their children need direction and they look to us to provide discipline and to set high academic expectations.

As you know, we do not support the rule changes affecting student suspensions and grade-level retentions. Tolerating disruptive and emotionally unstable behavior and socially promoting students are bad ideas that only deter learning and long-term academic success.

Although it is true that Mr. Lattimore initially asked us how we felt about the rule changes, you need to know that we responded and he ignored our input. In the end, he simply did what he always intended to do. Equally disappointing, he made the changes during the summer, anticipating that we could not resist collectively.

We regret that we have lost confidence in our principal, and we request that he be reassigned to another position as soon as possible.

> *Respectfully,*
>
> *[signed by 16 school employees and 42 parents]*
> *cc: Dr. Gray, superintendent*
> *School Board members*
> *Ms. Hutchins, president of the local teachers' union*

Principal Lattimore first learned of the petition from Dr. Danton. She read the content to him during a telephone conversation. He was surprised and saddened to learn that so many parents had signed it. Several parents who signed the petition had always been warm and friendly to him and he suspected that staff members had intimidated them. Dr. Danton asked him to not confront the staff members or to say anything about the petition for at least several days. She wanted him to cool down before responding to his critics.

The next morning, Lattimore went to the district administrative offices and met with Danton. They had been friends and colleagues for years and he trusted her implicitly. His anger about the petition had not subsided. He told Danton that the teachers who signed it acted unethically both by coercing parents to do likewise and by failing to inform him of the petition.

"You mean you had no idea that the teachers were passing around a petition?" she asked.

"No," Lattimore answered. "I believe I have acted correctly. If I were the dictator they describe, I would have changed these rules immediately after being named principal. I knew the school was a mess before I took the job and tried my best to collaborate in bringing about change. Most teachers simply smiled and said they opposed any type of change. A small group of teachers has been running this school for a long time and they have gotten rid of numerous principals. No principal can raise the effectiveness of Holmes if they remain in power. I repeatedly asked myself, who is more important, the students or the teachers? The answer always was and remains, the students. Apparently, I underestimated how brazen these teachers can be."

"So you allowed them to have input before you made changes?" Danton inquired.

"I had proposed the changes during my second year at Holmes. We never voted but that was not necessary. It was clear that most teachers were opposed to my proposal. Only two teachers told me they supported my ideas—and they relayed this information to me in private conversations. As you well know, this school is a mess. For most of the students, Holmes is another unpleasant experience. Kicking kids out of school and flunking them have only added to the misery. We can't help the students unless they remain in school and develop self-confidence. Negative reinforcement may not be the main problem, but it certainly is not the answer."

"Why do you believe that retaining students in first grade is a mistake?" she asked.

"Failing children who are already at risk of not succeeding academically does not work. The teachers prefer to say that I favor social promotions. I don't. But when you look at the data objectively, failing a child in first grade doubles the probability that he or she will never graduate from high school."

Before their conversation ended, Danton asked, "John, would you consider another assignment? I can arrange for you to have a district-level position. Dr. Gray and I discussed this matter briefly last night. He already has gotten calls from two board members about the petition. We can appoint you to be the assistant director of pupil personnel services. This spring, Sheila Macey is retiring, and you could replace her. Dr. Gray has said he would approve the reassignment immediately if you agree. I want to be clear, however; we are not forcing you to leave Holmes. If you stay, we will work with you to resolve the problems."

"Roberta, you probably know my answer. I've had other opportunities to assume district-level positions. I prefer to be around students. No, I'm not going to cut and run. I'm right on this issue, and if you give me time, I think I can turn the parents and hopefully the teachers around."

"John, the superintendent has two fears. One is that parents will be drawn into this conflict even to a greater degree in the next few months. The other is that the teachers' union will get involved. So, what happens over the next 2 or 3 months is critical."

Lattimore got up from his chair and nodded that he understood. He shook Danton's hand and left. The assistant superintendent realized that she was dealing with an explosive issue because Lattimore also belonged to a union, the highly influential principals' union. Removing him from his current position against his wishes would only elevate political turmoil.

Problem Framing

1. Assume you are Principal Lattimore. First determine the main issue (problem) in this case. Then describe the current state and the desired state of this issue. (The section on problem framing in the Introduction section of this book defines the problem framing process.)

2. Based on evidence provided in the case, describe the difficulty associated with eliminating the gap between the present state and desired state.

Questions and Suggested Activities

1. Share and critique the problem statements prepared by students in your class.
2. Do you agree with the teachers who describe Principal Lattimore as an autocratic principal? Why or why not?

3. What contextual variables contributed to the conflict between a majority of the teachers and the principal in this case?

4. Do you believe that assigning Principal Lattimore to a district-level position is a good way to resolve the conflict at Holmes? Why or why not?

5. Did Principal Lattimore behave prudently in recommending the rule changes knowing that many employees opposed them? Provide a rationale for your response.

6. What contextual variables in the case study provide evidence regarding the nature of the institutional culture at Holmes Elementary School?

7. Many of the teachers believe that schools like Holmes must provide strict discipline and high academic expectations. To what extent do you agree or disagree with them?

8. Did the teachers act ethically in getting some parents to sign the petition? Did they act ethically in not informing the principal that they were circulating the petition? Did they act ethically in sending the petition to the assistant superintendent without informing the principal?

9. What is socialization? What occurs to employees who are socialized?

10. Principal Lattimore contends that students retained in first grade are twice as likely to not graduate from high school as those who are not retained. Do you agree with him? What is the basis of your agreement or disagreement?

11. Evaluate the two rule changes that Principal Lattimore recommended and the school board approved.

Suggested Readings

Bali, V. A., Anagnostopoulos, D., & Roberts, R. (2005). Toward a political explanation of grade retention. *Educational Evaluation and Policy Analysis*, 27(2), 133–155.

Berlin, A. (2008). Social promotion or retention? *Education Week*, 28(9), 28–29.

Bertram, V. M. (2004). Reinventing a school. *Principal Leadership (High School Ed.)*, 4(6), 38–42.

Bestwick, J. F., Sloat, E. A., & Douglas, W. J. (2008). Four educational myths that stymie social justice. *The Educational Forum*, 72(2), 115–128.

Bowman, L. J. (2005). Grade retention: Is it a help or hindrance to student academic success? *Preventing School Failure*, 49(3), 42–46.

Copland, M. A. (2001). The myth of the superprincipal. *Phi Delta Kappan*, 82(7), 528–533.

David, J. L. (2008). Grade retention. *Educational Leadership*, 65(6), 83–84.

Emmons, C. L., Hagopian, G., & Efimba, M. O. (1998). A school transformed: The case of Norman S. Weir. *Journal of Education for Students Placed at Risk*, 3(1), 39–51.

Fullan, M. (2002). The change leader. *Educational Leadership*, 59(8), 16–20.

Houston, W. R. (1998). Innovators as catalysts for restructuring schools. *Educational Forum*, 62(3), 204–210.

Jimerson, S. R., Graydon, K., & Pletcher, S. M. W. (2006). Beyond grade retention and social promotion: Promoting the social and academic competence of students. *Psychology in the Schools*, 43(1), 85–97.

Johnson, P. E., Holder, C., Carrick, C., & Sanford, N. (1998). A model for restructuring governance: Developing a culture of respect and teamwork. *ERS Spectrum*, 16(2), 28–36.

Mendez, L. M., & Knoff, H. M. (2003). Who gets suspended from school and why: A demographic analysis of schools and disciplinary infractions in a large school district. *Education and Treatment of Children*, 26(1), 30–51.

Prestine, N. (1993). Shared decision making in restructuring essential schools: The role of the principal. *Planning and Changing*, 22(3–4), 160–177.

Protheroe, N. (2004). Professional learning communities. *Principal*, 83(5), 39–42.

Rosen, M. (1993). Sharing power: A blueprint for collaboration. *Principal*, 72(3), 37–39.

Sikes, P. (1992). Imposed change and the experienced teacher. In M. Fullan & A. Hargreaves (Eds.), *Teacher development and educational change* (pp. 36–55). Bristol, PA: Falmer Press.

Thomas, C., & Fitzhugh-Walker, P. (1998). The role of the urban principal in school restructuring. *International Journal of Leadership in Education*, 1(3), 297–306.

VanSciver, J. H. (2007). Resisters in our midst. *The American School Board Journal*, 194(10), 33.

Wager, B. (1993). No more suspension: Creating a shared ethical culture. *Educational Leadership*, 50(4), 34–37.

References

Datnow, A., & Castellano, M. E. (2001). Managing and guiding school reform: Leadership in success for all schools. *Educational Administration Quarterly*, 37(2), 219–249.

Fullan, M. (2002). The change leader. *Educational Leadership*, 59(8), 16–20.

Goldman, E. (1998). The significance of leadership style. *Educational Leadership*, 55(7), 20–22.

Hallinger, P., & Heck, R. H. (1998). Exploring the principal's contribution to school effectiveness: 1980–1995. *School Effectiveness and School Improvement, 9*(2), 157–191.

Hoy, W. K., & Miskel, C. G. (2005). *Educational administration: Theory, research, and practice* (7th ed.). New York: McGraw-Hill.

Kowalski, T. J. (2003). *Contemporary school administration: An introduction* (2nd ed.). Boston: Allyn and Bacon.

Kowalski, T. J. (2010). *The school principal: Visionary leadership and competent management.* New York: Routledge.

Kowalski, T. J., Petersen, G. J., & Fusarelli, L. D. (2007). *Effective communication for school administrators: An imperative in an information age.* Lanham, MD: Rowman and Littlefield Education.

Langer, S., & Boris-Schacter, S. (2003). Challenging the image of the American principalship. *Principal, 83*(1), 14–18.

Sergiovanni, T. J. (2004). *Strengthening the heartbeat: Leading and learning together in schools.* San Francisco: Jossey-Bass.

8 | SCHOOL IMPROVEMENT THROUGH BETTER GRADING PRACTICES

BACKGROUND INFORMATION

The relationship between student academic success and student behavior at school has been a subject of debate for some time. Many studies (e.g., Brigman & Campbell, 2003; Hattie, Biggs, & Purdie, 1996) have found that interventions, such as those provided through school counselors, can improve both student grades and student behavior. Logically, students who are consistently unsuccessful with their studies are more likely to find school an unpleasant experience and to behave in unacceptable ways.

Many scholars (e.g., Bandura, 1977, 1997; Guskey, 1994, 2006) posit that grading practices affect student motivation and ultimately academic success and personal behavior. As a primary example, students who receive a very low grade on an assignment or quiz in the first few weeks of a course may find it difficult or impossible to earn enough points to get a high course grade. Once students incur this problem, they may lose their motivation to study, and their excess energy gets expressed negatively—for example, they disrupt classes to gain attention. In an effort to counteract this situation, teachers and principals have been encouraged to adopt evaluation practices that enhance rather than curtail student motivation. One such idea is commonly known as *minimum grading policy* (Carifio & Carey, 2009). This concept's intent is to prevent students from receiving very low assessments early in a course, thus making it impossible for them to receive a higher final grade.

Especially in high schools, the extent to which principals control, supervise, or otherwise influence student grades is another matter that has received considerable discussion (O'Connor, 2001). In most cases, principals walk a fine line between ensuring that a fair and an effective grading system is in place and being used and respecting the professional status of teachers. Professionalism implies that teachers should have considerable discretion in making important decisions that affect their students (Kowalski, Lasley, & Mahoney, 2008). At the same time, principals are held accountable for school improvement and ensuring that students are not treated unfairly or in other ways that deter their academic and social growth (Kowalski, 2010).

This case takes place in a high school that has experienced considerable demographic change in the past 25 years. Dissatisfaction with the school's performance has led to instability in the principalship. A relatively young and inexperienced administrator, the fourth principal in 10 years, is employed with hopes that he can accomplish what his predecessors have failed to do—reduce discipline problems and raise academic achievement. The new principal proposes the adoption of an alternative grading policy as one strategy for achieving this goal. Unlike his predecessors, he believes that attacking academic progress problems is the most effective way to reduce unsatisfactory student behavior. His proposal, however, is met with skepticism and overt opposition. Thus, he must decide to implement, delay, or abandon his preference.

Key Areas for Reflection

1. Grading practices in high schools
2. A nexus between student academic success and student behavior
3. Student motivation to succeed academically
4. Principal-teacher relationships
5. Fair and objective ways to evaluate student academic progress

---

THE CASE

Tucker developed as a suburb shortly after World War II. During the 1950s and 1960s, the community's public schools were recognized as being among the state's best. Beginning in the late 1970s, however, many of the middle-class and upper middle-class families left the community, opting to build houses in newer and more affluent areas. As a result, the community and school system experienced substantial change as evidenced by demographic data. As an example, in the 1960 Census, only 2% of Tuckers' residents were identified as racial-ethnic minorities. In 2010, the figure was 61%. As early as 1984, Tucker High School had a minority-majority student body. Currently across the district, approximately 50% of the school's students qualified for free or reduced-price lunches.

Today, Tucker High School is classified by the state department of education as a low-performing school. Nearly 40% of the students taking the state's mandated 10th-grade high school graduation test (an exam that failing students retake in subsequent years) scored below standard in mathematics, science, and reading. Equally troubling, only 18% of the school's graduates over the past 5 years enrolled in 4-year colleges.

Six months ago, Jordan Johnson, a 36-year-old assistant principal in an urban high school, became Tucker's fourth principal in 10 years. His immediate predecessor, who had resigned before completing 2 years in the position, had been directed by the superintendent, Michelle Watson, to restore discipline at the school. In response, he developed new rules and regulations for student conduct that not only failed to improve student behavior, they resulted in a substantial increase in out-of-school suspensions. Moreover, many school employees disliked him because of his autocratic leadership style and inflexibility.

Prior to becoming an administrator, Jordan Johnson taught biology for 9 years. After interviewing him, Superintendent Watson realized that he was quite different than the high school's three previous principals. Johnson was considerably younger, much less experienced as an administrator, and focused on academics more than student discipline. At first, the superintendent could not decide whether these characteristics were advantageous. She remained convinced that discipline at the school remained a priority, but failed previous attempts to improve student conduct made her more willing to employ a principal with a different philosophy.

In a second employment interview she asked Johnson to clarify his conviction about the nexus between academics and student behavior. He told her, "Students focused on their studies are more successful academically. Often, it is hard to tell whether greater focus results from success or vice-versa. Regardless, students who experience success academically are less likely to exhibit behavior problems. Therefore, my goal is to create more opportunities for students to experience academic success."

Although the superintendent was skeptical of Johnson's belief, her options for selecting a new principal were very limited. Only three applicants had been invited for a second interview and two of them appeared to share the same characteristics of the school's three previous principals. Knowing that the school board was becoming impatient with the lack of progress at the high school, Superintendent Watson decided to gamble and selected Johnson.

Principal Johnson's primary strategy for applying his philosophy was a concept known as "minimum grading." The approach is intended to give low-performing students a second, third, or even fourth chance to do well. In presenting the idea to the faculty, Johnson shared data showing that students exhibiting unacceptable behavior usually did poorly in their studies. Moreover, their poor academic performance usually began early in a school term—for example, on the first quiz or test in a course. He argued that once students received low assessments, their motivation to study and improve diminished because they concluded that getting a good grade had become impossible. The minimum grading concept Johnson proposed had two facets.

1. *A minimum threshold component.* This provision set a floor for student scores on assessments used for grading. For example, on a 100 point quiz, the lowest score that could be given to a student was set at 50. Thus, even if a student actually scored 35, he or she would receive a score of 50. The purpose of this provision was to prevent students from getting into a situation in which earning a higher course grade was impossible.
2. *Adjusted scores.* This provision involved weighting assessments based on when they occurred during an academic term. For example, assessments made in the first half of a semester would carry less weight than those made in the last half of a semester. The intent here was to provide hope to students who got a poor start that they could rectify their performance by working harder in the second half of the course.

Most Tucker High School faculty members were unfamiliar with the grading paradigm. Josh McGill, the never bashful chairperson of the mathematics and science department, asked the first question.

"You showed us data indicating that students with behavior problems don't do well academically. What data do you have showing that the program you are proposing reduces behavior problems?"

Johnson responded, "You raise an important question. Although I am unaware of compelling evidence regarding the effects of minimum grading on student conduct, I don't see how it could make things any worse."

McGill immediately said, "Doesn't the minimum threshold simply give an unfair boost to poor students? If I study for my biology test and get a score of 85, my recorded score remains 85. But if I don't study and get a 25, the teacher gives me an extra 25 points. Tell me, how is that fair?"

Before Johnson could answer, Sharon Beasley, an English teacher, spoke "Would the end effect of this concept be grade inflation? If we gave all our students A's and B's, fewer would likely drop out of school. But would doing so have any positive effect on the school's pass rate on the state's high school exit exam? Would it reduce discipline problems? I'm willing to learn more about your idea, but at this point, I'm skeptical."

Johnson's hope was to convince the faculty to adopt minimum grading at the beginning of the second semester. After hearing the faculty comments, he asked for five volunteers to serve with him on an ad hoc committee to study the advantages and disadvantages of adopting the model at Tucker High School. He then said that the committee would present reports to the faculty at monthly meetings in October and November, and a decision to adopt the new grading program would be made no later than December 15.

The six-member committee began the assignment by examining existing policies and rules on student grading. Most were surprised to learn that beyond requiring students to receive grades and providing a grievance procedure for contesting grades, there were no substantive guidelines. In essence, teachers independently determined how they would grade students. This discovery led the committee members to examine how teachers graded students and the actual grades they assigned. This data showed disparate practices and outcomes. Some teachers based grades entirely or almost entirely on tests; others based grades primarily on homework and effort. Some routinely gave 85% or more of the students A's and B's; others routinely gave fewer than 40% of the students these grades.

At the October faculty meeting, Principal Johnson shared the committee's findings. He was optimistic that most teachers would view the status quo as being unorganized and unfair to students. Instead, several teachers voiced outrage that the committee was spending time examining and comparing teachers based on the grades they had given students. One social studies teacher said the data were misleading because the committee members failed to take into account the nature of the courses. He further contended that the data could be manipulated to the advantage of those who favored minimum grading. Several other teachers voiced similar sentiments but no teacher voiced a favorable opinion of the minimum grading concept at the October meeting.

Over the next month, the committee collected information from four high school principals who had implemented some iteration of minimum grading. Although all of them spoke favorably of the model, each said that it was too early to tell whether the approach would have a long-term, positive effect on reducing discipline problems, reducing drop-out rates, and improving school performance on the state's high school graduation examination. Moreover, three of the four principals reported that teachers, including some who had initially opposed the model, had adapted to the new grading system and were pleased with it. The other principal indicated that the faculty members at his school remained divided.

Prior to presenting an update at the November faculty meeting, Johnson met with Superintendent Watson. He had been keeping her apprised of the committee's progress, but now he wanted to know what her position would be if a majority of the faculty rejected his recommendation to implement the model at the start of the second semester. Previously, she had indicated that she was optimistic about minimum grading and thought the idea could produce positive results. However, she expressed this sentiment prior to learning that many teachers opposed the recommended change. The two administrators discussed three possibilities:

1. Implement the model regardless of teacher support
2. Implement the model only if and when a majority of teachers supported it
3. Not implement the model and seek other ways to improve school performance

Rather than stating a preference, Watson told Johnson she would support any decision he would make on the matter. She warned him, however, that mandating the approach in the presence of widespread teacher opposition would likely result in a political battle with the teachers' union—a group that had considerable influence with two school board members.

Problem Framing

1. Assume you are Principal Johnson. First determine the main issue (problem) in this case. Then describe the current state and the desired state of this issue. (The section on problem framing in the Introduction section of this book defines the problem framing process.)

2. Based on evidence provided in the case, describe the difficulty associated with eliminating the gap between the present state and desired state.

Questions and Suggested Activities

1. Share and critique the problem statements prepared by students in your class.
2. Do you believe that the teachers' fears of grade inflation are warranted? Why or why not?
3. Do you believe that the minimum grading policy proposed by the principal is fair? Why or why not?
4. What are the advantages and disadvantages of mandating the proposed concept regardless of teacher support?
5. Based on your knowledge of teaching and your experience as a teacher, do you agree that low scores in the early stages of a course reduce student motivation substantially? What evidence do you have to support your conclusion?
6. Evaluate the information the ad hoc committee received from the four principals using a minimum grading rule. If you were a teacher at Tucker High School, would you consider the information to help or hinder the principal's effort to implement the concept?
7. How do you evaluate the superintendent's position that she is relegating the decision to the principal?
8. The superintendent realizes that she gambled in hiring a young and relatively inexperienced principal for a very difficult assignment. Should she have allowed him to propose the controversial grading concept so early in his tenure? Why or why not?
9. If you were Principal Johnson, how would you interpret the superintendent's warning that political problems are likely to surface if the program is mandated?
10. What effect, if any, is the minimum-grading rule likely to have on student performance on the state-mandated high school graduation test?
11. Do you agree or disagree with the contention that there is a discernible nexus between academic success and student behavior? What evidence do you have to support your position?

Suggested Readings

Carifio, J., & Carey, T. (2009). Critical examination of current minimum grading policy recommendations. *The High School Journal, 93*(1), 23–37.

Dunham, L. (2008). Why zeros should not be permitted. *Principal, 87*(3), 62.

Dunleavy, J. (2009). The zero sum game. *Education Canada, 49*(4), 49.

Friess, S. (2008, May 19). At some schools, failure goes from 0 to 50. *USA Today.* Retrieved, from http://www.usatoday.com/news/education/2008-05-18-zeroes-main_N.htm

Guldin, M. (2009). Please respect me! *Principal Leadership, 9*(5), 24–27.

Guskey, T. R. (1994). Making the grade: What benefits students? *Educational Leadership, 52*(2), 14–20.

Guskey, T. R. (2004). 0 alternatives. *Principal Leadership, 5*(2), 49–53.

Guskey, T. R. (2006). Making high school grades meaningful. *Phi Delta Kappan, 87*(9), 670–675.

Reeves, D. B. (2004). The case against the zero. *Phi Delta Kappan, 86*(4), 324–326.

Resh, N. (2009). Justice in grades allocation: Teachers' perspective. *Social Psychology of Education, 12*(3), 315–325.

Sanders, D. (2001). A caring alternative to suspension. *The Education Digest, 66*(7), 51–54.

Willingham, W. W., Lewis, C., & Pollack, J. M. (2002). Grades and test scores: Accounting for observed differences. *Journal of Educational Measurement, 39*(1), 1–37.

Zirkel, P. A. (2007, March 28). Grade inflation: High schools' skeleton in the closet. *Education Week, 26*(29), 40, 30.

Zoeckler, L. G. (2007). Moral aspects of grading: A study of high school English teachers' perceptions. *American Secondary Education, 35*(2), 83–102.

References

Bandura, A. (1977). Self-efficacy: Toward a unifying theory of behavioral change. *Psychological Review, 84*(2), 191–215.

Bandura, A. (1997). *Self-efficacy: The exercise of control.* New York: W. H. Freeman and Company.

Brigman, G., & Campbell, C. (2003). Helping students improve academic achievement and school success behavior. *Professional School Counseling, 7*(2), 91–98.

Carifio, J., & Carey, T. (2009). Critical examination of current minimum grading policy recommendations. *The High School Journal, 93*(1), 23–37.

Guskey, T. R. (1994). Making the grade: What benefits students? *Educational Leadership, 52*(2), 14–20.

Guskey, T. R. (2006). Making high school grades meaningful. *Phi Delta Kappan, 87*(9), 670–675.

Hattie, J., Biggs, J., & Purdie, N. (1996). Effects of learning skills interventions on student learning: A meta-analysis. *Review of Educational Research, 66*(2), 99–130.

Kowalski, T. J. (2010). *The school principal: Visionary leadership and competent management.* New York: Routledge.

Kowalski, T. J., Lasley, T. J., & Mahoney, J. (2008). *Data-driven decisions and school leadership: Best practices for school improvement.* Boston: Allyn and Bacon.

O'Connor, K. (2001). The principal's role in report card grading. *NASSP Bulletin, 85*(621), 37–46.

9 | SALLY'S SOCIALIZATION

BACKGROUND INFORMATION

All organizations have cultures consisting of shared values and beliefs and providing an invisible framework of norms that guide employees as they encounter confusion, ambiguity, uncertainty, and other problems (Deal & Kennedy, 1982). Often, it is difficult to accurately diagnose a school's culture because artifacts and espoused beliefs do not always reveal basic and shared assumptions that have considerable influence on behavior. As an example, teachers may believe they cannot help students burdened by social, economic, or intellectual disadvantages. Admitting to this belief, however, would be precarious because many stakeholders would view as being unprofessional, irresponsible, and politically unacceptable. In order to accurately diagnose a school culture, therefore, a principal should not rely solely on surface evidence; instead, he or she needs to observe behavior over a protracted period and establish a trusting relationship with faculty that leads to open and candid communication.

Three characteristics can be used to describe school cultures (Kowalski, 2003):

1. *Strength.* School cultures fall along a continuum from strong to weak. In strong cultures, values and beliefs are shared by all or nearly all employees; in weak cultures, they are fragmented and thus less influential.
2. *Value.* School cultures fall along a continuum from positive to negative. In positive cultures, shared values and beliefs are congruous with the professional knowledge base; in negative cultures, they are not.
3. *Alignment.* School cultures fall along a continuum from aligned to misaligned. In aligned cultures, shared values and beliefs are congruous with the values and beliefs espoused by the formal organization (e.g., by district policy and school philosophy); in misaligned cultures, they are not.

Organizational members protect culture by attempting to socialize newcomers (Van Maanen & Schein, 1979). Socialization involves routine and social pressure intended to result in conformity (Hart, 1991). These pressures are delivered through formal (e.g., faculty orientation, staff meetings) and informal (e.g., social interaction) experiences. Basically, socialization informs new teachers about how to deal with common problems of practice (Hanson, 2003). In misaligned cultures, the accepted way of doing things differs from espoused solutions found in policy manuals and philosophy statements. Consequently, protectors of the prevailing culture (e.g., experienced teachers) continuously remind newcomers, "Ignore the policy manual. This is the way we really deal with this type of problem."

Many novice teachers encounter role-related or value-related conflict during socialization. The former pertains to inconsistencies between two or more role expectations. As an example, a new teacher struggles between being an independent professional and being an obedient member of a school's culture. The latter pertains to philosophical inconsistencies. As an example, the values and norms of a school's culture are incompatible with the accepted values and norms of the teaching profession.

Teacher empowerment has been interpreted in different ways but definitions essentially are anchored in professionalism; that is, empowerment focuses on professional independence as the preferred orientation to teaching (Ponticell, Olson, & Charlier, 1995). Scholars writing about school improvement (e.g., Fullan, 2001; Hall & Hord, 2001) conclude that meaningful improvement is much more likely when teachers function as professionals and change agents. Empowerment, however, often contradicts beliefs and norms entrenched in many schools (Kowalski, 1995). As examples, professionalism increases independence and reliance on professional knowledge to guide practice; conversely, strong negative cultures demand conformity and obedience—even in situations where the school's norm is not supported by established theory (Kowalski, Lasley, & Mahoney, 2008).

Many principals have been apprehensive about allowing teachers to chart their own pedagogical and classroom management agendas, largely for two reasons.

1. *Aversion to risk.* Principals may have a negative disposition toward risk taking, and consequently they view teacher empowerment as a threat to their authority and job security. If teachers make independent decisions about homework and discipline, for example, practices in the school may become highly inconsistent—a condition that could produce political and possibly legal problems.
2. *Protection of school culture.* Principals, especially those who have been employed in the same school for more than 2 or 3 years, are often key figures in a school's culture. If the culture is strong, teachers and other employees expect a principal to protect and foster dominant beliefs and norms. Empowerment essentially redefines the parameters for acceptable teacher behavior because greater importance is placed on personal responsibility for professional practice and less importance is placed on social acceptance.

Administrator behavior is also analyzed on the basis of leadership style. For example, the literature suggests that principals can be transactional or transformational, autocratic or democratic. A transactional style is characterized by exchanges between leader and follower for purposes of achieving personal objectives; it often entails a bargaining process focused on self-interests (Sergiovanni, 2001). In essence, a transactional principal believes that people are motivated by self-interests, and therefore their behavior can be controlled through rewards and punishment. Conversely, transformational principals tend to create an environment in which they and employees (a) share common goals, (b) are guided by ethical and moral principles, and (c) are motivated by higher-order needs (Burns, 1978). In essence, transactional leadership is a political process involving a quid pro quo, and transformational leadership is an ethical, moral, and professional process involving commitments to personal and organizational growth (Kowalski, 2003).

In this case, a novice first-grade teacher refuses to recommend the retention of two pupils. Her decision generates considerable tension as conflicting elements of school culture, teacher empowerment and principal leadership style converge.

Key Areas for Reflection
1. School culture
2. Teacher empowerment
3. Principal leadership style
4. Ethical behavior

THE CASE

Sally Vasquez sat alone in her first-grade classroom in Westside Elementary School. It was 4:30 P.M. and the students had departed more than an hour ago. As she stared aimlessly out the window at the empty playground, her thoughts meandered between her recollections of her role model, Mrs. Eagan, and the difficult decision she would have to make the next day.

Sally's intention to become an educator developed in the fourth grade. Her teacher, Mrs. Eagan, was young, energetic, kind, and consistently positive with students. Over the course of that year, Sally developed self-confidence and a positive attitude toward school. Years later as she formally prepared to be a teacher, her role model remained Mrs. Eagan.

Ten months ago, after graduating from college, Sally was employed as a first-grade teacher at Westside Elementary School. The school is in Maplewood, a 70-year-old suburb with a rapidly changing demographic profile. Currently, 27% of the students are eligible for free or reduced-price lunches and 42% are persons of color.

In addition to Sally, Martha Bigler, April Musilich, and Sharon Quigly, all highly experienced teachers, teach first grade at the school. Moreover, the three other first-grade teachers have been employed at Westside for at least 11 years. In this small group, Mrs. Quigly was the most experienced, oldest, and most influential.

The first-grade teachers meet once a month to discuss curriculum and common concerns. Their meetings are held after school on the third Tuesday of each month in Mrs. Quigly's classroom. They typically last about an hour. Initially, Sally looked forward to the sessions because she believed she could learn a great deal from her peers.

Three years prior to Sally's arrival, the first-grade teachers adopted academic progress and social development criteria for determining whether students should be retained in grade. Though the criteria were never formally approved by the school, they were known to the principal and the teachers had agreed to abide by them. As the demographic profile of Westside students changed, the retention rate increased. Approximately 4% of the students repeated first grade.

The topic of grade retention was first raised with Sally in the October first-grade teachers' meeting. Mrs. Quigly gave her a copy of the retention criteria and explained their purpose. As a college student, Sally had been told that the negative aspects of retaining students far outweighed the benefits—a contention that was supported by several research articles she was required to read. Specifically, the literature indicated that any gains attributable to repeating first grade usually dissipated after just 1 or 2 years; however, the harmful effects to a student's self-efficacy and self-esteem tended to endure even through high school. Therefore, she was surprised to learn that her colleagues apparently held dissimilar beliefs.

At the February first-grade meeting, Mrs. Quigly told Sally that she needed to identify students who might be retained by applying the criteria she had been given in October. To that point, Sally had elected to neither challenge nor overtly support student retention, largely because she felt inferior in the group. Now, however, she had to make an important and uncomfortable decision. She decided to share her dilemma with the principal, Carmen Pelfrey.

Mrs. Pelfrey has been principal at Westside for 6 years. She is well liked by the teachers and supported by most parents. Sally also had become fond of her and judged her to be a competent leader.

When she met with Principal Pelfrey, Sally revealed that she opposed retaining first-grade students and explained why she believed the practice was ineffective. She also said that she had not shared her belief with the other first-grade teachers. Mrs. Pelfrey emphasized that teachers were permitted but not required to retain students. She also pointed out that a student was never retained if his or her parents objected. Based on the comments, Sally felt somewhat relieved. Then, however, the principal began praising the other first-grade teachers and defending the criteria they adopted. She called Mrs. Quigly an ideal teacher-leader and the most influential employee in the school. Although Mrs. Pelfrey never expressed her position on the topic, it was clear to Sally that she condoned the criteria and the retentions. The meeting ended with the principal advising Sally to reveal her opposition to grade retention to the other first-grade teachers.

At the March first-grade meeting, Sally told the others that she did not believe in retaining students and explained why she had developed this stance. Mrs. Quigly responded by saying that Sally's apparent inflexibility on the matter was surprising in light of the fact that she was a novice teacher.

"You need to keep an open mind about retention," she told Sally. "Apparently, you have only heard one side of the argument. Some students simply are not ready academically or socially to enter second grade. And with the support of parents, repeating first grade has often proven to be a beneficial experience."

The other two teachers supported Mrs. Quigly's comments. Sally understandably was uncomfortable. Yet, she felt her colleagues would permit her to be guided by her convictions—that is, until Mrs. Quigly said, "Regardless of your personal beliefs, you still must apply the criteria and identify students who might be retained."

After the meeting, Sally and Mrs. Bigler walked to the parking lot together. She told Sally that she, too, once had been apprehensive about grade retentions. She explained that experience had changed her perspective; she now was convinced that some students were not prepared to be promoted to second grade.

The following morning, Sally again met with Principal Pelfrey and described the discussion that occurred the previous afternoon. She emphasized that despite Mrs. Quigly's insistence that she develop a list of potentially failing students, she did not intend to comply.

Mrs. Pelfrey acted surprised. "The other teachers are not asking you to identify students who will be retained; they only expect you to identify students who qualify for retention based on the criteria. By refusing to apply the criteria, you will appear to be stubborn and uncooperative."

Despite the principal's warning, Sally stood by her convictions. She informed the other three teachers that she would not apply the criteria nor recommend any students for retention. Her declaration prompted Mrs. Quigly to meet with the principal.

"Sally has many fine qualities, and she could become a great teacher. She loves children, and is bright. But she can be stubborn, as we have discovered. I and the other first-grade teachers are beginning to question whether Sally can be successful at this school."

Mrs. Quigly's veiled suggestion that Sally not be re-employed bothered Principal Pelfrey. On three occasions, she had conducted formal observations of Sally's teaching, and in each instance her assessments were positive. Moreover, comments from parents had been consistently complimentary. Not re-employing a teacher simply because she did not "fit in" would be problematic—especially if Sally resisted efforts to terminate her employment. On the other hand, protecting Sally could prove to be detrimental to the principal's relationships with staff.

Weighing the dilemma she faced, Principal Pelfrey again appealed to Sally to reconsider applying the criteria. Sally said she would not change her position. After a moment of silence, the principal spoke.

"I admire your conviction, but you should know that this issue could be detrimental for you. I will have to weigh the consequences of this conflict before I complete your annual performance evaluation."

After the conversation, Sally made an appointment to see the district superintendent, Dr. Frank Jobet. She had met him during her employment interview and remembered his comments about teacher professionalism and empowerment. She reminded him of those comments before detailing the conflict with the other teachers and the warning she received from the principal. She also pointed out that neither district policy nor school regulations directed teachers to take a position on grade retention. Dr. Jobet listened attentively and told Sally he would respond to her concerns after discussing the matter with Mrs. Pelfrey.

Several days later, Sally received a message that Principal Pelfrey wanted to meet with her later that day. As she walked into the principal's office, Sally immediately detected tension. Mrs. Pelfrey appeared angry, a demeanor that Sally had not seen previously.

The principal stared into Sally's eyes and said, "You went to see the superintendent without my permission? Maybe the other teachers are correct about you. I tried to advise you so that you could be successful at this school. But apparently, you have your own agenda."

"You hinted that I might not be re-employed just because I refused to apply criteria to determine students who should be retained. Neither my position on retention nor my refusal to apply the criteria violate policy. I sought your support and all you did was essentially tell me to be a team player. My position, not theirs, is supported by the professional knowledge base. If I offended you by seeing the superintendent, I'm sorry. But what other option did I have?"

"You could have been more cooperative. Look, I am not going to recommend your dismissal. However, I can't control how you may be treated by other teachers. You have put both of us in a difficult position. Though I will not recommend dismissal, I could recommend that you be transferred to another school in the district."

Problem Framing

1. Assume you are the principal. First determine the main issue (problem) in this case. Then describe the current state and the desired state of this issue. (The section on problem framing in the Introduction section of this book defines the problem framing process.)

2. Based on evidence provided in the case, describe the difficulty associated with eliminating the gap between the present state and desired state.

Questions and Suggested Activities

1. Share and critique the problem statements prepared by students in your class.
2. Do you believe that the principal has the primary responsibility to resolve the conflict between Sally and the other first-grade teachers? Why or why not?
3. Is Sally correct in saying that her position on retaining students is supported by the professional knowledge base? What evidence would validate or invalidate her position?
4. Based on evidence presented in the case, do you believe the principal has been an effective instructional leader? Why or why not?
5. Why are teachers and administrators pressured to conform to existing school culture?
6. Did Sally act responsibly by remaining silent on the issue of the criteria and grade retention until February?
7. Determine whether the school district in which you are employed (or reside if you are not currently practicing as an educator) has a policy addressing grade retention. Share the outcomes in class and identify differences in such policies.
8. Reflecting on your own experiences as a novice teacher, identify critical incidents that you believe were part of your socialization to a workplace. Then determine whether these experiences were beneficial. Share the incidents in class.
9. School officials commonly will not retain students if parents object. What information should parents be given when a teacher is recommending retention?
10. Is the principal justified in being angry because Sally met with the superintendent? Why or why not?

Suggested Readings

Beck-Frazier, S. (2005). To stay or not to stay: That's the dilemma. *Delta Kappa Gamma Bulletin, 71*(2), 28–33.

Bullough, R. V. (2005). Teacher vulnerability and teachability: A case study of a mentor and two interns. *Teacher Education Quarterly, 32*(2), 23–39.

Burk, D. I., & Fry, P. G. (1997). Autonomy for democracy in a primary classroom: A first year teacher's struggle. *Teaching and Teacher Education, 13*, 645–658.

Flores, M. A., & Day, C. (2006). Contexts which shape and reshape new teachers' identities: A multi-perspective study. *Teaching and Teacher Education, 22*(2), 219–232.

Johnson, P. E., & Short, P. M. (1998). Principal's leader power, teacher empowerment, teacher compliance and conflict. *Educational Management and Administration, 26*(2), 147–159.

Kowalski, T. J. (1995). Preparing teachers to be leaders: Barriers in the workplace. In M. O'Hair & S. Odell (Eds.), *Educating teachers for leadership and change: Teacher Education Yearbook III* (pp. 243–256). Thousand Oaks, CA: Corwin Press.

Mauer, E., & Zimmerman, E. (2000). Mentoring new teachers. *Principal, 79*(3), 26–28.

McCoy, A. R., & Reynolds, A. J. (1999). Grade retention and school performance: An extended investigation. *Journal of School Psychology, 37*(3), 273–298.

Normore, A. H., & Floyd, A. (2005). A roller coaster ride: The twists and turns of a novice teacher's relationship with her principal. *Phi Delta Kappan, 86*(10), 767–771.

Potter, L. (2003). Between a rock and a hard place. *Principal Leadership (Middle School Ed.), 3*(8), 46–48.

Short, P. M., & Short, R. J. (1998). Teacher empowerment and principal leadership: Understanding the influence process. *Educational Administration Quarterly, 34*, 630–649.

Weiss, E. M. (1999). Perceived workplace conditions and first-year teachers' morale, career choice commitment, and planned retention: A secondary analysis. *Teaching and Teacher Education, 15*(8), 861–879.

References

Burns, J. M. (1978). *Leadership.* New York: Harper Torchbooks.

Deal, T. E., & Kennedy, A. A. (1982). *Corporate cultures: The rites and rituals of corporate life.* Reading, MA: Addison-Wesley.

Fullan, M. (2001). *Leading in a culture of change.* San Francisco: Jossey-Bass.

Hall, G. E., & Hord, S. M. (2001). *Implementing change: Patterns, principles, and potholes.* Allyn and Bacon.

Hanson, E. M. (2003). *Educational administration and organizational behavior* (5th ed.). Boston: Allyn and Bacon.

Hart, A. W. (1991). Leader succession and socialization: A synthesis. *Review of Educational Research, 61*(4), 451–474.

Kowalski, T. J. (1995). Preparing teachers to be leaders: Barriers in the workplace. In M. O'Hair & S. Odell (Eds.), *Educating teachers for leadership and change: Teacher education yearbook III* (pp. 243–256). Thousand Oaks, CA: Corwin.

Kowalski, T. J. (2003). *Contemporary school administration: An introduction* (2nd ed.). Boston: Allyn and Bacon.

Kowalski, T. J., Lasley, T. J., & Mahoney, J. (2008). *Data-driven decisions and school leadership: Best practices for school improvement.* Boston: Allyn and Bacon.

Ponticell, J. A., Olson G. E., & Charlier, P. S. (1995). Project MASTER: Peer coaching and collaboration as catalysts for professional growth in urban high schools. In M. J. O'Hair & S. J. Odell (Eds.), *Educating teachers for leadership and change: Teacher education yearbook III* (pp. 96–116). Thousand Oaks, CA: Corwin.

Sergiovanni, T. J. (2001). *The principalship: A reflective practice perspective* (4th ed.). Boston: Allyn and Bacon.

Van Maanen, J., & Schein, E. H. (1979). Toward a theory of organizational socialization. In B. Staw (Ed.), *Research in organizational behavior* (pp. 209–264). Greenwich, CT: JAI Press.

10 | A MATTER OF HONOR

BACKGROUND INFORMATION

Authors examining administrator decision making (e.g., Begley, 2000; Kowalski, Lasley, & Mahoney, 2008; Willower, 1994) have commonly found that emotion, personal values, and political contexts contribute to subjectivity. Sergiovanni (1992) observed that three leadership dimensions may influence decisions. He labeled them the heart, the head, and the hand. The *heart* pertains to personal beliefs, values, dreams, and commitments; the *head* pertains to theories of practice that evolve by integrating theoretical and craft knowledge; and the *hand* has to do with actions and behaviors used as strategies institutionalized in district policies and normative procedures. When these dimensions are discordant, administrators almost always experience personal conflict because they must make a choice between doing what is appropriate professionally or doing what is expedient politically (Kowalski et al., 2008).

Principals also encounter conflict when trying to balance the need to give teachers professional autonomy and the need to exert authority to protect the school's interests (Kowalski, 2010). Administrators who allow employees considerable discretion often discover that they are still held accountable if employees make poor choices resulting in problems for students or other stakeholders.

In this case, a student is accused of plagiarizing a book report in a senior honors English class. The teacher, invoking school district policy, informs the principal that she intends to give the student a failing grade for the semester. The principal is apprehensive about enforcing the policy, given the student's past performance and reputation. The student, the first African American from the school to receive an appointment to a national military academy, had an unblemished academic record and had received numerous athletic awards prior to this incident. If the student received a failing grade in English, her appointment to the military academy would almost certainly be rescinded; if that occurred, some stakeholders would likely be furious.

As the case unfolds, the principal has to choose between enforcing the policy, as demanded by the teacher, and forging a political compromise, as suggested by the school system's attorney and the student's attorney. Though the principal much prefers the compromise option, he recognizes the teachers' association is supporting the position taken by the English teacher.

The decision the principal must make in this case has moral and ethical aspects—a situation common to administrative decisions. Hodgkinson (1991) noted that "values, morals, and ethics are the very stuff of leadership and administrative life" (p. 11). Morality focuses on "right" and "wrong" and may or may not involve illegalities (Kowalski, 2006). Ethics, however, "begin where laws and doctrines of right and wrong leave off" (Howlett, 1991, p. 19), and these standards are commonly encapsulated in professional codes of conduct.

Student discipline is a stressful aspect of school administration because it almost always involves an intricate mix of political, professional, moral, and ethical issues. Ideally, district policies and school rules reduce stress and ensure consistency. In fact, however, even good policy and rules rarely eliminate uncertainty and the risk that decision outcomes will negatively affect the school and the decision maker. At the same time, however, having too many policies and rules can be detrimental. Most notably, this condition often leads to "mock rules" (i.e., rules that are neither enforced nor followed) and diminishes the stature of teachers and principals as professionals (e.g., educators have little or no discretion to decide what is best for students). In essence, mandatory policies and rules (e.g., zero-tolerance policy) often preclude educators from being able to consider the moral and ethical aspects of student misconduct (Kowalski, 2003, 2006).

Key Areas for Reflection

1. Rational versus subjective decision making
2. Ethical and moral dimensions of student discipline
3. Mandatory versus discretionary policy
4. Political contexts and their effect on administrative decisions
5. Plagiarism and appropriate penalties

THE CASE

Community

Newton is an industrial town that has fallen on hard times in recent years. The local economy was devastated by the closing of two automobile-related factories, a transmission plant and a battery plant. Union strife, lower domestic automobile sales, high labor costs, and automation contributed to their demise. The parent companies diverted much of the work from Newton to new operations in Mexico—a pattern that has become all too common and exasperating for many residents in auto-producing communities.

Newton had grown rapidly after World War II. High salaries in local factories attracted a steady stream of new residents between 1950 and 1970, and Newton quickly became a large and demographically diverse community. During that period, the vast majority of new residents were either of Eastern European extraction or African extraction. The former group of new residents had migrated primarily from large Midwestern cities, such as Chicago, Detroit, and Pittsburgh. The latter group had migrated primarily from Southern states, such as Alabama, Mississippi, and Tennessee. Since the mid-1990s, the community has become even more diverse because of the in-migration of Hispanics.

Union Influence

When factories related to the auto industry were booming, virtually every nonmanagement employee was a loyal member of a local union. In the mid-1960s, labor unions, especially the one for auto workers, were the most powerful political, social, and economic force in Newton. Union leaders, either by virtue of holding public office or by virtue of exercising power over those who did, essentially controlled the community. When a resident wanted a pothole fixed, for example, he or she was more likely to call a union official than to call the mayor or street commissioner.

Local union officials also assumed an important community social role. Recognizing the importance of racial harmony in a city where persons of color lived in their own neighborhoods and attended their own churches, they operated the auto workers' union hall as if it were a community center. On a day-to-day basis, the hall was the one location in Newton where racial and ethnic groups interacted socially.

Economic and political conditions began to change in Newton circa 1980. Factory jobs dwindled as the companies struggled to compete with foreign manufacturers. A loss of factory jobs resulted in fewer active union members. In 1985, the two largest factories closed completely and membership in the local auto workers' union dropped to its lowest point since 1948. The loss of membership dues was devastating for the unions; even the once-a-month socials held at the union hall, gala events featuring free beer and music, were no longer held.

A New Mayor

The 1990s remained a difficult time for Newton residents. The city had lost more than 20% of its population and property values plummeted. In the midst of the downturn, residents desperately tried to recapture the past by electing a 65-year-old retired tool-and-dye maker, Stanley Diviak, mayor. He had been president of the local auto workers' union from 1965 to 1978, and in the eyes of many older residents, he remained a hero. He personifies the community's dominant values; he is devoted to his family, he goes to church regularly, and he keeps his word.

When he ran for mayor, Stanley faced token opposition from a Republican candidate, a 28-year-old lawyer. The election's outcome was never in doubt. Rather than comparing the merits of the candidates, residents who routinely gathered at Gloria's Diner and Kelsey's Bar reminisced about the good old days when Stanley Diviak "got things done." Many deluded themselves into believing that Newton's fate would have been different had there been more Stanley Diviaks to combat the auto company executives.

Following his election, Stanley appointed former union associates to key administrative posts in city government. He took special care to select individuals who represented the various publics. He also appointed a special committee to develop a plan for attracting new industry. Though he could not secure funds to resurrect the monthly socials at the union hall, he did re-establish the city's Fourth of July parade and picnic, an event that had not been held in 12 years.

Newton High School

Ask Newton residents about the local public schools and inevitably they talk about athletics. The high school, just four blocks from the center of town in a two-story building now nearly 50 years old, is adorned with dozens of trophy cases and pictures, artifacts of an era when the school's athletic teams were dominant regionally and often statewide.

The principal, Nick Furtoski, graduated from Newton High School. After college and 2 years of military service, he returned as a faculty member. He and his wife still live in the house his parents had built. While a Newton High School student, he played on a state championship football team and was captain of the baseball team.

Principal Furtoski's love for Newton High School is never more apparent than when he reminisces about past athletic victories. Those who visit his office, including students and school employees, rarely leave without hearing at least one story about a former athlete, an important game, or a state championship. Despite having lost nearly one-third of its enrollment since 1975, athletics remain moderately successful; last year, 13 students received full or partial athletic scholarships to attend college.

Newton School District

Overall, the school district's enrollment has declined from about 8,500 in 1975 to a present level of just over 6,000 students. Superintendent Andrew Sposis has survived 7 difficult years in office. During his tenure, two elementary schools have been closed, resulting in the reduction of 21 teaching positions, three administrative positions, and 14 support staff positions. Superintendent Sposis has also had to manage three employee strikes, two involving the teachers' union and one involving the custodians' union.

Historically, the local school board has had an unwritten policy of promoting persons to administrative positions from within the system. Superintendent Sposis benefited from that policy; he has never worked in another school system. During his 32 years of employment in the district, he has been a teacher, elementary school principal, assistant superintendent for business, and now superintendent.

The school board has five members, each elected to serve a 3-year term. In the past 10 years, the entire composition of the board has changed. Consequently, there is only one member remaining in office who was on the board when Mr. Sposis was elevated to superintendent. The current board includes three persons of color: two African American and one Hispanic. The board president, married to Mayor Diviak's sister, is not one of them.

Incident

Sheila Allison is a senior at the high school. She is a good student (slightly better than a *B* average), an outstanding athlete, and highly popular. She also is an African American. For the past 2 years, she was named to the all-state basketball team. Not unexpectedly, she received scholarship offers from more than 10 colleges and universities. And in the fall of her senior year, she was elected homecoming queen. However, her most notable honor came on March 1 during her senior year, the day she received a congressional appointment to one of the national military academies. The news spread throughout Newton quickly after her picture appeared on the front page of the local newspaper.

Sheila's life, however, took a dramatic turn a few weeks later. On March 17, Janice Durnitz, an English teacher, entered the principal's office requesting to see Mr. Furtoski. Upon returning to his office, Principal Furtoski asked, "Janice, what's the problem?"

"I've got bad news," she responded.

At that point, he motioned for her to have a seat and closed the office door. As soon as the principal sat down, Mrs. Durnitz said, "Sheila Allison is in my honors English class and she had been performing quite well. A few days ago, however, she turned in a book review that is required for the course. As I read her assignment last night, I found the style and quality of writing to be atypical of her previous work. The content of the review also seemed familiar. So I conducted an Internet search and found a review nearly identical to the one she submitted. The review had appeared in a literary magazine about 2 years ago and is archived on the magazine's Web page. In summary, she apparently plagiarized."

"You are absolutely sure about this?" asked the principal.

"I estimate that 65% of Sheila's paper was copied from the published book review. And as you know, there is a zero-tolerance policy for cheating and plagiarizing in an honors class. Students found guilty automatically receive a failing grade and must repeat the course."

"Have you confronted Sheila with this issue?" the principal asked.

"Yes. She admits taking the material from the Web site but contends that she did not know doing so constituted plagiarism. She said she read the book she critiqued and agreed with the review she found on the Web. Therefore, she thought it was permissible to write the same things."

A pained look came over Mr. Furtoski's face and he stared across the room as though in deep thought. After a few seconds, his eyes turned to Mrs. Durnitz.

"What do you plan to do about this?" he asked.

"District policy gives me no choice. I have to give her a failing grade and she must retake the course."

"Janice, we have worked together for over 15 years. We have never had a student at Newton High School flunk a course because of plagiarism. Hell, half the people in this town don't even know what the word means. Isn't there another solution? Can't we give Sheila the benefit of the doubt? Maybe she is telling the truth and didn't know she was breaking a rule. You know that if you give her an *F*, and especially an *F* for plagiarism, her appointment to the military academy is likely to be rescinded. At the very least, she will have to go to summer school in order to graduate, and I'm not sure she can do that in time to report to the academy in late June. What if I talk to the superintendent and recommend an alternative penalty? For example, Sheila could do a different book review and have her grade in the course reduced."

"Nick, this policy was recommended by teachers assigned to honors courses and you, and the superintendent, endorsed it. Plagiarism is cheating, and cheating has no place in an honors class. Not enforcing the policy because of Sheila's circumstances in essence nullifies the policy. I, too, empathize with Sheila, but my duty and your duty is to follow policy. Even if Sheila is telling the truth, ignorance does not excuse her behavior. Plagiarism is defined in the student handbook." At that point, the teacher got up from her chair and walked out of the principal's office.

Mr. Furtoski slumped in his chair and stared at the picture hanging on the wall across the room; it was a picture of the state championship football team of which he had been a member. About 15 minutes later, he called Superintendent Sposis and conveyed the bad news. He anticipated the superintendent would want a specific recommendation. Perhaps the easiest choice would be for him to hide behind the policy and let the superintendent or school board make an exception if they wished to do so. But Principal Furtoski was not inclined to do this, largely because he did not believe the punishment fit the offense. Yet, he had supported the policy after it was proposed by the teachers.

After being briefed, Superintendent Sposis said, "This is just what I need, Nick! Do you know what will happen if Sheila's appointment to the academy is withdrawn? The mayor has been bragging about her every chance he gets. The Allison family was just at city hall 2 days ago taking pictures with the mayor and city council. We need to find a way out of this. Don't forget, you recommended this policy."

"Mrs. Durnitz does not appear flexible. I don't know about her personal relationship with Sheila, but I don't think it is an issue in her decision. She made it clear that she is going to follow the policy and give Sheila an *F*. Janice's influence in the teachers' union is a factor to consider. As you recall, the policy in question was endorsed by the union and us. At this point, Janice is not willing to back off."

"You're the principal. Can't you override a teacher decision about a grade?" Mr. Sposis asked.

"And you're the superintendent. Can't you do the same? I don't think either of us wants to be in that position. One other option is to circumvent the policy because Sheila did not understand the nature of plagiarism. If we can prove this point, a lesser punishment might be acceptable. Another option would be to get the school board to rescind the policy."

The conversation between the two administrators continued for another 10 minutes. It concluded when the superintendent told the principal he would inform the school board and then get back to him. After ending his conversation with the superintendent, Mr. Furtoski spoke to both Mrs. Durnitz and Sheila Allison, asking them to keep the matter confidential until the school board had been briefed.

After learning about the situation, the school board turned to its attorney, June VanSilten, for advice. She made three suggestions to the board and the superintendent:

1. Following the policy literally would result in serious conflict in the community and possibly in the school. She did not specify, however, whether the nature of this conflict would be legal or political.
2. Board members should not discuss the matter with the media or anyone else. If the policy was enforced and the student appealed, the due process procedure required board members to judge the merits of the appeal.
3. The superintendent and board should not take any action until the teacher had submitted a formal recommendation to fail the student and the principal had either endorsed or rejected the recommendation.

The board agreed to follow her advice.

After the meeting, Superintendent Sposis briefed Principal Diviak. He emphasized that the board was not going to act until they saw the principal's formal recommendation. He added that the recommendation should not be made until Mrs. Durnitz submitted a written statement providing a rationale for enforcing the policy. The superintendent also warned that everyone involved in this matter needed to act appropriately since Sheila's parents would likely pursue legal recourse if Sheila received a failing grade.

The next day, the principal again met with Mrs. Durnitz to examine evidence. She showed him Sheila's assignment and copies of the published review, as it appeared in the magazine and as it appeared on the Web page. Although there was not indication that the review was copyrighted, the fact that Sheila had extracted content from the published review without giving credit to the author was apparent. Admitting that the evidence appeared to support the accusation of plagiarism, Diviak raised the possibility that Sheila did not violate policy because she, as claimed, did not understand the concept of plagiarism. Durnitz responded by reiterating that plagiarism is defined in the school's student handbook. She then handed the principal a letter detailing her assessment of the situation; the letter included a recommendation that Sheila be excused from the class for the remainder of the semester and receive a failing grade. As per a notation at the bottom of the letter, a copy had been sent to the teachers' association president.

The next morning, Principal Furtoski received a telephone call from the teachers' association president, Janelle Thompson, informing him that the association's executive board had voted unanimously to support Mrs. Durnitz's position on this matter. She also said that the association members expected the administration and school board to do the same.

Knowing that the issue could be made public at any time, Principal Furtoski decided it was time to speak to Sheila's parents about the problem. He has known Mr. And Mrs. Allison for more than 20 years and his previous interactions with them had been positive. Deloris Allison, Sheila's mother, answered the telephone. She affirmed that Sheila had told her and her husband about the problem the previous day. She then said that she and her husband believe that Sheila did not knowingly violate the plagiarism policy. The brief conversation ended after Mr. Furtoski pointed out that he was working with other school officials to investigate the matter fully and to arrive at a resolution that was in the best interests of all parties.

After his conversation with Mrs. Allison, the principal met with two teachers he trusted implicitly. His purpose was to determine whether faculty members knew about the situation. The two teachers told him that the incident and teachers' association position on it had been reported to all teachers by the association via e-mail that morning.

Shortly before leaving his office that day, Principal Furtoski learned that the local newspaper would report the plagiarism charge the next day. The information came from the reporter writing the story. He wanted the principal to comment on the matter. Principal Furtoski told the reporter, "There has been an accusation of plagiarism, and I and other officials are looking into the matter. In fairness to the student, I don't think you should publish this story, at least not at this time. At this point, the charges have not been verified and therefore, I have no further comments."

"When will you have results of the investigation?" asked the reporter.

"No comment."

The next morning, the newspaper published an article revealing that Sheila had been accused of plagiarism. Appearing on page 2, the headline read, "Honor Student Accused of Cheating." The article included the following quote from Sheila's mother, Mrs. Allison:

> My husband and I believe our daughter has been wrongly accused. She did not knowingly violate the policy on plagiarism. She never tried to hide what she did because she did not think her work violated any rules. If plagiarism is such an important issue, why didn't the principal and teachers instruct students on this matter?

The article also noted that the superintendent was unavailable to comment and that the principal simply stated that the matter was under review.

As he arrived at school that morning, Principal Furtoski found Superintendent Sposis waiting for him in his office.

"Have you read the paper?" the superintendent asked.

"Yes. I asked the reporter to wait until our investigation was completed, but he said the incident already was being discussed widely in the community."

The superintendent stood up and stared directly at the principal and said, "This is an absolute mess. I had hoped that we could avoid the public controversy, but now we are headed for a crisis. You need to make your recommendation quickly—and my advice is to be creative."

Not waiting for a response, the superintendent walked to the office door; instead of leaving, he turned and said, "You better find a way for us to get out of this mess."

Problem Framing

1. Assume you are Principal Furtoski. First determine the main issue (problem) in this case. Then describe the current state and the desired state of this issue. (The section on problem framing in the Introduction section of this book defines the problem framing process.)

2. Based on evidence provided in the case, describe the difficulty associated with eliminating the gap between the present state and desired state.

Questions and Suggested Activities

1. Share and critique the problem statements prepared by students in your class.

2. The policy not allowing for any exceptions, such as the one in this case, is known as a "zero-tolerance policy."

What are advantages and disadvantages of such policies?

3. Should emotions and ethics influence decisions we make as educators? Why or why not?

4. Assume that the student is telling the truth about not understanding the nature of plagiarism. Does this fact absolve her of responsibility? Why or why not?

5. The material the student copied appeared originally in a literary magazine and then on the Internet. Therefore, the book review almost certainly was copyrighted. What is the difference between copyright infringement and plagiarism? Why did the teacher not charge the student with copyright infringement?

6. As noted in the introduction for this case, administrative decisions often involve ethical and political considerations. What are the ethical and political issues in this case?

7. Given the principal's reactions in this case, does he have a responsibility to recommend that the plagiarism policy be rescinded? Why or why not?

8. As a principal, would you try to get the teacher to be more understanding? If so, what would you do?

9. What are some possible compromises that could be recommended to resolve this issue?

10. Given the nature of the plagiarism policy, should Sheila's cumulative record as a student be relevant to the punishment she receives? Why or why not?

Suggested Readings

Bartlett, L. (1987). Academic evaluation and student discipline don't mix: A critical review. *Journal of Law and Education, 16*(2), 155–165.

Casella, R. (2003). Zero tolerance policy in schools: Rationale, consequences, and alternatives. *Teachers College Record, 105*(5), 872–892.

Corey, S. F., & Zeck, P. A. (2003). *Combating plagiarism.* Fastback #514. Bloomington, IN: Phi Delta Kappa Educational Foundation.

Dempster, N., Carter, L., Freakley, M., & Parry, L. (2004). Conflicts, confusions and contradictions in principals' ethical decision making. *Journal of Educational Administration, 42*(4), 450–461.

Dowling-Sendor, B. (2001). What did he know, and when did he know it? *American School Board Journal, 188*(3), 14–15, 51.

Fennimore, B. S. (1997). When mediation and equity are at odds: Potential lessons in democracy. *Theory-into-Practice, 36*(1), 59–64.

Fris, J. (1992). Principals' encounters with conflict: Tactics they and others use. *Alberta Journal of Educational Research, 38*(1), 65–78.

Goldman, E. (1998). The significance of leadership style. *Educational Leadership, 55*(7), 20–22.

Goldring, E., Huff, J., May, H., & Camburn, E. (2008). School context and individual characteristics: What influences principal practice? *Journal of Educational Administration, 46*(3), 332–352.

Gorman, K., & Pauken, P. (2003). The ethics of zero tolerance. *Journal of Educational Administration, 41*(1), 24–36.

Hayes, N., & Introna, L. D. (2005). Cultural values, plagiarism, and fairness: When plagiarism gets in the way of learning. *Ethics and Behavior, 15*(3), 213–231.

Henault, C. (2001). Zero tolerance in schools. *Journal of Law and Education, 30*(3), 547–553.

Hobbs, G. J. (1992). The legality of reducing student grades as a disciplinary measure. *Clearing House, 65,* 284–285.

Holloway, J. H. (2002). The dilemma of zero tolerance. *Educational Leadership, 59*(4), 84–85.

McGregor, J. H., & Williamson, K. (2005). Appropriate use of information at the secondary school level: Understanding and avoiding plagiarism *Library and Information Science Research, 27*(4), 496–512.

Militello, M., Schimmel, D., & Eberwein, H. J. (2009). If they knew, they would change: How legal knowledge impacts principals' practice. *NASSP Bulletin, 93*(1), 27–52.

Saunders, E. J. (1993). Confronting academic dishonesty. *Journal of Social Work Education, 29*(2), 224–231.

Skiba, R., & Peterson, R. (1999). The dark side of zero tolerance: Can punishment lead to safe schools? *Phi Delta Kappan, 80*(5), 372–376, 381–382.

Verdugo, R. R. (2002). Race-ethnicity, social class, and zero-tolerance policies: The cultural and structural wars. *Education and Urban Society, 35*(1), 50–75.

References

Begley, P. T. (2000). Values and leadership: Theory development, new research, and an agenda for the future. *Alberta Journal of Educational Research, 46*(3), 233–249.

Hodgkinson, C. (1991). *Educational leadership: The moral art.* Albany: State University of New York Press.

Howlett, P. (1991). How you can stay on the straight and narrow. *Executive Educator, 13*(2), 19–21, 35.

Kowalski, T. J. (2003). *Contemporary school administration: An introduction* (2nd ed.). Boston: Allyn and Bacon.

Kowalski, T. J. (2006). *The school superintendent: Theory, practice, and cases* (2nd ed.). Thousand Oaks, CA: Sage.

Kowalski, T. J. (2010). *The school principal: Visionary leadership and competent management.* New York: Routledge.

Kowalski, T. J., Lasley, T. J., & Mahoney, J. (2008). *Data-driven decisions and school leadership: Best practices for school improvement.* Boston: Allyn and Bacon.

Sergiovanni, T. J. (1992). *Moral leadership: Getting to the heart of school improvement.* San Francisco: Jossey-Bass.

Willower, D. J. (1994). Values, valuation and explanation in school organizations. *Journal of School Leadership, 4*(5), 466–483.

11 | INDIVIDUALIZING STAFF DEVELOPMENT

BACKGROUND INFORMATION

As professionals, principals and teachers need to engage in lifelong learning to ensure that they have knowledge and skills to deal with emerging problems. Historically, staff development has been the preferred process for meeting this requirement. For example, most school systems designate a certain number of in-service days each school term, and employees are required to attend workshops or other activities planned by the superintendent and principals. Fullan (2007) notes that traditional staff development has been little more than a few half-days of disconnected presentations provided annually to passive participants. Cole (2004) adds that such approaches to professional improvement are not only ineffective, they deter necessary improvement by diverting attention away from real individual and school needs.

Describing a principal's responsibilities for teacher development, Kowalski (2010) noted that individual professional growth and school improvement should be viewed as integrated, long-term, and vision-driven objectives. Further, effective staff development is (a) rooted in validated needs (Hirsh, 2009), (b) designed for continuous and sustained learning (Elmore, 2004), (c) interwoven into the daily practice of teachers (Fullan, 2007), (d) grounded in empirical and tacit knowledge of best practices (Loucks-Horsley & Stiegelbauer, 1991), (e) guided by relevant and measurable goals (Little, 1993), and (f) adequately funded (Eady & Zepeda, 2007).

Criticisms of staff development have increased in the context of sustained pressures to produce school improvement. Historically, in-service programs have been the preferred strategy for pursuing positive change in schools. As an example, a principal seeking to adopt a new instructional strategy would expose teachers to knowledge via workshops, conferences, or other learning opportunities with the expectation that teachers would learn and accept what they were taught. Often these expectations were not met; and even when they were, the changes being pursued often failed to be institutionalized. Reversion usually stemmed from the realization that staff development did not account for either individual professional growth needs or the extent to which the promoted program or process was incongruent with the prevailing school culture (Sarason, 1996).

This case study describes the effort of a new principal to move a middle school away from traditional staff development. He promotes the idea of individual career plans that are integrated with teacher teams and the school's vision. Teachers' reactions to his idea are mixed and he must decide whether he should move forward knowing that approximately half of the teachers oppose his plan.

Key Areas for Reflection

1. Principles of effective staff development
2. Advantages and disadvantages of staff development
3. Alternative approaches for teacher growth
4. Principal's responsibility for teacher growth
5. Linking individual growth to school improvement
6. Individual professional growth plans

THE CASE

Timberlake Middle School opened in 1983. Located in a city with a population of approximately 18,000, the school enrolls just over 650 students in Grades 6, 7, and 8. One year ago, Andy Harper, the assistant principal, was promoted after Principal Weggler retired.

During his 5-year tenure as assistant principal, Harper frequently urged Weggler to experiment with new approaches for teacher staff development. As per the school district calendar and policy, all professional employees had to participate in four half-day, in-service programs. Each school was given a budget to support the activities, and principals had the leeway to determine the nature of the programs, either independently or collectively (e.g., principals at two or more schools deciding to collaborate on the same programs). Weggler, as his predecessor had done, opted to collaborate with the high school and allowed the high school principal to select the programs.

After attending in-service sessions during his first 2 years as assistant principal, Harper concluded that the programs were perfunctory and treated as such by both administrators and teachers. The topics were general and usually more relevant for high school teachers. The afternoon sessions had a standard agenda: a luncheon for attendees and a 90-minute presentation by an invited speaker that was followed by small-group discussions of the speech. The topics appeared to be determined by speaker availability since they were not connected thematically nor linked to defined problems being addressed by the district's or schools' strategic plans. Further, no type of evaluation was conducted to determine if the in-service was effective.

After reaching these conclusions, Harper recommended to Weggler that the middle school should conduct its own staff development programs. Principal Weggler agreed that the joint programs had not been productive, but he believed that severing the long-standing arrangement with the high school would not ensure that the sessions would be more beneficial. Expressing skepticism toward all types of staff development, he said, "Professional improvement is an employee's responsibility. But, the state and school board require us to have staff development. Doing what we do now doesn't hurt anyone. Besides, everyone gets a free lunch."

Disappointed by Weggler's attitude, Harper decided that pursuing the matter further would be futile. Likewise, he chose not to share his concerns about staff development with teachers, fearing that his comments eventually would be revealed to Weggler.

When Principal Weggler announced that he would retire, he and many of the teachers urged Harper to pursue the job. Although there were 22 applicants, the superintendent and selection committee interviewed just three of them—Harper and two others. Harper, enjoying widespread support from the school's faculty, was the selection committee's first choice, and his appointment was approved unanimously by the school board.

After he became principal on July 1, revamping the staff development program was one of his top priorities. Making changes for the upcoming school term, however, was not possible. Outgoing principal Weggler had already agreed to continue the standing arrangement with the high school principal. Nevertheless, Harper wanted to engage the faculty in conversations about staff development, hoping that a new approach could be planned for the following school term.

Principal Harper shared his concern about staff development at the opening faculty meeting in mid-August. He said that he would be presenting suggested changes in the near future. The topic was not discussed in the September faculty meeting, but in October, Harper outlined a proposal for a radically different approach to staff development—one that included the following alterations:

- Staff development would not be conducted jointly with the high school. Rather, future programs would focus exclusively on middle school education and the professional development of middle school teachers.
- Instead of the entire faculty attending the same sessions, teachers would engage in individual or small-group activities during the designated time periods.
- Each teacher would develop a professional-growth plan based on personal needs and objectives. The plans had to be relevant to the middle school's vision statement; that is, personal development was to be pursued in the context of institutional goals and objectives.
- Each plan had to be approved by the principal within 3 weeks after the start of a new school term.
- Teachers could collaborate and develop identical or similar growth plans if they could demonstrate why such an arrangement is beneficial. The middle school instructional program is organized by teacher teams rather than academic departments, thus team development plans could be advantageous.
- Money allocated by the district for staff development and previously used to support the joint half-day sessions with the high school would now be appropriated for individual teachers or small groups to fund activities in their growth plans (e.g., purchasing a book, attending a professional meeting).
- The principal would meet with each teacher or small group once each semester to assess progress. The assessments would be formative and summative; that is, they would be used to assist teacher professional growth and they would be used to determine whether stated objectives were met.
- Summative assessments of professional growth would be infused into a teacher's annual performance evaluation.

After finishing the outline, Principal Harper said he wanted everyone to reflect on his proposal prior to next month's faculty meeting. "I prefer that you give my proposal considerable thought before commenting or making up your mind."

Between the October and November meetings, Harper's proposal was a primary topic in the teachers' lounge. Teachers clearly were divided over his proposal, and only a few were neutral.

Discussion of the proposed change was the third item on the November faculty meeting agenda. Once teachers started commenting, it seemed like the conversation might never end. Opponents were concerned that the amount of personal time required to develop and evaluate the individual plans would outweigh possible benefits. They also doubted that funds provided by the district would be sufficient to support revised approach to staff development. Their greatest concern, however, was the effect the growth plans would have on their annual performance evaluations.

Proponents countered by commenting the current half-day sessions were irrelevant, ineffective, and controlled by the high school. They also commented that personal or small group growth plans could make staff development learner-centered, goal-oriented, and connected to the school's vision.

Generally, the older and more experienced teachers opposed the proposed change and the younger, less experienced teachers favored it. One of the more tense exchanges occurred between a veteran language arts teacher and Principal Harper. The teacher asked, "Are you going to help us construct these plans? I have never done this, and if I must, I need someone to help me."

"I can help you procedurally, but the substance of the plan comes from you," Harper responded. "You are in the best position to decide what you need to do to grow professionally." The nonverbal reactions of some teachers indicated that they were not pleased with his answer.

Because only about half of the attendees revealed their sentiments at the meeting, Principal Harper did not know the exact number of proponents and opponents; he guessed, however, that those opposed to the change constituted a majority. And even if that were not true, the known opponents had considerable political influence, especially with parents and possibly with the school board. Because the allocated meeting time expired, the principal said the discussion would have to continue at the next faculty meeting.

Hoping his approach to staff development would eventually be accepted, Harper informed the high school principal that the middle school might opt to conduct its own staff development in the future. The two principals agreed that a decision on this matter had to be made by March 15.

At the December faculty meeting, comments made by the middle school teachers revealed that they remained divided on the proposed change to staff development. Believing that consensus was impossible and tiring of the discussion, one of the teachers suggested that the matter be resolved by voting. Several others immediately agreed. The suggestion caught the principal off-guard. He had hoped to avoid this alternative fearing that nearly half the faculty would find the outcome unacceptable.

"I know that voting would be easy and quick, but this matter is too important to be decided politically. At the same time, I support democratic decision making. So even though I prefer to reach consensus, I will consider the suggestion. I will let you know what I decide at least 1 week before the January faculty meeting. If I decide to follow the suggestion, then the vote will take place at the January meeting. If I decide against the suggestion, I will either seek the superintendent's approval of the proposed change or inform the high school principal that we will continue with the standing arrangement."

After the meeting, five teachers, all opposed to individual growth plans, made an appointment to see the superintendent, Estelle McFee. They asked her whether she knew about Harper's proposal and if so, they wanted to know if she supported it. She told them that she was aware of the proposal and was inclined to support it. She added that she had encouraged other principals to consider requiring individual growth plans. One teacher then asked, "If you are in favor of the growth plans, why don't you make the proposal a district requirement?" The superintendent said that the principals had not had ample opportunity to discuss the matter and that changing the existing policy without such discussions was not prudent.

Another teacher asked, "Don't you think that Mr. Harper should allow us to vote on this matter? Most of the teachers oppose the change, and forcing us to develop these growth plans could be very divisive."

"Principals have a responsibility to lead," the superintendent answered. "Sometimes they must make difficult decisions in the best interest of the school, students, and the community. Voting will tell us what the teachers want but it does not ensure that what they want is the best course of action."

At that point, the superintendent was asked if she would approve Harper's proposal if a vote were not taken or if the vote is taken and the proposed change is defeated.

Superintendent McFee thought about the question for a moment and then answered. "I don't like to answer hypothetical questions. My approval could depend on a vote count. For example, there is a big difference between a one-vote margin and a 20-vote margin. As to what I might do if a vote is not taken, I can tell you that I favor individual growth plans for staff development. I believe they would be a much better alternative than what we have been doing. Unless someone can prove otherwise, I am inclined to approve Principal Harper's proposal."

The teachers left the meeting disappointed. The superintendent's comment about the vote count led them to believe that she was sensitive to possible political repercussions; yet, the superintendent clearly supported the idea of individual growth plans.

The next morning, the superintendent briefed Principal Harper about her conversation with the teachers. She voiced concern about possible political problems. For example, the teachers' association might get involved or the teachers opposed to the growth plans might attempt to involve parents in the conflict. She suggested a compromise.

"Instead of taking a vote or instead of seeking approval without a vote, why don't you consider conducting a pilot study? If this were done, you could require the individual growth plans for 1 or 2 years. The outcomes could then be evaluated and we would be better informed as to whether the approach is effective. The findings from this study could be extremely valuable with respect to changing our current district staff development policy."

Harper indicated he would consider the suggested compromise. Later that day, he sent an e-mail to all the middle school professional staff seeking their reaction to conducting a 2-year pilot study of the individual growth plans. Only about 17 of the 37 teachers responded; among them, 11 supported a pilot project and six did not.

Problem Framing

1. Assume you are Principal Harper. First determine the main issue (problem) in this case. Then describe the current state and the desired state of this issue. (The section on problem framing in the Introduction section of this book defines the problem framing process.)

2. Based on evidence provided in the case, describe the difficulty associated with eliminating the gap between the present state and desired state.

Questions and Suggested Activities

1. Share and critique the problem statements prepared by students in your class.
2. What are the advantages and disadvantages of continuing the traditional approach to staff development?
3. What is an individual growth plan? Why is it considered essential for teachers?
4. As principal, should you be responsible for helping teachers to develop individual growth plans? Why or why not?
5. Assume that Superintendent McFee decides to recommend new policy that requires all teachers in the district to develop individual growth plans and requires principals to assist teachers to do so. As a principal, what specifically would you do to help teachers?
6. By attending staff development, teachers are exposed to new ideas. Often they return to school enthused about the ideas, but after a period of time, their fervor wanes and the change initiative is discarded. What are some possible reasons for this outcome?
7. One of the points the principal makes is that individual growth plans need to be tied to the middle school's vision statement. Do you agree with him? Why or why not?

8. The principal had hoped that he could get the faculty to reach consensus. What is consensus?

9. What are the advantages and disadvantages of voting to resolve the conflict?

10. Infusing the summary assessments from the individual growth plans into the annual performance evaluation is a concern voiced by teachers opposing the principal's

proposal. Should the two documents be connected? Why or why not?

11. The principal indicates that the periodic assessments of the growth plans will be both formative and summative. What are formative and summative assessments?

12. As a new principal, describe what you want in terms of a working relationship with the superintendent?

Suggested Readings

Arnau, L. (2008). NSDC's standards ease the shift from isolation to collaboration. *Journal of Staff Development, 29*(3), 49–50.

Danielson, C. (1996). *Enhancing professional practice: A framework for teaching.* Alexandria, VA: Association for Supervision and Curriculum Development.

Davis, S. H. (1997). The principal's paradox: Remaining secure in a precarious position. *NASSP Bulletin, 81,* 73–80.

Edwards, M. A. (1998). Turbo-charging professional development. *School Administrator, 55*(11), 34–36.

Dietz, M. E. (1995). Using portfolios as a framework for professional development. *Journal of Staff Development, 16*(2), 40–43.

Hirsh, S. (2009). A new definition. *Journal of Staff Development, 30*(4), 10–14, 16.

McNelly, T. (2002). Evaluations that ensure growth: Teacher portfolios. *Principal Leadership, 3*(4), 55–60.

Peine, J. M. (2003). Planning, measuring their own growth. *Journal of Staff Development, 24*(1), 38–42.

Randi, J., & Zeichner, K. M. (2004). New vision of teacher professional development. *Yearbook* (National Society for the Study of Education) Part 1, 180–227.

Steiny, J. (2009). A work in progress. *Journal of Staff Development, 30*(3), 32–37.

References

Cole, P. (2004). *Professional development: A great way to avoid change.* Melbourne, Australia: Center for Strategic Education.

Eady, C., & Zepeda, S. J. (2007). Evaluation, supervision, and staff development under mandated reform: The perceptions and practices of rural middle school principals. *Rural Educator, 28*(2), 1–7.

Elmore, R. (2004). *School reform from the inside out.* Cambridge, MA: Harvard University Press.

Fullan, M. (2007). Change the terms for teacher learning. *Journal of Staff Development, 28*(3), 35–36.

Hirsh, S. (2009). Before deciding what to do, determine what is necessary. *Journal of Staff Development, 30*(1), 71–72.

Kowalski, T. J. (2010). *The school principal: Visionary leadership and competent management.* New York: Routledge.

Little, J. W. (1993). Teachers' professional development in a climate of educational reform. *Educational Evaluation & Policy Analysis, 15*(2), 129–151.

Loucks-Horsley, S., & Stiegelbauer, S. (1991). Using knowledge of change to guide staff development. In A. Lieberman & L. Milkler (Eds), *Staff development for education in the '90s: New demands, new realities, new perspectives* (pp. 15–36). New York: Teachers College Press.

Sarason, S. B. (1996). *Revisiting the culture of the school and the problem of change.* New York: Teachers College Press.

12 | BREAK THE RULES AND PAY THE PRICE

BACKGROUND INFORMATION

Role theory addresses variables that shape work behavior. Theoretical models provide conceptual frameworks that assist analysts to study work behavior in the context of performance expectations (Gaynor, 1998). Such analysis often uncovers *role conflict,* disharmony between actual and ideal behavior. Commonly experienced by most school principals, this problem may be attributable to several factors. One is role ambiguity—a condition in which a formal role designated by the employer is either not clearly defined or not interpreted accurately (Hanson, 2003).

Even clearly written job descriptions do not ensure that prescribed roles will be interpreted correctly and uniformly. This is because school stakeholders hold dissimilar values, beliefs, and needs, and their dispositions shape informal role expectations (Kowalski, 2003). During a strike, for example, teachers may expect the principal to be sympathetic to their cause; the school board and superintendent may expect the principal to be a loyal member of the administrative team.

Role conflict also can be intrapersonal, as when a principal accepts two or more discordant roles as being appropriate (Owens, 2001). For example, she believes that she should closely and objectively supervise teachers to ensure school effectiveness; at the same time, she believes that she should treat teachers as colleagues and friends. The resulting internal conflict leads to inconsistent behavior, and teachers typically feel uncomfortable when a principal's behavior is unpredictable (Kowalski, Lasley, & Mahoney, 2008).

Principals can react in several ways to role conflict. Using the example in which a principal encounters competing expectations during a teachers' strike, the following are possible choices:

- *Picking one expectation over others.* The principal chooses either to meet the teachers' expectations or to meet the superintendent's/school board's expectations.
- *Withdrawing.* The principal retreats from the conflict; for example, he resigns or tries to hide in his office without expressing support for either side.
- *Seeking reconciliation.* The principal attempts to reconcile the differing expectations; for example, he tries to get both parties to accept his difficult positions in hopes that they will lessen their expectations.
- *Trying to satisfy everyone.* The principal attempts to be all things to all parties; for example, he wants the teachers to believe that he is completely on their side and he wants the superintendent and school board to believe that he is completely on their side.
- *Seeking protection for supervisors.* The principal attempts to gain relief by having the superintendent (or a designee) intervene. As an example, the principal asks the superintendent

to explain to the teachers that principals are only following orders by trying to keep schools operational during a strike.

- *Ignoring the situation.* The principal avoids decisions or comments that would reveal whether he supports the school board's position or the teacher association's position. The anticipation is that the strike will end before the principal has to be decisive.

This case involves a principal prone to suspending middle school students for what he considers serious violations of the school's code of conduct. An out-of-school suspension is a disciplinary sanction that excludes a student for a specified period of time; historically, it has been used commonly in secondary schools to punish unacceptable student behavior. Research, however, indicates that a temporary exclusion from school rarely reduces the negative behavior being punished; it does, however, usually have an adverse effect on academic performance (Christle, Nelson, & Jolivette, 2004). Many stakeholders in this case believe otherwise as evidenced by their approval of the principal's leadership style. Supporters believe that his tough disciplinary actions have contributed to an effective learning environment and a positive school image. Detractors, including several teachers, contend that the principal's stance toward student discipline is injudicious and ineffective. Tensions resulting from the divergent opinions are heightened when a student leaves school without permission after the principal tells him that he will be suspended for speaking to a teacher inappropriately.

Key Area for Reflection

1. Role expectations
2. Role conflict
3. School and community cultures
4. Student learning and discipline
5. Zero-tolerance policy

THE CASE

School Profile

Rogers Middle School, in a major city in a Southwestern state, was built less than 4 years ago to accommodate population growth. The attractive and well-maintained building is a source of pride for local families, some of whom live in public-housing projects and some of whom live in inexpensive prefabricated houses that were constructed about 20 years ago.

Many Rogers Middle School students are bilingual. A statistical report prepared for district administration provided the following racial-ethnic profile:

Hispanic: 41%

African American: 15%

Caucasian: 24%

Native American: 9%

Asian American: 9%

Other: 2%

The demographic profile of the school's professional staff, however, is quite different. Nearly 70% of the teachers, counselors, and administrators identify themselves as Caucasian.

Rogers Middle School contains Grades 6, 7, and 8 and serves approximately 1,150 students. Data for the last 3 years show that the school's students have made greater gains on the state proficiency test than students enrolled in the district's other six middle schools. At the same time, however, Rogers has the highest suspension rate among the district's middle schools. Both outcomes are commonly attributed to the school's principal, Hector Sanchez.

Principal Profile

Ever since he was in the third grade, Hector Sanchez wanted to be a teacher. One of nine children reared in a lower-middle-class family, he pursued his dream by working in a local factory and driving 45 miles twice a week to take night classes at the nearest state university. After 6 years, he had completed three-fourths of the degree requirements and saved enough money to allow him to finish his senior year as a full-time student.

Subsequently, Mr. Sanchez was employed as a mathematics teacher in a small high school. He also served as an assistant football coach and head track coach. Two years later, he began studies to complete his master's degree as a part-time student. Once he completed the degree and obtained a principal's license 4 years later, he was employed as an assistant principal in a large high school. There his primary responsibilities were student discipline and extracurricular activities. The principal, Carl Brown, became his mentor. Mr. Brown was a traditional administrator—stern, forceful, and decisive. Sanchez embraced his leadership style without reservation.

Over the next 3 years, Principal Brown molded his protégé and told him he was ready to be a principal. Heeding the advice, Sanchez applied for the principalship in a newly built middle school in the same district. While interviewing Hector, the assistant superintendent for pupil services, familiar with Principal Brown's discipline philosophy, asked him whether he shared his mentor's values and beliefs. Hector answered immediately, "Absolutely." He then added, "A principal's primary responsibility is to maintain a safe school. When I discipline students, and especially when I exclude them from school, I'm thinking about the welfare of all students. Contrary to popular thought, the typical student does not want to be suspended or expelled. The behavior of most students improves after they return to school."

Student discipline and school safety were pervasive concerns in this 24,000-student school district. Although policy required principals to suspend or expel students for certain infractions (e.g., possession or use of an illegal drug or possession of a weapon), considerable discretion was allowed for punishing lesser offenses. Support for existing policy among the district's administrators, including the principals, was mixed. In light of this fact, the assistant superintendent asked Hector: "Do you favor current district policy toward excluding students from school? Or, do you believe the school board should revise policy by specifying all offenses that merit suspensions?"

"I support current policy. Principals should have discretion. A single incident of misbehavior may appear minor, but when considered in relation to a student's cumulative record, it may justify a suspension."

Only four of the six-member selection committee voted to recommend Mr. Sanchez for the job. However, neither of the other two interviewees received more than three favorable votes. Consequently, Mr. Sanchez was recommended for and received the position.

Student Suspensions at Rogers Middle School

As Rogers Middle School commenced its second school year, Principal Sanchez decided to establish the Student Discipline Advisory Committee (SDAC), a group of seven parents and four teachers. The SDAC met periodically to review discipline practices in the school and to make recommendations for improvements. Approximately 6 months after it was formed, a member of the SDAC, a teacher, suggested that the group review student suspension records. The teacher made this suggestion knowing that among the district's five middle schools, Rogers had the highest percentage of suspensions.

The group first reviewed district policy for student suspensions. The policy statement included the following provisions:

- A school principal (hereafter including an assistant principal, acting principal, or a legitimate designee) may suspend a student when, in the principal's judgment, the action is required. In the exercise of this authority, the principal is subject to all provisions of law and school board policy.
- Students may be suspended from school for up to five (5) school days by the school principal without concurrence from the superintendent or his/her designee.
- Prior to imposing a suspension, the principal must inform the student of the intent to suspend and provide an explanation of charges. The student is required to sign a form indicating he or she has been informed of these matters.
- If the student denies the charges, a written explanation of facts is given to the student and to his or her parent or guardian. Students whose presence poses a continuing danger to persons or property or an ongoing threat of disruption may be removed from school immediately.
- After a decision is made to suspend a student for five (5) school days or less, the principal shall report the facts of the case in writing to the superintendent or his or her designee, the student's parent or guardian, and the student as soon as practicable.
- Appeals of out-of-school suspensions are governed by board policy concerning suspensions and expulsions.

Next, the group reviewed school records that listed the reasons why students had been suspended. They learned that the cause of approximately one-third of the suspensions was listed as "recurring misbehavior." Uncertain as to the precise meaning of this term, the SDAC invited Principal Sanchez to meet with them. He explained that the term described a pattern of misbehavior as evidenced by a student's cumulative record. When asked about the higher rate of suspensions at Rogers, he said, "I can't explain suspension rates at the other four middle schools. You should know, however, that our student achievement test scores improved this year and our overall safety record is excellent. I believe discipline, student achievement, and school safety are interrelated." After meeting with the principal, the SDAC members, though not unanimously, decided to discontinue their review of student suspensions.

By its third year of operation, Rogers Middle School was receiving public recognition. The city's major newspaper published several columns praising improvement in student scores on the state proficiency tests. Various media reports portrayed Principal Sanchez as a model administrator, and the superintendent publicly announced that he had nominated Mr. Sanchez for the state's "Middle School Principal of the Year" award.

Not everyone agreed with the portrayal of Mr. Sanchez as an effective principal. His most outspoken critic was a social studies teacher at Rogers, Aaron Carson. An experienced educator, he considered the principal to be a bully who used his authority recklessly. After learning about the SDAC's review of student suspensions, he challenged the principal's views in a faculty meeting. He said, "Contrary to what Mr. Sanchez told the SDAC, excluding students from school, especially for minor infractions, is ineffective punishment. You are really penalizing students academically while ignoring positive interventions that could improve behavior." Although several colleagues agreed with him, none did so openly at the faculty meeting.

After the meeting, Principal Sanchez invited Mr. Carson to meet with him to discuss their divergent beliefs. They met on two occasions; though their conversations were candid and civil, they ended up agreeing to disagree.

Conflict Intensifies

Most everyone at Rogers Middle School either knew or knew about Jimmy Malenga. He was a good athlete with a knack for finding trouble. His father was deceased and he lived with his mother and two sisters. Unfortunately, Jimmy's performance in the classroom did not mirror his performance on the athletic field. However, he did better in social studies than he did in other subjects, possibly because his favorite teacher was Mr. Carson.

Unlike many middle schools, Rogers did not organize instruction around teacher teams and block scheduling. Instead, the daily schedule was traditional—seven periods, each 43 minutes long. Jimmy's first period class, language arts, was taught by his least favorite teacher, Mr. Draycroft. Jimmy found diagramming sentences, studying grammar, and reading poetry to be unexciting. But he disliked the teacher even more than he disliked these activities. One day, Mr. Draycroft was reprimanding Jimmy for not having completed his homework. When he asked him why he failed to do his assignment, Jimmy answered, "Because this stuff is boring. Why don't we do something useful?"

Other students in the class laughed loudly, but Mr. Draycroft was not amused. Instead, he shook his finger at Jimmy. "Young man, I have had it with you. You and I are going to see the principal at the end of the period." Then Jimmy shouted back, "And, I've had it with you."

The class period ended a few minutes later and Mr. Draycroft escorted Jimmy to the principal's office. Jimmy was told to wait in the reception area as Mr. Draycroft talked to the principal. After a few minutes, Mr. Draycroft exited the office and went to his second-period class without looking at or speaking to Jimmy. At that point, Principal Sanchez took Jimmy into his office.

Jimmy already had been suspended from Rogers twice: once the previous school term and once during the current school term, each time for 3 days. "Jimmy," Mr. Sanchez began, "when are you going to learn? Mr. Draycroft told me what you said to him." After repeating the statements, the principal asked, "Did you say these things to Mr. Draycroft?"

Jimmy answered, "Yes. I said them because they are true. He's not a good teacher."

"Jimmy, you are in no position to judge teachers. Your remarks were disrespectful, and there are consequences for being disrespectful. In addition to being suspended previously this term, you have had after-school detention twice. Your persistent misbehavior is unacceptable, and clearly you have learned little from your previous suspensions. So, I am going to suspend you again for 3 days. Hopefully, this time it will have a positive effect. Before you go back to class, you need to sign this form indicating that I've told you of my intent to suspend you and then I'll inform your mother that you are entitled to have an informal hearing if you contest the suspension."

Jimmy responded angrily, "I'm not signing the form." He then ran out of the principal's office. Principal Sanchez tried to catch him, but Jimmy was too quick. Within seconds, he was out of the building and still running. Mr. Sanchez telephoned Jimmy's mother, who was at work at the time. He told her about the incident, reported that Jimmy had left school without permission, and informed her of the impending suspension.

Mrs. Malenga left work immediately in hopes of finding her son at home. She did not find him there nor did he return home that evening. At 11:30 P.M., she contacted the police and reported that he was missing.

Various accounts of the incident spread quickly through the school. Aaron Carson found out about Jimmy bolting from the principal's office as he was leaving school that day. The next morning, he learned that Jimmy's mother had filed a missing person report. Angry about the way the matter had been handled, he confronted Principal Sanchez in the hallway before first period. Unlike their previous discussions, this one was not civil. Harsh words were exchanged and Mr. Carson promised to express his feelings to Dr. Penelope Mackee, the assistant superintendent for secondary education and Mr. Sanchez's immediate supervisor. He telephoned Dr. Mackee during his preparation period. After listening to his concerns, she said she would look into the situation.

Disappointed with the response he received from Dr. Mackee, Carson wrote the following letter to the city's major newspaper and hand delivered it that same day. It appeared on the editorial page the next day.

The public needs to know the story of Jimmy Malenga, a young Native American student at Rogers Middle School who apparently is now a runaway. Jimmy is one of my students and over the past few months, he has been making progress in my class. He was going to be suspended from school for expressing a viewpoint about another teacher. Though his behavior was undeniably improper, so was the disciplinary action imposed by the principal. Jimmy is now somewhere on the streets because his principal believes it is more important to punish him than it is to help him. What happened to Jimmy unfortunately is not unusual at our school. The principal routinely suspends students, at times for petty issues. Yet, he ignores possible interventions such as counseling or constructive behavior modification. I urge the superintendent and school board to revise policy so that principals will be unable to indiscriminately exclude students from schools. Hopefully, parents and other teachers will do the same.

Sincerely,
Aaron Carson
Social studies teacher,
Rogers Middle School

After the letter was published, the superintendent, Dr. Fred Lopson, and school board members received numerous e-mails supporting Mr. Carson's views. They also were contacted by reporters. Late that afternoon, the superintendent issued a statement saying that he would investigate the matter and issue his finding at the next board meeting to be held in 4 days.

Two days after he ran from the principal's office, Jimmy Malenga returned home. His mother, relieved to have him back, informed the police and the media. Mrs. Malenga also called Principal Sanchez and told him she would not request a hearing. She said Jimmy would accept the punishment, apologize to Mr. Draycroft, and return to school after serving his suspension.

Controversy over suspensions at Rogers, however, did not wane. Now Mr. Sanchez's supporters were politically active. The following petition, signed by more than 200 Rogers Middle School parents and teachers, was given to the superintendent before the school board meeting at which he was to issue his report:

> We the undersigned fully support the leadership of Principal Hector Sanchez. He has made Rogers Middle School the most successful and safest middle school in this district. We are relieved that Jimmy Malenga is safe and pleased that he will continue as a Rogers student, and we believe that Mr. Sanchez acted responsibly. We urge the school board to join us in supporting a great principal of an outstanding school.

Many of the people who signed the petition were at the board meeting.

During the meeting, Superintendent Lopson reported the outcome of his investigation. He concluded that Principal Sanchez had acted within the parameters of existing policy. He also pointed out that after the school's SDAC had investigated concerns about suspensions the previous school term, it concluded that current practices were acceptable. In closing, the superintendent said he would not recommend a change to existing policy. He explained that principals were professionals and should have discretion when disciplining students.

After he concluded his comments, George Manulita, a board member, was recognized.

"We are all aware that Mr. Sanchez is popular. In my opinion, he deserves some credit for operating a successful middle school. But the real issue is suspending students, not his popularity or influence. I believe the reasons why students get suspended should be specified in policy and policy should be enforced consistently across our schools. Therefore, I favor a policy change."

A few attendees applauded, but their reaction was quickly eclipsed by shouts of "no" from Sanchez supporters.

Darren Marshall, another board member, spoke next. "I disagree that a policy change is needed. As for Mr. Sanchez, he is doing a great job."

The principal's supporters stood, applauded, and then chanted, "Mr. Sanchez, Mr. Sanchez."

Problem Framing

1. Assume you are Superintendent Lopson. First determine the main issue (problem) in this case. Then describe the current state and the desired state of this issue. (The section on problem framing in the Introduction section of this book defines the problem framing process.)

2. Based on evidence provided in the case, describe the difficulty associated with eliminating the gap between the present state and desired state.

Questions and Suggested Activities

1. Discuss the intended purposes and merits of student suspensions. What does research on this topic reveal?
2. Do you agree with Principal Sanchez's contention that the effectiveness of discipline needs to be considered in relation to student learning? Why or why not?
3. What is the policy for suspensions in your school district? How does your district's policy differ from the one described in this case?

4. What alternatives could have been used by Principal Sanchez to discipline Jimmy given the incident and his previous record of misbehavior?
5. To what extent are student learning and discipline connected? What evidence do you have for your response?
6. What purposes should be served by policies and rules for student discipline?

7. The superintendent contends that specifying conditions for suspensions restricts principal discretion. Do you agree? What are the advantages and disadvantages of restricting employee discretion?

8. Did Mr. Carson, the teacher who wrote the letter to the editor of the local newspaper, behave professionally in criticizing Principal Sanchez publicly? Why or why not?

9. If you were a principal in this school district, would you prefer the current policy on student suspensions or a policy that would prohibit suspensions except for specified offenses? Defend your response.

10. Is Principal Sanchez an effective administrator? Why or why not?

Suggested Readings

Carey, M. (1986). School discipline: Better to be loved or feared? *Momentum, 17*(2), 20–21.

Christle, C., Nelson, C. M., & Jolivette, K. (2004). School characteristics related to the use of suspension. *Education and Treatment of Children, 27*(4), 509–526.

Costenbader, V., & Markson, S. (1998). School suspension: A study with secondary students. *Journal of School Psychology, 36*(1), 59–82.

Denney, K. A., & Van Gorder, C. H. (2004). A team approach to exclusionary sanctions. *Principal Leadership (Middle School Ed.), 4*(5), 52–55.

Henley, M. (1997). Why punishment doesn't work. *Principal, 77*(2), 45–46.

Mukuria, G. (2002). Disciplinary challenges: How do principals address this dilemma? *Urban Education, 37*(3), 432–452.

Nichols, J. D. (2004). An exploration of discipline and suspension data. *Journal of Negro Education, 73*(4), 408–423.

Pantesco, V. (2005). An immediate response protocol for addressing intolerant behavior. *Principal Leadership (Middle School Ed.), 6*(3), 8–9.

Raffaele-Mendez, L. M., & Knoff, H. M. (2003). Who gets suspended from school and why: A demographic analysis of schools and disciplinary infractions in a large school district. *Education and Treatment of Children, 26*(1), 30–51.

Raffaele-Mendez, L. M., Knoff, H. M., & Ferron, J. M. (2002). School demographic variables and out-of-school suspension rates: A quantitative and qualitative analysis of a large, ethnically diverse school district. *Psychology in the Schools, 39*(3), 259–277.

Rosen, L. (1997). *School discipline: Best practices for administrators.* Thousand Oaks, CA: Corwin Press.

Scott, T. M., & Nelson, C. M. (1999). Universal school discipline strategies: Facilitating positive learning environments. *Effective School Practice, 17*(4), 54–64.

Stader, D. L. (2004). Zero tolerance as public policy: The good, the bad, and the ugly. *Clearing House, 78*(2), 62–66.

Sughrue, J. A. (2003). Zero tolerance for children: Two wrongs do not make a right. *Educational Administration Quarterly, 39*(2), 238–258.

References

Christle, C., Nelson, C. M., & Jolivette, K. (2004). School characteristics related to the use of suspension. *Education and Treatment of Children, 27*(4), 509–526.

Gaynor, A. K. (1998). *Analyzing problems in schools and school systems: A theoretical approach.* Mahwah, NJ: Lawrence Erlbaum Associates.

Hanson, E. M. (2003). *Educational administration and organizational behavior* (5th ed.). Boston: Allyn and Bacon.

Kowalski, T. J. (2003). *Contemporary school administration* (2nd ed.). Boston: Allyn and Bacon.

Kowalski, T. J., Lasley, T. J., & Mahoney, J. (2008). *Data-driven decisions and school leadership: Best practices for school improvement.* Boston: Allyn and Bacon.

Owens, R. (2001). *Organizational behavior in education* (7th ed.). Boston: Allyn and Bacon.

13 | AN AMBITIOUS ASSISTANT PRINCIPAL

BACKGROUND INFORMATION

Research on administrator career patterns has focused on regularities in the ascension from lower-level to higher-level positions. Although many administrators began at the principal level, the modal entry-level position, especially in secondary schools, has been the assistant principalship (Miklos, 1988; Weller & Weller, 2001). Turnover in the latter position has been relatively high for several reasons. Consider three of them:

1. Many assistant principals want to be principals; and therefore, they actively pursue a job change after a few years (Kowalski, 2010).
2. The position is less standardized than the principalship; that is, the duties assigned to assistant principals are dissimilar across districts and schools. Assistant principals may become dissatisfied if their duties are narrow and mundane (Moore, 2009).
3. Some principals fail to serve as mentors and others discourage assistant principals from seeking promotions. Frequently, the behavior of these principals is self-serving; for example, they try to convince their assistants not to seek promotions simply because they do not want to be inconvenienced by staff turnover. Rather than succeeding, such behavior more often than not encourages assistant principals to seek another position after a relatively short period of time (Porter, 1996).

More recently, however, setting the assistant principalship as an ultimate career goal has become relatively common. From a professional perspective, research shows that many assistant principals find the position as fulfilling their needs and interests (e.g., Chen, Blendinger, & McGrath, 2000; Sutter, 1996). From a personal perspective, increasing numbers of assistant principals appear unwilling to sacrifice family and quality-of-life interests in order to become a principal; as an example, they are unwilling to relocate to receive a promotion (Kowalski, 2010).

Legal and ethical issues also can influence career decisions. As examples: Are administrators legally and ethically bound to fulfill the terms of an employment contract before accepting another position? Should they mislead their employer about their career intentions? Upwardly mobile applicants (i.e., those viewing the assistant principalship as a stepping stone) realize that telling an employer the truth about their career aspirations may prevent them from being selected. Conversely, employers also face ethical problems such as not being candid about prospects for being promoted to the principalship.

As the locus of school improvement has shifted gradually to the school level, stability in both the principal and assistant principal positions has become a greater concern. Leadership instability often has a detrimental effect on change initiatives, especially those that may take 4 or 5 years to fully implement (Fullan, 2010). Moreover, instability diminishes the probability that attainable, shared visions and strategic plans will be developed and pursued (Kowalski, 2003).

This case describes a dilemma faced by an ambitious young teacher who becomes an assistant principal in a small, rural secondary school. As an applicant, he makes a commitment to remain in the position for at least 5 years. Actually, he wants to become a principal as quickly as possible and prefers to work in a city or suburb.

Key Areas for Reflection

1. Administrator career patterns
2. Ethical and legal dimensions of career decisions
3. The assistant principalship
4. Principal and assistant principal relationships

THE CASE

Bentonville, in northern Iowa, is a farming community. Many of the 2,500 residents have never lived elsewhere, and the level of community pride is exceedingly high. The downtown area is just a few blocks of old stores and commercial buildings, including a bank, a Sears outlet store, a restaurant, a grocery store, several taverns, and a farm equipment business. A Catholic church is at the eastern edge of downtown, and a Lutheran church is at the western end.

There are few secrets in Bentonville. Though families are divided religiously by their membership in the two churches, the community's social, political, and cultural structure is homogeneous. In some fashion, nearly all the families are engaged in farming or farm-related businesses.

Bentonville Junior/Senior High School

Bentonville Community School District spans two townships and operates just two schools: a combined junior and senior high school and an elementary school. The Bentonville Junior/Senior High School enrolls approximately 450 pupils in Grades 7 to 12. The building, less than one mile outside the town of Bentonville in a rural setting, was constructed 16 years ago. Oscar McCammick, the principal, has never been employed in another school. Having just completed his 10th year as principal, he previously served as the assistant principal for 6 years and as science and mathematics teacher for 7 years.

Hiring a New Assistant Principal

When Mr. McCammick was promoted to be principal, he convinced the superintendent and school board to hire George Stileke, a close friend, a teacher, and a coach at the school, to be assistant principal. Although Superintendent Becky Potter favored employing a younger person, she honored the principal's wishes and recommended Stileke for the position. He served in it for 10 years before retiring.

Initially, an internal job search was conducted because the superintendent and principal thought several current employees who held principal licenses would apply. None of them did. In early June, Superintendent Potter broadened the search to include external applicants. By the deadline, July 15, she had received only six applications. One was eliminated from consideration because he did not qualify for the required administrative license. The remaining five files were sent to Principal McCammick for his consideration. After completing reference checks, the principal eliminated three of the five; the two remaining applicants, Norman Emons and Raymond Tyler, were invited to Bentonville to interview for the position.

Emons was the first to be interviewed. Fifty-one years old and a middle school teacher from Des Moines, he only recently had received a license qualifying him to be an assistant principal. When asked why he had waited so long to pursue an administrative career, he explained that until recently he and two other teachers owned a small house painting company. Because the venture was successful and consumed his summer months, he was unwilling to accept a position that would require him to work beyond the standard school year. Recently, however, the business was dissolved.

Tyler, the other finalist, was only 29 years old. A teacher employed in Davenport, he had moved to Iowa to attend college; previously, he lived with his family in a relatively affluent Chicago suburb. His employment interview was conducted by the superintendent and principal. Shortly after it began, the principal asked, "If you are selected for this job, what are your intentions about remaining in the position for more than a couple of years?" Rather than answering the question, Raymond asked a question. "How long do you want a person to remain in this job"

Principal McCammick answered, "At least 5 years; hopefully, longer."

Raymond said, "That would not be a problem for me. I want to work for a highly experienced principal for at least 5 years. Regardless of whether I get this job, I am planning to enroll in a doctoral program in school administration. Pursuing my studies on a part-time basis, it will take me at least 5 years to complete the degree. At that point, my plans are either to become a principal or to teach in a university."

The superintendent then asked him to express his feelings about living in a rural community.

"I love Iowa and although I've not lived in a town as small as Bentonville, I look forward to having the experience. A month ago, my application for the Ph.D. program at a state university 45 miles from here was approved. My intent is to begin the program as a part-time student as soon as possible. I'm also planning to get married in about a year and my fiancée will be a full-time Ph.D. student at the same university beginning in August. Between going to school and working, I'll be very busy. My only real concern would be finding a place to live."

After the interview ended and Raymond departed, the superintendent turned to the principal and said, "This fellow is a really good prospect. He's well-groomed, confident, and articulate." In a letter of reference, Raymond's current principal described him as "one of the best young teachers I have ever supervised." Principal McCammick, however, was skeptical. He was not convinced Raymond would be a "good fit" for either the school or the community. "I'm not sure he realizes what it is like to live in a small community; despite what he said, I doubt that he would remain here for more than a few years. Yet, he is undeniably a better applicant than the first person we interviewed."

The two administrators agreed that Raymond should be offered the position. When he received a telephone call a few days later from the superintendent, Raymond immediately accepted the job.

First Year

Raymond officially became assistant principal on August 10 and rented a small apartment in the basement of a home owned by a retired teacher. The first 2 months were hectic. For example, he was not used to having weekend responsibilities, such as attending Friday night football games. Moreover, he enrolled in a Wednesday evening class and began the Ph.D. program.

Initially, Principal McCammick was very pleased with Raymond's performance, and he even questioned whether his earlier reservations were warranted. Raymond related well with students, and his job performance seemed to please everyone, especially the superintendent and school board members. In early December, Principal McCammick told Superintendent Potter, "I think you were completely correct about Raymond. He's proving to be an excellent assistant principal."

The following week, Raymond informed the principal that he was moving to Lincoln, the county seat, about 16 miles away. He explained that the small apartment he was renting did not meet his needs. The principal's doubts about Raymond resurfaced. In recent decades, virtually all Bentonville administrators resided in the school district. With a declining population, residents were very sensitive about public employees living elsewhere. The principal reminded Raymond of this fact and added, "I hope living in Lincoln will not affect your job performance."

Raymond had become friends with two Bentonville teachers who were also coaches. The three were approximately the same age, and during the fall semester, they had attended several college football games together. During casual conversations, Raymond told them that he had underestimated how uncomfortable it would be for him to live and work in a rural community. He added that after he finished his Ph.D., he definitely wanted to work in a larger community.

In early April, Raymond received his annual performance evaluation during a conference with the principal. Before being given the evaluation form, the principal told him that some parents, including a couple of school board members, were displeased with his decision to reside outside the school district. Raymond did not respond to the comment. He was then shown the evaluation report and it included seven ratings; four were marked "above average" and three were marked "average." In the comment section of the document, the principal wrote that Raymond needed to act more maturely when dealing with students—but neither evidence to support the judgment nor an explanation as to why it was made was included in the report.

Raymond was surprised and displeased with the evaluation for two reasons. First, he was not used to receiving mediocre ratings. All of his previous teaching evaluations described his performance as being "excellent." Second, Principal McCammick's comments about his performance became less positive after he moved out of the community; thus, he assumed he was being punished for an issue unrelated to his job performance. He told the principal, "I am not pleased with the evaluation, and I disagree with the satisfactory ratings."

McCammick responded, "This is a pretty good evaluation for a first-year assistant principal. And I am recommending that you be re-employed with a salary increase."

Raymond signed the evaluation form as required by district policy but did not make a formal objection to its content. He concluded that being cooperative was prudent. A few weeks later he received and signed an employment contract for the next school term.

Conflict Intensifies

As the second semester was drawing to a close in late May, Raymond and two friends on the faculty had lunch together at school. One of them informed Raymond that the principal was asking questions about him. Specifically, he was asking teachers if they knew whether Raymond planned to leave before the next school term. The teacher sharing this information added that McCammick was under the impression that Raymond had become dissatisfied with his job. Raymond thanked his friend for the information but did not comment further.

A week later, Principal McCammick received a telephone call from a high school principal in suburban Chicago. She was inquiring about Raymond Tyler. She told McCammick that she had interviewed Raymond for an assistant principal's position the previous day. McCammick responded, "Did he interview for a position that begins this summer?"

"That's correct."

"Did Raymond tell you he signed an employment contract here for the next school term?"

"He did."

"Then, aren't you curious why he is looking for a new job after just 1 year?"

"Not really because it is not unusual for administrators under contract to seek new employment," she said. "Our high school has 2,100 students, four assistant principals, and the salary is substantially higher than the one he is now receiving. The fact that Mr. Tyler wants to advance his career does not bother me. I am interested in knowing, however, your assessment of his performance as an assistant principal. Obviously, my impressions of him to this point are positive. Otherwise, I would not be contacting you."

"When we hired Raymond a year ago," McCammick responded, "he assured the superintendent and me that he would remain in the position for at least 5 years. Given the fact he has applied for other jobs already, he was not being truthful. He also moved out of our school district after being employed here a few months. As you might detect, I'm not pleased to learn he is seeking another position. Given the fact that he did not have the courtesy to tell me he was applying for other jobs, I prefer not to comment on his job performance."

The inquiring principal thanked McCammick for his time, and then ended the conversation. Without putting down the phone, McCammick called Superintendent Potter, shared the information he had just received, and asked whether they could prevent Raymond from taking another job.

"Even if there were a legal constraint," the superintendent responded, "would you want to force him to stay here?"

McCammick said he would talk to Raymond about his candidacy for another job and would update her after he did so.

About an hour later, McCammick saw Raymond in the hallway and told him about the telephone call he had received earlier that day from the principal in Illinois.

"You promised that you would stay in Bentonville for at least 5 years. Today I find out that you're applying for other jobs. Why didn't you tell me what you were doing?"

"First, I never promised I would stay here for 5 years. I said I wanted to work under a highly experienced principal for 5 years. The opportunity in suburban Chicago is not something I directly pursued. I'm getting married in a few months and my fiancée has accepted a teaching position at the same high school. She told the principal about me and things evolved. So I wasn't actively seeking another position. If I don't get the job in Illinois, I'll stay here and do my best. Obviously, it won't be an ideal situation with my wife living in Chicago and me being here."

McCammick was not pleased with the explanation. "You signed a contract to work here next school term. If you do not honor that contract, I'll be very disappointed. Integrity is important."

Problem Framing

1. Assume you are Raymond. First determine the main issue (problem) in this case. Then describe the current state and the desired state of this issue. (The section on problem framing in the Introduction section of this book defines the problem framing process.)

2. Based on evidence provided in the case, describe the difficulty associated with eliminating the gap between the present state and desired state.

Questions and Suggested Activities

1. Share and critique the problem statements prepared by students in your class.
2. Discuss the legal dimensions of an administrator's employment contract, especially with respect to the rights of both the employer and employee.

3. Given the content of this case, did Raymond promise to remain at Bentonville High School for at least 5 years? What evidence in the case supports your answer?

4. Did Raymond err in not telling Principal McCammick that he would be interviewing for another position? Why or why not?

5. Divide into two groups and debate the advantages and disadvantages of employers demanding that assistant principals remain in that job for a specified period of time.

6. After receiving his annual performance evaluation, Raymond presumes that he is being punished for moving out of the school district. What evidence in this case is relevant to this presumption?

7. Assume you were Principal McCammick. Would you try to force Raymond to stay in his current position for another year? Why or why not?

8. Should employers in rural districts weigh an individual's cultural background in making hiring decisions? Why or why not?

9. Assume that Raymond does not get the job in suburban Chicago. What advice would you give him about remaining at Bentonville High School?

Suggested Readings

Calabrese, R. L., & Tucker-Ladd, P. R. (1991). The principal and the assistant principal: A mentoring relationship. *NASSP Bulletin, 75,* 67–74.

Fields, L. J. (2005). Patterns of stress and coping mechanisms for novice school administrators. *Essays in Education, 14,* 1–10.

Gerke, W. (2004). More than a disciplinarian. *Principal Leadership (Middle School Ed.), 5*(3), 39–41.

Glanz, J. (1994). Dilemmas of assistant principals in their supervisory role: Reflections of an assistant principal. *Journal of School Leadership, 4*(5), 577–590.

Goodson, C. P. (2000). Assisting the assistant principal. *Principal, 79*(4), 56–57.

Hart, A. (1991). Leader succession and socialization: A synthesis. *Review of Educational Research, 61,* 451–474.

Hartzell, G. N. (1993). When you're not at the top. *High School Magazine, 1*(2), 16–19.

Hibert, K. M. (2000). Mentoring leadership. *Phi Delta Kappan, 82*(1), 16–18.

Kwan, P. (2009). Vice-principals' dilemma–career advancement or harmonious working relationship. *International Journal of Educational Management, 23*(3), 203–216.

Murray, K. T., & Murray, B. A. (1999). The administrative contract: Implications for reform. *NASSP Bulletin, 83*(606), 33–38.

Oliver, R. (2003). Assistant principal job satisfaction and desire to become principals. *Education Leadership Review, 4*(2), 38–46.

Tooms, A. (2003). The rookie's playbook: Insights and dirt for new principals. *Phi Delta Kappan, 84*(7), 530–533.

Winter, P. A., & Partenheimer, P. R. (2002). *Applicant attraction to assistant principal jobs: An experimental assessment.* (ERIC Document Reproduction Service No. ED471 558)

Sutter, M. R. (1996). What do we know about the job and career satisfaction of secondary school assistant principals? *NASSP Bulletin, 80*(579), 108–111.

References

Chen, K., Blendinger, J., & McGrath, V. (November 2000). *Job satisfaction among high school assistant principals.* Paper presented at the annual meeting of the Mid-South Educational Research Association, Bowling Green, Kentucky.

Fullan, M. (2010). *All systems go: The change imperative for whole system reform.* Thousand Oaks, CA: Corwin Press.

Kowalski, T. J. (2003). *Contemporary school administration: An introduction* (2nd ed.). Boston: Allyn and Bacon.

Kowalski, T. J. (2010). *The school principal: Visionary leadership and competent management.* New York: Routledge.

Miklos, E. (1988). Administrator selection, career patterns, succession, and socialization. In N. Boyan (Ed.),

Handbook of research on educational administration (pp. 53–76). New York: Longman.

Moore, T. (2009). Let's end the ambiguous role of assistant principals. *Principal, 89*(1), 66.

Porter, J. J. (1996). What is the role of the middle level assistant principal, and how should it change? *NASSP Bulletin, 80*(578), 25–30.

Sutter, M. R. (1996). What do we know about the job and career satisfaction of secondary school assistant principals? *NASSP Bulletin, 80*(579), 108–111.

Weller, L. D., & Weller, S. J. (2001). *The assistant principal: Essentials for effective leadership.* Thousand Oaks, CA: Corwin Press.

14 | LET'S GET STRATEGIC

BACKGROUND INFORMATION

Educators are told repeatedly that authentic school improvement is unlikely unless change is guided by a strategic plan. Done properly, this document details a school's responsibility, existing and emerging needs, a description of a desired future state, goals for achieving that future state, and strategies for goal attainment. Definitions of strategic planning vary, with some including all of these components; others are narrow, focusing solely on goals and strategies. In the realm of school reform, the comprehensive definition has been the norm.

A school's overall responsibility should be described accurately in a *mission statement.* This document expresses a school's purpose—its reason for existing. Mission statements for public schools are largely determined by state constitutions, laws, and policies, but they may be augmented by local commitments (Coleman & Brokmeier, 1997). Missions should be written in present tense and usually are not modified substantially over time. They serve multiple purposes including informing the public and employees, cultivating unity of purpose, providing a frame of reference for strategic planning goals, and guiding difficult decisions such as resource allocation (Kowalski, 2011).

In addition to knowing why a school exists, educators need to be aware of emerging needs and wants. A need is a gap between what is and what is not required. For instance, if a high school's graduation rate is 53% and the state benchmark for accreditation is 85%, improving the rate by 32% points is a real need. In strategic planning, needs and wants are identified through *environmental scanning* (Poole, 1991)—a process in which school officials periodically collect and analyze data pertinent to the school's mission (Kirst & Kelley, 1995). Examples include opinion polls, enrollment projections, analysis of community development plans, and changing requirements for student enrollment in higher education.

One of the most essential and difficult aspects of strategic planning is *visioning.* Properly pursued, a school's vision statement should be developed collectively by primary stakeholders such as school employees, civic leaders, and other community residents. Reaching consensus, even in small schools, requires open and candid communication and skilled conflict management so that the principal is able to "effectively monitor, interact, and react to key groups within the organizational environment" (Lamb & McKee, 2005, p. 1). Written in future tense, a vision statement should provide a clear picture of what the school is intended to look like in meeting its mission at some designated point in the future (Kowalski, 2011). As such, the statement provides a guide for long-term action, a symbolic statement that gives meaning to action (Conger, 1989), and it is a sociological force that generates shared commitment essential to intended change (Björk, 1995). Visioning, however, is an enigma for many, as evidenced by the fact that some school vision statements are written as mission statements (Rozycki, 2004). Since the purpose of visioning is to describe what a school will look like in meeting its mission, both an accurate mission statement and environmental scanning should be completed prior to visioning.

Once a common vision is adopted, strategic planning focuses on achieving the desired future state. Specifically, *short-term goals* (incremental steps for reaching the vision) and *goal attainment strategies* are essential (Cunningham & Gresso, 1993; Sergiovanni, 2001). Strategy development encompasses both process and technique; the former details the sequence of steps to be taken whereas the latter identifies tactics (or approaches) used at each step (Kowalski, Petersen, & Fusarelli, 2007).

Lastly, strategic planning requires periodic assessments and annual evaluations. Assessment entails measurement: for example, determining how many students met a benchmark for an improvement goal. Evaluation entails judgments about assessments: for example, determining why more students did not meet the benchmark (Kowalski, 2010). Assessment and evaluation data serve two purposes: They determine the extent to which goals have been met and they provide information used to make periodic modifications to a strategic plan.

In summary, strategic planning is a long-range activity that relies on a mission statement and environmental scans to produce a collective vision statement, short-term goals, goal attainment strategies, and assessment and evaluation data.

This case is about a novice principal who assumes leadership of a low-performing urban school. She accepts the position knowing that her predecessor was dismissed for failing to conduct strategic planning appropriately and knowing that many of the teachers were displeased because of his dismissal. As you read this case, consider how the prevailing school culture is pivotal to school improvement generally and strategic planning specifically.

Key Areas for Reflection

1. Strategic planning and school improvement
2. Mission and vision statements
3. Collaborative planning
4. Group decision making
5. School culture and change
6. Managing conflict in collaborative decision making

THE CASE

The District and the School

Averton City School District grew rapidly after World War II because the city of Averton attracted numerous manufacturers, resulting in an 80% increase in population from 1950 to 1970. The district's peak enrollment, 24,788, was recorded in 1968. Since then, the enrollment has declined incrementally to 14,393, and approximately 30% of the schools have been closed.

Monroe Elementary School is about two miles from Averton's business district. Housed in a two-story brick building that was originally constructed in 1962 and renovated in 1998, it serves about 350 pre-school to fifth-grade students. The demographic profiles of the student body and faculty are typical of those in the district's other elementary schools. Approximately 55% of the students qualify for free or reduced-price lunches; 74% of the students and 56% of the school employees are persons of color; the average age of the teachers is 56.

Sheila Adams

With the exception of the 4 years she spent in college, Sheila Adams has lived in Averton all her life. She began teaching second grade in one of Averton's other elementary schools. During her 9 years of teaching, she completed a master's degree in school administration and several additional courses required for a principal's license. She had applied for two other principal vacancies in the school system before being selected as Monroe Elementary School's new leader.

Strategic Planning

The state requires all public elementary and secondary schools to engage in strategic planning as part of a comprehensive accountability program. Although plans were developed and filed for Monroe Elementary School in each of the last 3 years, the superintendent had received warnings from the state department of education indicating that they were flawed and needed to be improved. Specifically, the plans were criticized for the following reasons:

- They did not include any type of needs assessment.
- There was no evidence that an effort was made to involve primary stakeholders.
- The vision statement was ambiguous and did not meet the criteria established by state policy.
- The short-term goals were general and not measurable.
- There was no evaluation component in the plans.

The previous principal, Malcolm Easlow, had been warned by the associate superintendent for instruction that he had to devise an acceptable plan or face dismissal. Rather than trying to resolve the concerns voiced by state officials, he argued that Monroe's previous plans were typical of those developed for the district's other elementary schools and enlisted the faculty to echo that sentiment. Although the associate superintendent assigned one of his assistants to work with Easlow, the plan did not improve. The assistant told the associate superintendent that Principal Easlow had neither the knowledge nor the inclination to engage in strategic planning. After the fourth attempt to develop an acceptable plan failed, the principal was dismissed.

Principal Adams

Two factors weighed heavily in the decision to employ Sheila Adams as Monroe's principal: She had been teaching in the elementary school that had the best strategic plan in the district and she had an accurate understanding of the planning process. Adams assumed the position at Monroe knowing that her timeframe for successfully completing a strategic plan was limited—probably no more than 2 years.

She began by reading the existing plan and the state's criticisms of it. She then investigated what had or had not been done to produce an acceptable plan. The following are several of the primary conclusions she reached:

- Easlow openly and consistently expressed a negative attitude toward strategic planning. He contended that the notion that school employees could control Monroe's future was a myth. His attitude was to do as little as necessary to mollify the associate superintendent and state officials.
- Many faculty members shared and supported Easlow's convictions. For them, not having to participate in planning was a reward, and as long as he did not require them to be actively involved they were satisfied.

- Much of the last plan Easlow developed he had copied from a principal in one of the district's other elementary schools. He did so even though the plan he duplicated also had been judged unacceptable by the state department of education previously.
- There was no evidence that Easlow had involved parents or other stakeholders in any phase of planning.
- Once written, the last plan was presented to the school's employees and they approved it unanimously, most voting without having read the document.
- After learning that this plan too was unacceptable, Easlow only made minor modifications and resubmitted it. He contended that the state would eventually soften its demands regarding strategic planning.

Principal Adams was disappointed but not surprised by the facts she had uncovered. She informed school employees that the strategic plan would be revamped substantially and that they had to be involved in shaping the document. Expectedly, the employees, especially teachers, wanted to know the nature and extent of their involvement. Adams told them they would be involved continuously and they would be collaborating with her and other stakeholders, especially to develop a meaningful vision statement, short-term goals, and goal attainment strategies.

Almost immediately, several teachers reacted negatively. The following were comments they made:

"You can't make us do this. Planning is an administrative responsibility."

"Who is going to teach my class while I'm doing all these things?"

"Mr. Easlow never made us get involved. He knew how busy we were."

"What if we don't participate? What are you going to do?"

At age 35, Adams was considerably younger and less experienced than almost all of the teachers. In her mind, the negative comments and questions were intended to intimidate her. She decided not to surrender to political pressure. After listening to the teachers' objections, she stated her position.

"Being involved is not an option any longer. My hope, however, is that you will collaborate because of your commitment to students and not because I force you or threaten you. We are more likely to succeed in constructing an effective plan if we work together as professionals. But let me be clear, if you elect not to cooperate, I will rectify the situation. Developing a meaningful strategic plan is extremely important and it no longer can be ignored simply because you don't want to do it."

Most of the teachers were staggered by their new principal's candidness. No previous principal had ever spoken to them in this manner. Principal Easlow, in particular, always went out of his way to mollify teachers. He considered their collective support to be a form of job security.

Planning Begins

Principal Adams began redesigning the strategic plan by reviewing the mission statement. All the other district's elementary school mission statements were virtually identical, and she concluded that it did not need to be revised. The last plan did not address needs assessment directly. Adams proposed establishing a needs assessment committee. It would include two teachers, two parents, and her, and the group's primary assignments would be to conduct an opinion poll with parents, collect existing data pertinent to the school, and build an integrated database to facilitate planning.

After reading the vision statement in the present plan, Adams agreed with state officials that the document was a general statement of purpose that failed to provide a meaningful image of the school's future. She proposed a visioning process that would begin with individual vision statements.

Teachers would be required to submit them and other stakeholders would be invited to do so. Public discussions would then be held to amalgamate the individual statements into a collective vision.

After she shared her thoughts on needs assessment and visioning with the school's employees, negative feedback occurred immediately. Fourteen teachers sent e-mails to the principal stating their objections. Some said that they had no idea what the school should be like in the future; others said they did not care what the school would look like in 10 years because they would be retired by then. And others said that visioning was an administrative responsibility.

Adams decided to discuss the concerns by meeting with grade-level teams (all the teachers assigned to a given grade level). She listened carefully to the assumptions teachers expressed and recorded notes immediately after the discussions ended. After the last group meeting, she analyzed her notes in an effort to understand why many of the teachers were reluctant to develop individual vision statements. She arrived at the following conclusions.

- Many teachers believed that they had limited ability to help students who were struggling academically. Most notably, they blamed social and economic conditions and not themselves for low academic performance.
- The attitudes of many teachers toward planning were influenced by the belief that a high percentage of students in the school were incapable of succeeding academically. Thus, visioning and planning were viewed as politically correct but otherwise meaningless assignments.
- Many teachers did not understand strategic planning and they showed little interest in acquiring this knowledge.
- Many teachers viewed school reform as a political initiative and they believed that pressures to reform would subside in the near future.
- Many teachers were convinced that, if they remained cohesive, the principal would be unable to take punitive actions against them.

The conversations made Principal Adams realize her personal knowledge of strategic planning would have limited value unless she could convince teachers and other stakeholders to participate in the process. The key questions in her mind were: How should I seek teacher engagement? Should I appeal to the teachers' sense of duty and professionalism? Should I remind the teachers that they would jeopardize their job security by refusing to participate? Or, should I seek assistance from the associate superintendent, thus admitting that I cannot achieve teacher engagement alone?

Problem Framing

1. Assume you are Principal Adams. First determine the main issue (problem) in this case. Then describe the current state and the desired state of this issue. (The section on problem framing in the Introduction section of this book defines the problem framing process.)

2. Based on evidence provided in the case, describe the difficulty associated with eliminating the gap between the present state and desired state.

Questions and Suggested Activities

1. Share and critique the problem statements prepared by students in your class.
2. Obtain the mission and vision statements for your school. Based on background information provided before this case, are they written properly? Why or why not?

3. Based on your experiences in schools, are the attitudes and assumptions of the teachers at Monroe Elementary School typical? What evidence do you have to support your response?
4. How do the attitudes and assumptions voiced by the teachers relate to school culture?

5. How does school culture relate to school improvement?
6. Principal Adams suggests that every teacher be required to write a personal vision statement and that other stakeholders be invited to do so. Do you agree with these suggestions? If not, what is your suggestion?
7. As Monroe's principal, what would you do to engage parents in strategic planning?
8. Why is strategic planning considered essential to school improvement? Do you agree that it is essential?
9. Would you involve various stakeholders in assessing and evaluating planning progress? Why or why not?

10. What purpose is served by a vision statement? What is the nexus between a mission statement and vision statement?
11. What purpose does environmental scanning serve in strategic planning?
12. As principal, do you believe that it is possible to engage the teachers in strategic planning by appealing to their sense of professionalism? If yes, how would you do this? If no, what would you do instead?

Suggested Readings

Auerbach, S. (2007). Visioning parent engagement in urban schools. *Journal of School Leadership, 17*(6), 699–734.
Cook, W. J. (2004). When the smoke clears. *Phi Delta Kappan, 86*(1), 73–75, 83.
DuFour, R., & DuFour, B. (2007). What might be: Open the door to a better future. *Journal of Staff Development, 28*(3), 27–28.
Joyce, B. (2004). How are professional learning communities created? History has a few messages. *Phi Delta Kappan, 86*(1), 76–83.
Killion, J. (2006). Strategies for assessing needs. *Principal Leadership, 6*(9), 45–46.

Patterson, W. (2000). Grounding school culture to enable real change. *The Education Digest, 65*(9), 4–8.
Poole, M. L. (1991). Environmental scanning is vital to strategic planning. *Educational Leadership, 48*(4), 40–41.
Reeves, D. (2006-07). How do you change school culture? *Educational Leadership, 64*(4), 92, 94.
Rutherford, C. (2009). Planning to change: Strategic planning and comprehensive school reform. *Educational Planning, 18*(1), 1–10.
Schmoker, M. (2004). Tipping point: From feckless reform to substantive instructional improvement. *Phi Delta Kappan, 85*(6), 424–432.

References

Björk, L. G. (1995). Substance and symbolism in the education commission reports. In R. Ginsberg, & D. Plank (Eds.), *Commissions, reports, reforms and educational policy* (pp. 133–149). New York: Praeger.
Coleman, D. G., & Brockmeier, J. (1997). A mission possible: Relevant mission statements. *School Administrator, 54*(5), 36–37.
Conger, J. A. (1989). *The charismatic leader. Behind the mystique of exceptional leadership.* San Francisco: Jossey-Bass.
Cunningham, W., & Gresso, D. (1993). *Cultural leadership: The culture of excellence in education.* Boston: Allyn and Bacon.
Kirst, M. W., & Kelley, C. (1995). Collaboration to improve education and children's services: Politics and policy making. In L. Rigsby, M. Reynolds, & M. Wang (Eds.), *School-community connections: Exploring issues for research and practice* (pp. 21–44). San Francisco: Jossey-Bass.

Kowalski, T. J. (2010). *The school principal: Visionary leadership and competent management.* New York: Routledge.
Kowalski, T. J. (2011). *Public relations in schools* (5th ed.). Boston: Allyn and Bacon.
Kowalski, T. J., Petersen, G. J., & Fusarelli, L. D. (2007). *Effective communication for school administrators: An imperative in an information age.* Lanham, MD: Rowman & Littlefield Education.
Lamb, L. F., & McKee, K. B. (2005). *Applied public relations: Cases in stakeholder management.* Mahwah, NJ: Lawrence Erlbaum Associates.
Poole, M. L. (1991). Environmental scanning is vital to strategic planning. *Educational Leadership, 48*(4), 40–41.
Rozycki, E. G. (2004). Mission and vision in education. *Educational Horizons, 82*(2), 94–98.
Sergiovanni, T. J. (2001). *The principalship: A reflective practice perspective* (4th ed.). Boston: Allyn and Bacon.

15 EVEN ON SATURDAYS

BACKGROUND INFORMATION

The legal doctrine of *in loco parentis* refers to assuming parental responsibility for a nonadult without legal adoption. In fact, the term means "in the place of a parent." The concept was first applied to public education in colonial times. Rooted in English common law, it "functioned as a doctrine for institutions to govern behavior" (Bowden, 2007, p. 482), and it gave school personnel authority over both education and moral development. Over time, legal challenges to the concept's application have weakened it, particularly as it relates to older students. During the 1960s, lawsuits regarding the authority of school officials to control pupil behavior resulted in legal precedent that students do not lose their constitutional rights at the schoolhouse door. The courts continued to permit the application of *in loco parentis*, however, but have limited the application of the concept to reasonable punishment in light of circumstances such as the nature of the infraction, the method of discipline, and the age of the student (Zirkel & Reichner, 1987).

This case is about a student initiation ritual that took place on a Saturday away from a high school campus. Over 40 students, mostly females, were arrested for underage drinking and several also for assault. The incident brings into question the legal responsibility of school officials to prevent and control incidents that are allegedly school-related but not school-sponsored.

Once the media become involved, school officials quickly realize they have a public relations crisis. Incidents, even those away from campus and clearly not part of the school curriculum, can damage a school's reputation and raise questions about administrator responsibility (Kowalski, 2011). In this case, the superintendent and principal take the position that neither they nor other school personnel were responsible for student behavior in this incident. They then declared that they would not comment further on the matter until the legal charges against the students are resolved. As is almost always the case, reporters are suspicious that their "no further comment" indicates that the administrators are attempting to conceal vital information (Kowalski, Petersen, & Fusarelli, 2007). As noted school safety expert, Kenneth Trump, warns, failure to communicate effectively during a crisis situation often produces a crisis after the crisis—that is, a second-level problem for school officials (Kowalski, 2002).

Key Areas for Reflection

1. Student discipline
2. Media relations
3. Dealing with a crisis situation
4. School public relations
5. Legal aspects of student punishment

THE CASE

Jim Marshfield and his wife, Angie, were attending a party at their daughter's sorority. It was parents' weekend, the Texas sun was shining, and everyone was celebrating the victory at the football game that had ended just hours earlier. Jim was finishing his second barbecue sandwich when his cell phone started vibrating.

Jim is principal of Melton High School, one of the most prestigious public schools in Texas. Located in an affluent suburb of Dallas, the school enrolls approximately 2,500 students; nearly 85% of the graduates enter a higher-education institution. Prior to being principal, Jim was an assistant principal at Melton High School for 6 years.

Looking at his phone, Jim saw the call was from Superintendent Rachel Gregory. He knew it was an emergency because Dr. Gregory did not usually call him on weekends. Gregory told him that 43 Melton students, almost all junior and senior girls, had been arrested several hours earlier at a local state park. All were charged with underage drinking and several were also charged with assault. Marshfield immediately knew what had occurred.

For at least the last 25 years, a touch football game between the senior girls and the junior girls had become a Melton tradition. School officials, though aware of the contest, did not interfere because the game occurred on a Saturday morning away from the school's campus. In fact, Principal Marshfield did not know that the game was on that Saturday. As a matter of record, he routinely advised school employees not to participate in this or other unsanctioned student events, especially those taking place off school property.

In recent years, however, the touch football game had become a prelude to the senior girls hazing the junior girls. Although social clubs and sororities were not permitted at Melton, it was widely known that the annual touch football game was sponsored by an elite social clique. A group of approximately 25 senior girls who had been initiated the previous year challenged an equal number of junior girls to a touch football game. The initiation to upper class standing, not the football game, was the event's purpose. Though rumors about the ritual were widespread throughout the school and the community, school officials had never intervened to prevent it.

Gregory told Marshfield that reporters were in a feeding frenzy about the arrests. Even a reporter from a national news service tried to speak with her. She alerted Marshfield that reporters also were seeking to contact him.

Apparently, there were several kegs of beer at the event, and some male students attended to cheer on the activities. The initiation turned into a minor riot. Several fights broke out, and a student was seriously injured when she tried to escape an assailant by climbing into a tree and then broke her leg in three places after she was pushed and fell to the ground.

The call for an ambulance brought police to the scene. They found several dozen students intoxicated. The junior girls were covered with honey and feathers and several had minor injuries ranging from facial bruises to cuts on their arms and legs.

Superintendent Gregory indicated that she was trying to reach the school board members to apprise them of the situation. She had told reporters that the initiation, while unfortunate and disgusting, was not a school-sponsored event. She added that school officials would investigate the matter and take disciplinary action if warranted. She also suggested that Principal Marshfield return to Melton as soon as possible.

The Marshfields returned home about 8:00 P.M. The answering machine was filled with messages, most from media representatives but some from angry parents. Less than 15 minutes later, Jim had his first conversation with a reporter about the incident. He reiterated what Superintendent Gregory had already told the media: The gathering at the state park was not a school-sponsored event, and school officials in no way condoned the activity.

By Sunday evening, the story had made national news. One network had obtained a video-tape from an unidentified male student who had left the scene before police arrived. The video shocked even Principal Marshfield. Several senior girls, obviously intoxicated, were repeatedly punching junior girls. The video also showed several students vomiting and making obscene gestures toward the camera.

On Monday morning, a special meeting of the school board was held in Superintendent Gregory's office, and Principal Marshfield was told to attend. The board members were outraged. Melton was an upscale community, and its high school had an outstanding reputation. The board members demanded to know how this could happen. Both the superintendent and the principal explained that the event was beyond their control. They argued that they could not be held accountable for student behavior that occurred on a weekend and away from campus. One board member asked whether the school officials knew that the initiation would be taking place. Both administrators indicated that they knew of the tradition but not the event's specific date and location.

After emotions subsided, the board members, at the urging of the two administrators, decided to schedule a press conference that afternoon. School officials would continue to take the position that the incident, though unfortunate, was not their responsibility. The superintendent and principal would tell reporters that they had no knowledge of the event's date and location and announce that they would refrain from further comments until the legal aspects of the case were resolved. At that point, they would decide whether they would take disciplinary action against any of the students.

The press conference drew a huge crowd of reporters. Principal Marshfield read a prepared statement that had been approved by the school's attorney and by the director of communication. The statement, only two paragraphs, summarized the decisions that had been made with the school board that morning. Reporters asked questions after the statement, but both the superintendent and the principal responded that as per the written statement, they would not comment further until the legal issues were resolved.

Over the next 24 hours, media coverage of the event did not cast school officials in a favorable light. Some reporters hinted that the superintendent, principal, and school board were essentially engaging in a cover-up. A Dallas newspaper reported that several unnamed teachers at Melton High School admitted that the initiation was a long-standing tradition at the school and many teachers, and probably the administrators, knew that it would be taking place.

Over the next week, media coverage of the initiation and arrests intensified. So did criticism of school officials. Several experts on school violence who were interviewed by reporters indicated that the principal should have taken steps to prevent the initiation because it centered on the school and affected the school's reputation and culture.

Exactly one week after they first met to discuss a strategy for dealing with the arrests, the school board met again. This time, several members directly criticized the principal for not having taken action to prevent the initiation and the superintendent for having mismanaged "the crisis after the crisis." The board then directed the superintendent to retain a public relations firm so that it could advise school officials on further action related to the matter.

The public relations consultant assigned to handle the school district advised the superintendent and principal to make public statements admitting that some mistakes were made. More importantly, they were advised to assure the public that steps were being taken to prevent such an incident from recurring. Both Superintendent Gregory and Principal Marshfield were uncomfortable with the recommendation. They felt that they were being asked to be the scapegoats for a situation that was beyond their control and responsibility. Dr. Gregory telephoned the board president about the consultant's recommendation. The board president, her staunchest supporter, told her, "Rachel, you better do what he advised you to do. If not, there could be additional consequences. We are paying this PR firm a big fee. We have confidence in the consultant's advice."

After that conversation, Dr. Gregory telephoned Principal Marshfield and shared the board president's comments. The superintendent then said that she would prepare a statement indicating that school officials could have done more to prevent this situation. She advised him to consider a similar statement.

Problem Framing

1. Assume you are Principal Marshfield. First determine the main issue (problem) in this case. Then describe the current state and the desired state of this issue. (The section on problem framing in the Introduction section of this book defines the problem framing process.)

2. Based on evidence provided in the case, describe the difficulty associated with eliminating the gap between the present state and desired state.

Questions and Suggested Activities

1. What is the legal concept of *in loco parentis*? Why may this concept be relevant to this case?
2. Evaluate the position taken by the principal that an event occurring on Saturday away from the school campus is not the school's responsibility.
3. This case has both a legal dimension and a public relations dimension. What is the legal dimension?
4. What is the public relations dimension of this case?
5. Do you agree that school officials should not take any action against the students until the legal charges against the students are resolved? Why or why not?
6. Evaluate the press conference held by the superintendent and principal. Did they handle the situation properly? Why or why not?
7. Evaluate the advice given to the superintendent and principal by the public relations consultant.
8. Determine whether the school district in which you work or reside has policy that would have been relevant

to situations such as the one described in this case. Discuss the policies in class.
9. Most of the students attending the initiation were arrested for underage drinking. Is such an arrest away from campus on a weekend grounds for expelling or suspending a student? Why or why not?
10. What actions could have been taken by the principal to prevent the initiation?
11. What actions can be taken by the superintendent, principal, and other school officials to repair the high school's reputation?
12. Is this incident likely to cause irreparable damage to the principal's relationship with the superintendent and school board? Why or why not?
13. Discuss possible lawsuits that may result from this incident. How might these lawsuits affect the school district, the superintendent, and the principal?

Suggested Readings

Eastridge, H. E. (1999). The do's and don'ts of coping with crises. *School Administrator, 56*(6), 31–32.

Dixon, M. (2001). Hazing in high schools: Finding the hidden tradition. *Journal of Law and Education, 30*(2), 357–363.

Kowalski, T. J. (2002). Working with the media during a crisis situation: Perspectives from school administrators. *Journal of School Public Relations, 23*(3), 178–196.

Kowalski, T. J. (2011). *Public relations in schools* (5th ed.). Upper Saddle River, NJ: Merrill, Prentice Hall (see Chapters 9 and 10).

Kowalski, T. J., Petersen, G. J., & Fusarelli, L. D. (2007). *Effective communication for school administrators: An imperative in an information age.* Lanham, MD: Rowman and Littlefield Education (see Chapter 9).

Lester, J. (2004). Crisis situations deserve more than a "no comment." *School Administrator, 61*(3), 34.

Rerrandino, V. (2002). Surviving a crisis. *Principal, 80*(4), 72.

Sauer, R. T. (2004, April 14). Discipline and off-campus behavior. *Education Week, 23*(31), 41, 43.

Sharp, H. M. (2005). After the fact. *Principal Leadership (High School Ed.), 5*(5), 39–41.

Sharp, H. M. (2006). *When a school crisis occurs: What parents and stakeholders want to know.* Lanham, MD: Rowman and Littlefield Education.

Watt, S. M., Peters, B. S., Hambrook, J., Bucy, A., Braun, R., & Trump, K. S. (2008). Schools need to improve safety. *American School Board Journal, 195*(2), 12–13.

Worley, V. (2003). The teacher's place in the moral equation: In loco parentis. *Philosophy of Education Yearbook,* 280–282.

Zirkel, P. A., & Reichner, H. F. (1986). Is the in loco parentis doctrine dead? *Journal of Law and Education, 15,* 271–283

References

Bowden, R. (2007). Evolution of responsibility: From in loco parentis to ad meliora vertamur. *Education, 127*(4), 480–489.

Kowalski, T. J. (2002). Working with the media during a crisis situation: Perspectives from school administrators. *Journal of School Public Relations, 23*(3), 178–196.

Kowalski, T. J. (2011). *Public relations in schools* (5th ed.). Upper Saddle River, NJ: Merrill, Prentice Hall.

Kowalski, T. J., Petersen, G. J., & Fusarelli, L. D. (2007). *Effective communication for school administrators: An imperative in an information age.* Lanham, MD: Rowman and Littlefield Education.

Zirkel, P., & Reichner, H. (1987). Is in loco parentis dead? *Phi Delta Kappan, 68*(2), 466–469.

16 APPROPRIATE PUNISHMENT VERSUS POLITICAL EXPEDIENCY

BACKGROUND INFORMATION

States grant local school boards the authority to set policy. This power, however, is not unlimited; all board policy decisions must conform to the limitations of relevant constitutional provisions, statutes, federal and state regulations, and common law (Imber & Van Geel, 1993). As part of the executive branch of government, administrators have the responsibility of developing rules and regulations that are extensions of policy and that aid policy implementation.

Over the past 2 decades, a series of violent acts perpetrated in schools across the country made the public aware that violence can and does occur in all types of schools (e.g., public and private, high schools and colleges) and communities. Highly publicized acts of violence have occurred in such places as Columbine, Colorado; Jonesboro, Arkansas; Paducah, Kentucky; and Lancaster, Pennsylvania. These and similar tragedies prompted an outraged public to demand that school officials take actions to elevate school safety. One of the outcomes has been the growing popularity of "zero-tolerance" policies. Some of these policies, though, were promulgated with little consideration of their unintended effects and potential pitfalls (Holloway, 2002).

Student-discipline policy may be influenced by federal and state laws, prevailing community values, local politics, and professional knowledge provided via superintendent policy recommendations (Kowalski, 2006). Frequently, policy intended to regulate pupil conduct often has sparked intense conflict because not all stakeholders in a district share the same philosophical and political dispositions toward restricting and punishing student behavior. Some parents, for example, believe that discipline's primary purpose is to protect the school and broader community, whereas other parents believe it is to correct improper behavior (Rasicot, 1999). These dissimilar views also may divide educators. Some teachers and administrators, for example, view zero-tolerance policies as being essential to school safety, whereas others see these policies as being unfair because they disregard a student's total record. Observing these tensions, several authors (e.g., Essex, 2000) argue that the challenge facing administrators and school board members formulating discipline policy and rules is to balance school safety and student rights.

In this case, several African American males are initially expelled for 2 years for engaging in violent acts while attending a football game at their high school. Segments of the local community react negatively, claiming the punishment is excessive and biased. After being expelled, the teenagers are charged with criminal offenses. A national civil rights leader gets involved and tensions worsen in a city that has had a history of racial strife.

Key Areas for Reflection

1. Race relations
2. Race and student discipline
3. The appropriateness of zero-tolerance policies
4. Violence in schools
5. Managing political conflict
6. Using conflict to produce positive change

THE CASE

Lincoln

Lincoln is an industrial community with a population of approximately 76,000. The three primary employers are a chemical plant, a stamping plant that makes truck fenders, and a candy company. Approximately 15% of the city's residents are African American and approximately 3% are Hispanic. In the past 2 decades, the city's population has declined about 11%, primarily because of job losses at the stamping plant.

The city has a history of segregation in housing patterns. Virtually all African American families reside in two neighborhoods just south and west of the city's business district; virtually all Hispanic families reside in a neighborhood just east of the city's business district. Less than 150 new single-family dwellings have been built in Lincoln in the last 20 years.

Prior to 1975, registered Republicans outnumbered registered Democrats by nearly a two-to-one margin. Now, however, the voter registration records show an almost equal number of Republicans and Democrats. The current mayor is the first Democrat to be elected to that office in over 25 years. His political base is a coalition of minority groups and union members. Since taking office 3 years ago, he has created a special advisory committee on race relations and sponsored a number of improvements in both the African American and Hispanic neighborhoods. Several months ago, the most prominent leader in the African American community issued a statement indicating that race relations in Lincoln had improved and that the mayor was largely responsible. He told a reporter, "Things aren't as bad as they were 25 years ago. Racism was very obvious back then. We are still trying to deal with the lingering effects of institutional racism but things certainly have improved." Just 2 weeks after this interview, a white policeman shot and killed an African American male who had shot at him. Reactions to the incident differed along racial lines, and many citizens questioned whether race relations were actually better now than in the past.

The School District

The Lincoln School District has a total enrollment of approximately 10,000. The peak enrollment, 12,300 students, occurred in 1985. The district operates 12 elementary schools (Grades K–5), four middle schools (Grades 6–8), and two high schools (Grades 9–12).

The district's two high schools are Lincoln Central and Lincoln North. The former, built in 1955, is just blocks from the city's business district. The school enrolls about 2,000 students, of whom 46% are African Americans and 5% are Hispanics. Lincoln North, built in 1979, is in the city's most affluent neighborhood and a quarter mile from the city's northern boundary line.

Enrollment at this school is about 1,800 students, of whom 18% are African Americans and 1% are Hispanics.

There are seven members on the district's school board: four elected from specific areas of the city and three elected at-large. Currently, two board members are African Americans. The superintendent, Dr. Thomas Yundt, and the principals of both high schools are white males. Dr. Yundt has been in his present position for 3 years, having moved to Lincoln after serving as superintendent in a smaller school district. Only one of the three assistant superintendents, Dr. Robin Daniels, is a person of color.

The Incident

The two Lincoln high schools belong to different athletic conferences; however, they compete against each other in football. The annual game, always scheduled for the third Friday of September, draws a huge crowd. During the most recent game, a brawl broke out in the bleachers midway through the second quarter, causing the game to be stopped. A group of African American students appeared to be engaged in a fistfight, the turmoil then spread indiscriminately through the crowd. School officials, including the principals of both schools, and several law enforcement officers attempted to intervene. One of the students involved allegedly grabbed the principal from Lincoln Central by the shirt and hit him in the chest with his fist. Although there were no hospital reports of injuries, there were conflicting stories as to whether people had been hurt.

The Lincoln School District had adopted a zero-tolerance policy with regard to violence at school or school events 18 months prior to the incident at the football game. The two principals identified nine African American teenagers whom they believed were part of the group initiating the fighting; seven of them were current students at Lincoln Central. The principals recommended a 2-year expulsion for the seven students. Their recommendation was based on provisions in the board's zero-tolerance policy.

Separate due process hearings were set for the students. Only one of them attended his hearing. He and his parents requested that he be allowed to withdraw from school to avoid being expelled—an act that would protect his permanent record. The hearing officer recommended that the request should be honored but argued that expulsion recommendations for the six students who did not appear at their hearings should be upheld. Dr. Yundt concurred with all of the hearing officer's recommendations and so informed the school board. He pointed out that the period of the expulsion, 2 years, was based on the egregious nature of the offense. However, the students could seek reinstatement after only 1 year if they produced evidence of positive behavior, such as staying out of trouble, pursuing tutoring and counseling, or performing community service. The board voted six to one to approve the superintendent's recommendation; one of the African American board members voted against the recommendation.

Fallout

During the weeks that followed the board's approval of the expulsions, police were careful not to label the brawl as "gang-related." Nevertheless, rumors flowed through the community that the fight was the continuation of an altercation that occurred between two groups of teenagers several days earlier. Eventually, criminal charges were filed against the nine teenagers identified as being part of the initial fight. Four were charged as adults with felony mob action and one of them, an 18-year-old, was also accused of aggravated battery and resisting a peace officer. The remaining five were charged in juvenile petitions.

Initially, many in the African American community believed that expelling the seven students for 2 years was excessive punishment. When the criminal charges were filed weeks later, their disapproval changed to anger. At that point, a national civil rights figure, the Rev. Arnold James, became involved. He spoke at a rally in Lincoln to protest the treatment of the students and to start a defense fund for them. James made the following points in his speech to the angry crowd:

- He condemned the action of the school board and superintendent, arguing that they had rushed to judgment and overreacted.
- He insisted that the key issue in this matter was fairness rather than race. He argued that African American students had been disproportionately the subjects of harsh discipline; he cited a statistic indicating that of the six students expelled the previous year, five were African Americans. He also noted that the board had expelled a white student who had committed what he considered to be a much more serious offense (sending a bomb threat note) for only 1 year.
- He contended that the punishment given to the students was excessive for a fistfight in which no weapons were involved.
- He condemned the filing of criminal charges, insisting that the school board was working in tandem with law enforcement. He noted that by making the students criminals, the board was in essence justifying the unusually long expulsions.

Within days of James's appearance in Lincoln, the controversy was covered by the national media. The governor, the state school superintendent, and local elected officials were drawn into the matter. Unrest in the African American community was getting progressively tense, and Superintendent Yundt decided to close the schools for 3 days, fearing an outbreak of additional violence.

In the midst of growing national interest, the board president issued a statement in which she noted, "I really resent the fact that we have outsiders telling us how to run our schools." The governor was able to get both sides to attend a daylong meeting that resulted in the school board's agreeing to reduce the punishment to an expulsion for the remainder of the school year. In addition, the expelled students would be allowed to attend the district's alternative high school program. James called the board's concession inadequate and pressured the governor and state superintendent to intervene directly. Both declined, indicating that they would facilitate a solution but would not usurp the authority of the local school board.

Key figures on both sides were inundated with requests for media interviews. Leaders in the local African American community met with reporters and restated many of the claims that James made in his initial speech in Lincoln. School officials who previously refused to disclose any information about the students now made selected data available to the media and public. For example, Dr. Yundt, appearing on a national news show, revealed that three of the students were third-year freshmen and that collectively the seven students had missed 350 days of school the previous year. In addition, school officials made available an amateur videotape of the incident. The camera captured the last third of the brawl, showing spectators scurrying to get away from a group of teenagers throwing punches and tossing each other down the concrete bleacher steps.

In the aftermath of the board's concession (reducing the length of the expulsion) and the viewing of the videotape, conservative media commentators and politicians criticized James for having misstated the facts and for having intensified tensions in Lincoln. They refuted James's contention that no one was hurt and declared that criminal activity was indeed an issue. They pointed to the video as clear evidence that James either erred in reporting the facts of this case or purposely misled the public.

Continuing Controversy

Despite the school board's decision to reduce the expulsion period, tensions did not subside. James and his supporters filed a 13-page civil rights complaint in U.S. District Court alleging that the school board had violated the students' constitutional rights in the following ways:

- By failing to have an explicit zero-tolerance policy in writing
- By labeling the conduct as "gang-related" without evidence
- By failing to notify the students about alternative education options
- By punishing them too harshly for a fistfight void of weapons

At the same time that anger lingered in the African American community, many white residents criticized the school board and superintendent for having reduced the expulsion periods.

James repeatedly warned community officials and the media that the matter had not ended just because the punishment was reduced. Moreover, he now accused school officials of having violated privacy laws by disclosing information about the case to the news media. He vowed to continue his activities in Lincoln until the teenagers were cleared of criminal charges. He announced that he would lead a march through the city the following week. Clearly, the matter was not resolved, and the superintendent, school board, and other school officials continued to be criticized by leaders in the African American community.

Problem Framing

1. Assume you are the superintendent. First determine the main issue (problem) in this case. Then describe the current state and the desired state of this issue. (The section on problem framing in the Introduction section of this book defines the problem framing process.)

2. Based on evidence provided in the case, describe the difficulty associated with eliminating the gap between the present state and desired state.

Questions and Suggested Activities

1. Share and critique the problem statements prepared by students in your class.
2. What racial and political characteristics of the community and school district are relevant to the problem presented in the case?
3. James cited a case in which a white student had been expelled for just 1 year for a bomb threat. Do you agree with him that the fistfight was a lesser offense? Do you agree with him that the lesser penalty given to the white student was evidence of discriminatory discipline practices?
4. Identify and discuss the advantages and disadvantages of zero-tolerance policy.
5. The one student recommended for expulsion who attended his hearing requested that he be permitted to withdraw from school. The hearing officer, superintendent, and school board concurred. Do you think this was a good decision? Why or why not?
6. Was James's claim of unequal treatment of African American students nullified when the school board reduced the expulsion period? Why or why not?
7. In the aftermath of this incident, identify actions you would recommend with regard to increasing security at school-sponsored events.
8. Some educators believe that student discipline should be primarily punitive and others believe it should be primarily remedial. Which position do you favor? Provide a rationale for your response.
9. Identify and discuss the advantages and disadvantages of excluding students from school for violent behavior.

Suggested Readings

Baker, J. A. (1998). Are we missing the forest for the trees? Considering the social context of school violence. *Journal of School Psychology, 36*(1), 29–44.

Bock, S. J., Savner, J. L., & Tapscott, K. E. (1998). Suspension and expulsion: Effective management of students? *Intervention in School and Clinic, 34*(1), 50–52.

Casella, R. (2003). Zero tolerance policy in schools: Rationale, consequences, and alternatives. *Teachers College Record, 105*(5), 872–892.

Clark, C. (1998). The violence that creates school dropouts. *Multicultural Education, 6*(1), 19–22.

Costenbader, V., & Markson, S. (1998). School suspension: A study with secondary school students. *Journal of School Psychology, 36*(1), 59–82.

Edmonson, H. M., & Bullock, L. M. (1998). Youth with aggressive and violent behaviors: Pieces of a puzzle. *Preventing School Failure, 42*(3), 135–141.

Edwards, C. H. (2001). Student violence and the moral dimensions of education. *Psychology in the Schools, 38*(3), 249–257.

Gable, R. A., Quinn, M. M., & Rutherford, R. B. (1998). Addressing problem behaviors in schools: Use of functional assessments and behavior intervention plans. *Preventing School Failure, 42*(3), 106–119.

Gordon, J. A. (1998). Caring through control. *Journal for a Just and Caring Education, 4*(4), 18–40.

Haynes, R. M., & Chalker, D. M. (1999). A nation of violence. *American School Board Journal, 186*(3), 22–25.

Holloway, J. H. (2001). The dilemma of zero tolerance. *Educational Leadership, 59*(4), 84–85.

Hoffman-Miller, P. (2009). The role of principals' ethnicity and gender in the suspension of African American students. *National Forum of Educational Administration & Supervision Journal, 26*(3), 62–80.

Hyman, I. A., & Perone, D. C. (1998). The other side of school violence: Educator policies and practices that may contribute to student misbehavior. *Journal of School Psychology, 36*(1), 7–27.

Jimerson, S. R., Brock, S. E., & Cowan, K. C. (2005). Threat assessment: An essential component of a comprehensive safe school program. *Principal Leadership (Middle School Ed.), 6*(2), 11–15.

Lashley, C., & Tate, A. S. (2009). A framework for educative, equitable, and empowering disciplinary practice. *Journal of Special Education Leadership, 22*(1), 24–35.

McEvoy, A., Erickson, E., & Randolph, N. (1997). Why the brutality? *Student Intervention Report, 10*(4).

Morrison, G. M., & D'Incau, B. (1997). The web of zero-tolerance: Characteristics of students who are recommended for expulsion from school. *Education and Treatment of Children, 20*(3), 316–335.

Roper, D. A. (1998). Facing anger in our schools. *Educational Forum, 62*(4), 363–368.

Skiba, R. J., & Peterson, R. L. (1999). The dark side of zero tolerance: Can punishment lead to safe schools? *Phi Delta Kappan, 80*(5), 372–376.

Stefkovich, J. A., & Guba, G. J. (1998). School violence, school reform, and the Fourth Amendment in public schools. *International Journal of Educational Reform, 7*(3), 217–225.

St. George, D. M., & Thomas, S. B. (1997). Perceived risk of fighting and actual fighting behavior among middle school students. *Journal of School Health, 67*(5), 178–181.

Toby, J. (1998). Getting serious about school discipline. *Public Interest, (133),* 68–83.

Zirkel, P. A., & Gluckman, I. B. (1997). Due process in student suspensions and expulsions. *Principal, 76*(4), 62–63.

References

Essex, N. L. (2000). Zero tolerance approach to school violence: Is it going too far? *American Secondary Education, 29*(2), 37–40.

Holloway, J. H. (2002). The dilemma of zero tolerance. *Educational Leadership, 59*(4), 84–85.

Imber, M., & Van Geel, T. (1993). *Education law.* New York: McGraw-Hill.

Kowalski, T. J. (2006). *The school superintendent: Theory, practice, and cases* (2nd ed.). Thousand Oaks, CA: Sage.

Rasicot, J. (1999). The threat of harm. *American School Board Journal, 186*(3), 14–18.

17 | THE PASSIVE PRINCIPAL

BACKGROUND INFORMATION

After-school reform again became a national issue in the early 1980s, policymakers attempted to improve schools by first making students do more of what they were already doing and, second, by raising standards for preparing and licensing administrators. Although these actions had some positive effects, they failed to improve underperforming schools sufficiently for at least three reasons.

1. Intensification mandates ignored the importance of school culture. Hence, requiring students and educators to do more of what they were already doing had little or no effect on educator shared values and beliefs (Sarason, 1996).
2. Intensification mandates had little or no effect on the way that schools were structured (Patterson, 2000). Therefore, the failure rate in them remained essentially unchanged (Schlechty, 1990).
3. Generic intensification mandates ignored the fact that districts and schools had different types and levels of needs (Kowalski, 2003).

Circa 1990, the locus of reform activity shifted to individual schools, as evidenced by the popularity of concepts such as site-based *management* (SBM). Revised strategies were intended to allow educators to make important changes based on the real needs of the schools in which they worked (Hoy & Miskel, 2005). To enable them to do this, teachers were to be treated as true professionals (Marzano, 2003), schools were to be given greater latitude to shape school-improvement initiatives (Kowalski, 2006), and local stakeholders were to be involved in strategic planning (Kowalski, Petersen, & Fusarelli, 2007).

In order to individualize reforms, schools had to become more flexible and adaptable. These attributes, however, heightened tensions between state authority and local district authority. Many state policymakers struggled to find ways to give districts and schools greater liberty without relinquishing accountability. One pervasive outcome was the adoption of *directed autonomy*—a strategy in which state policymakers set broad achievement benchmarks and then held local officials accountable for determining how they would be met (Weiler, 1990).

Principals arguably were affected more by the revised efforts to achieve school reform than were other educators (Brown, 1990). Specifically, their revised role included three school-improvement responsibilities:

1. They were to engage others in creating achievable and acceptable visions that detailed what needed to be done to improve their schools.
2. They were to engage others in building strategic plans for achieving the vision.
3. They were to garner political and economic support for change by communicating with a broad base of local stakeholders.

Concurrently, however, they were not relieved of extensive managerial responsibilities (Kowalski, 2010).

Although the strategy of tailoring reforms for individual schools has obvious merit, research has found that decentralizing authority, especially in schools that previously were highly centralized, often spawned unanticipated problems. Engaging in shared decision making, for instance, increased political behavior, divided faculty into factions, and stretched already inadequate budgets (Brown, 2001).

This case is about an experienced principal who volunteers to participate in a first phase of implementing SBM. In creating a school council, the principal determines that teachers, parents, and staff representatives should be elected. Although an ex officio member, the principal is passive during council meetings. After the council becomes mired in conflict, his laissez-faire attitude angers the council chair who has become frustrated with bickering between two factions of teachers.

Key Areas for Reflection

1. Problems associated with decentralized governance of schools
2. Social conflict among individuals and groups in schools
3. Dynamics of group decision making
4. Leadership style and participatory decision making
5. Leadership role in conflict resolution

THE CASE

Community and School District

The LaSalle County School District has three high schools, six middle schools, and 19 elementary schools. From 1980 to 2005, the population increased by nearly 25% resulting in the construction of six new schools. One of them, Elm Street Elementary, is in the city of Sunland, the seat of government for the county and location of the school district's administrative offices.

Superintendent and SBM

Three years ago, the school board employed Dr. Ursula Jones as superintendent. The 42-year-old administrator had been associate superintendent for instruction in a large-city school system in an adjoining state. Prior to coming to LaSalle County, Dr. Jones had established a reputation as a change agent. When the newspaper announced her employment, her former superintendent was quoted as saying, "LaSalle County is getting a top-notch superintendent. Dr. Jones is a creative and bold administrator and we will miss her leadership."

During her first year as superintendent, Dr. Jones developed a district decentralization plan calling for the incremental adoption of SBM. The initial phase included establishing pilot projects in one elementary and one secondary school. Six principals volunteered to have their schools become pilot projects, and after interviewing the principals, the superintendent selected the two schools.

The two participating schools received supplemental funding, including a $25,000 allocation for staff development. The additional resources had to be used for SBM-related activities. In addition, the two principals were allowed to control budgetary allocations for supplies, equipment, and staff travel—allocations that normally were controlled by the assistant superintendent for business.

Elm Street Elementary School

Elm Street Elementary is one of the district's newest buildings, having been made operational just 4 years ago. The school has three sections at each grade level, kindergarten to fifth grade. Albert Batz, previously a teacher and principal in the district, was selected to be the school's first administrator. An outgoing, friendly individual, he had been successful in his previous assignments.

Principal Batz's first major task at Elm Street Elementary was to select staff. He was inundated with applications, most from teachers already employed at other schools in the district. When the school opened, 75% of the teachers were people who had transferred from other district schools.

Mr. Batz describes his leadership style as "managing by walking around." He spends a great deal of time walking around the building, stopping to converse with employees and students when possible. It is not uncommon for him to walk into a classroom and join whatever activities are taking place. He usually makes two or three trips a day to the teachers' lounge, and one of his favorite midmorning hideaways is the kitchen. Teachers speculate as to whether his interaction with the cafeteria employees is motivated by his intense interest in the latest gossip or his intense interest in sampling the day's dessert. Most have concluded that the two motivators have equal influence on his behavior.

Teachers view Batz as an atypical principal. He appears to have a high need for social acceptance; for example, he often tells teachers that he is their peer and not their boss. Mrs. Lumans, his secretary, worked with him in his previous assignment; she was the first employee he selected after being named principal. The two complement each other; he does not like mundane management tasks and she has no problem when they are delegated to her.

Implementing SBM

In seeking to be part of the pilot project, Batz claimed that he had always embraced democratic decision making; his interest, however, was not restricted to administrative philosophy. Pragmatically, he hoped that a school council could resolve intense conflict that had emerged between two teacher factions. One group consisted of four teachers who previously worked together at Harrison Elementary School; their leader was Jenny Bales. The other group consisted of three teachers who previously worked together at Weakland Township Elementary School; their leader was Leonard Teel. While neither faction was large, each was cohesive. After just a few months in the new school, they were continuously vying for broader political support.

Principal Batz concluded that Mrs. Bales and Mr. Teel were political enemies with similar traits and needs. In their previous schools, each had been the "alpha" teacher—the faculty member with the greatest power over other teachers. Each was attempting to recapture that status at Elm Street Elementary School. Bales and Teel viewed Batz as a weak administrator and basically ignored him. Instead, they attempted to garner support from the 15 teachers not aligned with either faction.

The superintendent's SBM plan required the pilot school principals to (a) establish school councils, (b) serve as ex officio council members, (c) determine the size of the council, and (d) determine how other council members would be selected. Batz opted for an 11-member committee consisting of six teachers, three parents, one support staff employee, and himself. He decided that members should be elected by the faculty, the school staff, and the PTA (each group selecting its respective representatives). Nine teachers expressed interest in serving on the council; seven were members of either the Bales or Teel faction.

Amy Raddison and Tim Paxton, two novice teachers not aligned with either faction, received the most votes in the faculty election. The other four teachers elected were Jenny Bales, Arlene McFadden (aligned with Bales), Leonard Teel, and Lucille Isacson (aligned with Teel).

Mr. Batz initially was pleased with the election outcome. He hoped that Bales and Teel would reconcile their differences by working together on the council. After 4 months, however, he realized his optimism was unfounded. Rather than diminishing tensions, the council became a conduit for intense confrontations, some of which were malevolent. A dispute over an agenda item at the December council meeting was an example. A request to send five teachers, including Teel and a member of his faction, to a mid-January conference on SBM was submitted for approval. Bales and her collaborator immediately opposed the request.

"Just because we have a budget for staff development doesn't mean that we should send people to California to conferences," she said.

Teel shot back, "This conference focuses on effective SBM practices. Teachers from all over the United States will be there. We can learn a great deal. It's not my decision to have the conference in California. Why do you care where it is held?"

Bales answered. "There are plenty of good programs you could attend closer to home that would be less expensive. Stop thinking about what you want to do and think about what is best for the school. I will vote against this request and urge others to do likewise." The vote was delayed until the next council meeting.

Barbara Whitlow, president of the Parent and Teachers Association, a parent representative, and council chair, was surprised by Batz's indifference to the petty bickering. After the meeting, she expressed her feelings to him and suggested that he could have ended the conflict by expressing a professional opinion.

He answered, "You know that I don't like to take sides. As principal, I need to be neutral. I have to work closely with everyone. This is probably a good conference but there are also good conferences and workshops closer to home. So, there are merits to both arguments. I want to hear how other council members feel before I decide how I will vote."

Since becoming council chair, Mrs. Whitlow had questioned Batz regarding his responsibility to exercise authority on the council. However, his responses always were vague. Now in the midst of another argument between Bales and Teel, she again asked him to explain his role. He answered that his role was identical to other members'; he had one vote just as they did.

At the next council meeting, Whitlow told the others that she had asked Batz to take a position on the travel request because of his role as principal. She added that he refused to do so. Expectedly, Bales and Teel were comfortable with Batz's position and openly agreed that his authority was no greater or less than any other council member.

In light of Batz's unwillingness to state his position on the matter in question, Bales made a motion to deny the travel request. The motion was seconded by McFadden, her political ally. Teel requested that the vote be taken by secret ballot, a process that was becoming common and one that Whitlow saw as divisive. Nevertheless, other council members agreed to the secret ballot, perhaps because it provided a quick resolution and anonymity.

The motion to deny the travel request was defeated by a one-vote margin. A parent on the council then made another motion to approve the travel request, and it passed by one vote.

The next day, Whitlow again met with Batz privately to discuss his refusal to manage the destructive conflict between Bales and Teel.

"I just don't understand how you can sit back and allow Mrs. Bales and Mr. Teel to constantly take jabs at each other. Their behavior is destructive to the council and probably to the entire school. Don't you see that?" she asked.

"Barbara, I still hope they will reconcile their differences and begin to collaborate. If I intervene, I have to take sides. There will be a winner and loser. I don't want to do that."

Whitlow again was irritated with his lack of leadership and she told him how she felt. She added that if he remained passive, she would resign from the council. "You know, Albert, I have plenty to do besides spending 10 to 12 hours a week at the school. I will stop vol-unterring my time unless the council becomes a productive force, as intended by Dr. Jones. We spend much of our time in meetings listening to petty arguments that are more about power struggles than about school improvement. I'm not an expert, but I believe you have a responsibil-ity to deal with this negative behavior."

Batz pleaded with Whitlow to be patient. He told her that her continued leadership on the council was essential.

Two days after their private meeting, Whitlow wrote a letter to Batz resigning from the council. Copies were sent to Dr. Jones and each member of the LaSalle County school board. In her letter, she indicated that the SBM pilot project at Elm Street Elementary School was being undermined. She wrote:

> . . . If schools are given leeway and added resources, principals must be made accountable for these assets. Simply sharing power and authority does not ensure that our children receive a better education. I resign from the Elm Street Elementary School Council. My decision is based on two related issues. First, the council has been infected by conflict contaminants emanating from a power struggle between two teacher factions. I have become frustrated because of my inability to improve the situation. Second, I have repeatedly requested the principal to address the contaminants and he has been unwilling to do so. To this point, experimentation with SBM has not been successful at Elm Street Elementary School.

After reading the letter, Batz put it in his top desk drawer and worried about how the superintendent, school board, and Elm Street faculty would react to it. Shortly thereafter, he left his office and started toward the school cafeteria. A smile came over his face as he got close enough to smell freshly baked cookies. Two hours later, however, Mr. Batz received a telephone call from the superintendent notifying him he was being reassigned to a vacant position (assistant curriculum director) in the district's administrative office.

Problem Framing

1. Assume you are Mr. Batz. First determine the main issue (problem) in this case. Then describe the current state and the desired state of this issue. (The section on problem framing in the Introduction section of this book defines the problem framing process.)

2. Based on evidence provided in the case, describe the difficulty associated with eliminating the gap between the present state and desired state.

Questions and Suggested Activities

1. Did the superintendent's approach to selecting pilot schools to implement SBM contribute to the conflict at Elm Street Elementary School? Why or why not?

2. Do you agree with the principal's decision to permit council members to be elected? If you agree, what is your rationale? If you disagree, what would you have done differently?

3. As the new principal, you could remove the four teachers from the competing factions from the council. What are the advantages and disadvantages of taking this action?

4. Were members of the school council adequately prepared to assume their responsibility? What evidence do you have to defend your response?

5. As the new principal, what role would you play on a school council?

6. Was Mr. Batz's behavior indicative of a democratic leadership style? Why or why not?

7. To what extent is Barbara Whitlow (the PTA president and council chair) responsible for the conflict described in this case?

8. Based on your experiences in schools, how do non-administrators acquire power?

9. Based on the information in this case, did the superintendent act prudently by removing Mr. Batz as principal?

Suggested Readings

Bergman, A. (1992). Lessons for principals from school-based management. *Educational Leadership, 50*(1), 48–51.

Blasé, J. R., & Blasé, J. (1999). Shared governance principles: The inner experience. *NASSP Bulletin, 83*(606), 81–90.

Delaney, J. G. (1997). Principal leadership: A primary factor in school-based management and school improvement. *NASSP Bulletin, 81*(586), 107–111.

DuFour, R., & Marzano, R. (2009). High-leverage for principal leadership. *Educational Leadership, 66*(5), 62–68.

Epp, J. R., & MacNeil, C. (1997). Perceptions of shared governance in an elementary school. *Canadian Journal of Education, 22*(3), 254–267.

Ferris, J. (1992). School-based decision making: A principal-agent perspective. *Educational Evaluation and Policy Analysis, 14*(4), 333–346.

Fraze, L., & Melton, G. (1992). Manager or participatory leader. *NASSP Bulletin, 76*(540), 17–24.

Golarz, R. (1992). School-based management pitfalls: How to avoid some and deal with others. *School Community Journal, 2*(1), 38–52.

Henkin, A. B., Cistone, P. J., & Dee, J. R. (2000). Conflict management strategies of principals in school-based managed schools. *Journal of Educational Administration, 38*(2), 142–158.

Kowalski, T. J., Petersen, G. J., & Fusarelli, L. D. (2007). *Effective communication for school administrators: An imperative in an information age.* Lanham, MD: Rowman and Littlefield Education (see Chapter 11).

Kowalski, T., Reitzug, U., McDaniel, P., & Otto, D. (1992). Perceptions of desired skills for effective principals. *Journal of School Leadership, 2*(3), 299–309.

Lange, J. (1993). School-based, shared decision making: A resource for restructuring. *NASSP Bulletin, 76*(549), 98–107.

Laud, L. E. (1998). Changing the way we communicate. *Educational Leadership, 55*(7), 23–25.

Leithwood, K., & Menzies, T. (1998). A review of research concerning the implementation of school-based management. *School Effectiveness and School Improvement, 9*(3), 233–285.

Lovely, S. D. (2005). Making the leap to shared leadership. *Journal of Staff Development, 26*(2), 16–21.

Miles, W. (1982). The school-site politics of education: A review of the literature. *Planning and Changing, 12*(4), 200–218.

Minor, J. T., & Tierney, W. G. (2005). The danger of deference: A case of polite governance. *Teachers College Record, 107*(1), 137–156.

Patterson, W. (2000). Change for good: Staying the course. *High School Magazine, 7*(7), 5–6, 8–9.

Rodriguez, T. A., & Slate, J. R. (2005). Site-based management: A review of the literature part II: Past and present status. *Essays in Education, 15*, 186–212.

Smylie, M. (1992). Teacher participation in school decision making: Assessing willingness to participate. *Educational Evaluation and Policy Analysis, 14*(1), 53–67.

Sorenson, L. D., & Evans, R. D. (2001). Superintendent use of site-based councils: Role ambiguity and accountability. *Planning and Changing, 32*(3/4), 184–198.

Turk, R. L. (2002). What principals should know about building and maintaining teams. *NASSP Bulletin, 87*, 15–23.

Watkins, P. (1990). Agenda, power and text: The formulation of policy in school councils. *Journal of Education Policy, 5*(4), 315–331.

References

Brown, D. J. (1990). *Decentralization and school-based management*. London: Falmer Press.

Brown, F. (2001). School-based management: Is it still central to the school reform movement? *School Business Affairs, 67*(4), 5–6, 8–9.

Hoy, W. K., & Miskel, C. G. (2005). *Educational administration: Theory, research, and practice* (7th ed.). New York: McGraw Hill.

Kowalski, T. J. (2003). *Contemporary school administration: An introduction*. Boston: Allyn and Bacon.

Kowalski, T. J. (2006). *The school superintendent: Theory, practice, and cases* (2nd ed.). Thousand Oaks, CA: Sage.

Kowalski, T. J. (2010). *The school principal: Visionary leadership and competent management*. New York: Routledge.

Kowalski, T. J., Petersen, G. J., & Fusarelli, L. D. (2007). *Effective communication for school administrators: An imperative in an information age*. Lanham, MD: Rowman and Littlefield Education.

Marzano, R. J. (2003). *What works in schools: Translating research into action*. Alexandria, VA: Association for Supervision and Curriculum Development.

Patterson, W. (2000). Change for good: Staying the course. *High School Magazine, 7*(7), 5–6, 8–9.

Sarason, S. B. (1996). *Revisiting 'the culture of the school and the problem of change'*. New York: Teachers College Press.

Schlechty, P. C. (1990). *Schools for the twenty-first century: Leadership imperatives for educational reform*. San Francisco: Jossey-Bass.

Weiler, H. N. (1990). Comparative perspectives on educational decentralization: An exercise in contradiction? *Educational Evaluation and Policy Analysis, 12*(4), 433–448.

18 A DISILLUSIONED ASSISTANT PRINCIPAL

BACKGROUND INFORMATION

Administrative behavior is affected by a mix of personal, professional, and contextual variables. One of the most powerful variables is socialization, a process through which persons are pressured to learn and accept the behavioral norms of an organization or other social group. Workplace socialization begins when administrators are initially employed in schools, and the most critical values and beliefs typically pertain to problem solving and decision making (Kowalski, 2010). The process is especially intense in schools having strong cultures—that is, schools in which most organization members share the same values and beliefs about their work. Conversely, socialization is least intense in weak cultures where there is limited concurrence regarding values and assumptions.

Administrators almost always experience four levels of socialization:

1. *Socialization to teaching.* This process begins when a person enters college and more specifically a teacher education program. The intent is to provide normative standards for professional behavior. For example, students are usually taught to behave ethically, to serve their students, and to be caring and objective.
2. *Socialization to the workplace as a teacher.* This process begins when a person enters school as an employee and is most intense during the first year of employment. New-to-the-school teachers, including those who have previous experience in other schools, are directly and indirectly (symbolically) told which values and assumptions are most important and they are expected to embrace or at least tolerate them (Aiken, 2002). Frequently, a new teacher discovers that the core values of the teaching profession may not be the core values of a given school.
3. *Socialization to administration.* This process begins when teachers enter a school administration degree or licensure program. The knowledge, values, and assumptions they study are intended to influence their dispositions and behavior as administrators.
4. *Socialization to the workplace as an administrator.* This process begins when a person assumes an administrative position for the first time and recurs when the person moves to a different school or district. Again, the normative standards learned as a graduate student in administration classes may or may not be congruent with shared values and assumptions of a given school culture.

When the values and assumptions promoted at different levels are incongruent, administrators commonly experience conflict because they must choose between competing values and beliefs. These choices are pivotal because they determine how a principal or assistant principal will behave in a challenging situation (Hanson, 2003). An assistant principal, for example, may have been taught to treat teachers as peer professionals, but her immediate supervisor and the superintendent may expect her to treat teachers as subordinates. Negative school cultures—that is, cultures in which members share values and beliefs incongruent with the professional knowledge base—generate the most conflict because educators are pressured to accept norms that contradict evidence of best practices (Kowalski, 2003).

Novice administrators do not respond uniformly to socialization. Although most conform and accept or pretend to accept dominant workplace values, others do not, even at the risk of incurring sanctions (Heck, 1995). When an administrator overtly rejects the prevailing culture, one of three outcomes occurs: she will resign; she will be dismissed; she will remain and incur sanctions (e.g., poor evaluations, being ostracized).

This case is about a female teacher who becomes an assistant principal. As a novice administrator, she quickly discerns that she and the principal have different values and beliefs—a condition that affects her self-confidence and her relationship with the principal. Moreover, she recognizes that the principal's philosophy is shared by most of, if not all, the teachers at the school. She begins to weigh four possible options: (a) learning to live with the conflict so she can remain in her current position, (b) accepting the principal's values and beliefs, (c) seeking an administrative position in another school, or (d) returning to teaching.

Key Areas for Reflection

1. School culture
2. Socialization in organizations
3. Problems encountered by novice administrators
4. Professional knowledge, personal values, and ethical behavior
5. Determinants of administrative behavior

THE CASE

Amber Jackson sat in her office at Polk Middle School trying to finish work assigned by the principal. At nearly 9:30 P.M., the three night custodians were the only other people still in the building. Amber was tired and frustrated, making it difficult for her to focus on the work she had to complete. As she stared at the clock, she concluded that she was not going to get much sleep that evening.

Amber had started teaching English and physical education at a middle school in Southern California at age 22. Two years later, she began coaching volleyball and enrolled as a part-time student in a master's degree program at a local state university. She selected educational administration as a major because she wanted to be a school principal. Dr. Tom Appleton, formerly a principal in a suburban school district near San Diego, was her adviser. During her master's program, Amber completed two of his classes: "School Public Relations" and "The School Principal." He considered her to be the best student he had encountered since becoming a professor 4 years earlier.

As Amber was about to complete her master's degree, Professor Appleton told her that she could be a highly successful administrator. "You are intelligent and your work ethic is great. I think you should start applying for assistant principal jobs. And once you find the right position, you should think about pursuing a doctoral degree. You are an exceptional student and your future is unlimited."

Professor Appleton's career advice was flattering and the idea of becoming an assistant principal and a doctoral student was inviting. Amber, however, was hesitant to follow the advice because she had only 5 years of teaching experience and she had recently gotten engaged.

Amber told Professor Appleton that she had decided to wait at least a year before applying for administrative positions. "I'm getting married in November, and my fiancé is an Air Force officer currently stationed in Texas. His tour of duty will be over in about 8 months, and then he plans to be a commercial pilot. Therefore, I'm not sure where I'll be living a year from now. Once we get settled and he has a job, I would be more comfortable seeking an administrative position and entering a doctoral program."

Over the course of the following year, Amber got married and her husband became a pilot for an airfreight company based in Chicago. They rented an apartment in a suburb about 20 minutes north of the city. Amber applied for teaching and administrative positions in the Chicago area. In less than a month, she had two job offers: one a teaching position in an affluent suburban district and the other a middle-school assistant principal position in a predominately lower-middle-class suburban district. She accepted the administrative position.

Polk Middle School, constructed in the early 1960s, enrolls approximately 800 students in Grades 7 and 8. Twenty-eight percent of the students are identified as racial or ethnic minorities, equally divided between African American and Hispanic students.

The other two administrators employed at the school are Emil Denko, the principal, and Ernest Tarver, the other assistant principal. The former is white and has been in his role for 14 years and the latter is African American and has been in his role for 12 years. Mr. Denko and Mr. Tarver plan to retire in 3 years.

Amber found Polk Middle School to be substantially different from the middle school where she had previously been employed as a teacher. Given the differences in the communities served, she correctly assumed that there would be more academic and discipline problems at Polk. She did not anticipate, however, that relationships among teachers and administrators at the two schools would be substantially different. At her previous place of employment, the administrators had a collegial relationship with the teachers, and teachers were routinely involved in important decisions, especially those relating to curriculum and instruction. At Polk, relationships between teachers and administrators were primarily adversarial and virtually all important decisions were made by administrators and contested by teachers.

Conflict between administrators and the faculty was pervasive at Polk Middle School and it was almost always resolved in one of two ways. Either the principal brokered a negotiated settlement, or the dispute was adjudicated in accordance with the grievance procedures contained in the teachers' union master contract. Yet, Mr. Denko and Mr. Tarver were rarely criticized personally; on a day-to-day basis, their relationships with teachers were friendly. Essentially, the administrators and teachers behaved as members of opposing political parties; they could engage in bitter disputes at school but then have cocktails together after work.

Amber also discovered that many Polk teachers set low expectations for their students. For example, teachers often commented openly (e.g., at faculty meetings) that many of their students could never succeed academically. Even more disturbing, Principal Denko appeared to share this conviction. During a conversation between Denko and Amber about student homework, he essentially echoed the conviction that many Polk students would never do well as students, primarily because they were situated in families that cared little about education. To support his belief, he pointed out that only 24% of the district's high school graduates enrolled in post-secondary education and 19% of high school freshmen dropped out of school before they graduated.

After 3 months at Polk, Amber already was experiencing job dissatisfaction. Almost all of her assigned duties were related to discipline and routine management. Her preference was to be more involved in instructional issues. By the end of the first semester, she wrote a letter of resignation. But before submitting it, she telephoned her former professor and mentor, Dr. Appleton.

She shared her impressions of Polk Middle School and her doubts about continuing in her current position. After listening for nearly 10 minutes, he offered his advice.

"Before you make a decision, you need to have the conversation we are having with the principal. Share your impressions of the school; express your desire to be more involved with instructional programs. Find out how he will respond. If he is closed minded, maybe you should resign. If you decide to leave Polk, however, do so at the end of your current annual contract. Leaving in the middle of a school year may make it difficult for you to find another administrative position."

Heeding Appleton's advice, Amber met with Denko and shared her concerns. She told him, "I don't understand why the teachers have such a low opinion of students. They appear to be giving up on students who most need their help. High expectations usually affect students positively. One of my former professors said that it was especially important for administrators to believe that all students could succeed."

Denko stared at her with a cynical expression on his face. He was astonished by her comments, thinking to himself that she should be grateful for the opportunity he had given her. After a moment of silence, he responded verbally.

"How could you be dissatisfied? Here you are, not even 30 years old and you're already an administrator. You're making nearly twice as much as most teachers your age. Personally, I think you're doing a good job. Maybe there is something else bothering you and you do not want to tell me about it. Is that the case?"

Amber replied. "No. I'm being totally candid. I just feel uncomfortable in this school. The negative attitude about students and the pervasive conflict between administration and the faculty are draining. Many of the teachers leave school at the end of the day as if it was on fire. Even worse, they talk about the school's lack of effectiveness as if they were totally unaccountable for negative outcomes."

"Polk students don't come from wealthy families; many of them don't come from healthy families. People who have not worked in this type of community should not prescribe solutions. You cannot ignore the social environment. Being here and working with these social problems day after day have given the teachers a sense of reality. The teachers are being straightforward. Don't confuse their bluntness with indifference. They actually try to help students, but now and then they let off steam. They cannot ignore the fact that 20% of their students hate school and drop out when they turn 16 or shortly thereafter. I have lived in this type of community all my life. I, too, once dreamed that every one of my students would go to college and be successful. Unfortunately, dreams do not shape reality. Years ago, I also listened to idealistic professors. The problem then and now is that many of them are unaware of what it is like to be in the trenches, especially in a community like this one."

Amber disagreed with his comments, but instead of rebutting, she moved to her second concern.

"Emil, I'm also bothered by the fact that I have had no opportunity to work directly with teachers on instructional matters. I don't mind handling discipline problems, and I don't mind doing things like supervising students getting on and off buses. I expected to have these responsibilities—I just didn't expect them to be my entire job. I want to work closely with teachers. As a teacher, I benefited from the counsel of my principal; she always exhibited interest in my professional growth. She was a terrific role model. I am a good teacher and I can help other teachers."

"I'm sure you can," Mr. Denko answered. "And maybe next year, you can be assigned to evaluate several teachers, especially in language arts. Right now, I don't think you should be doing that. You're younger than most of the teachers, and some might resent being evaluated by a person with much less classroom experience. In addition, teachers in this district don't want administrators meddling in their classrooms."

"Why are they opposed to receiving instructional supervision?"

"I suppose because that has been the history in this district. This is a union-oriented community, and the teachers' union has clout. We have to live with the union whether we like it or not. The doubts you're having will fade with time. As I told you, I, too, once had grand ideas about saving poor teachers and helping troubled students. But reality takes hold. My primary concern as principal now is to keep this school operating efficiently and safely. I started teaching in this district 34 years ago. This once was a much more affluent area and our school statistics looked much better. We can't control the social deterioration around us. Play your cards right, and you could be the next principal 3 years from now."

Hours later, Amber was sitting at her desk finishing the monthly student discipline report. Her thoughts, however, kept drifting back to Denko's comments; the more she thought about his advice, the more she felt dissatisfied with her job. The thought that she might become Polk's principal and Denko's protégé actually frightened her.

At 10:15 that evening, Amber finally finished the report and drove home. While in her car, she called Professor Appleton on her cell phone. She told him about the conversation she had with Principal Denko.

"Clearly, these were not the answers you wanted," he told her. "Even so, I think you need to finish the school year at Polk before moving to another position."

Problem Framing

1. Assume you are Amber. First determine the main issue (problem) in this case. Then describe the current state and the desired state of this issue. (The section on problem framing in the Introduction section of this book defines the problem framing process.)

2. Based on evidence provided in the case, describe the difficulty associated with eliminating the gap between the present state and desired state.

Questions and Suggested Activities

1. Do you believe that Amber has a realistic perspective about her role as assistant principal? Why or why not?
2. If you were Amber, would you remain at Polk until the end of the school year? Why or why not?
3. When you began teaching, to what extent did you experience workplace socialization? How did you respond to socialization?
4. In what ways is workplace socialization for teachers different than workplace socialization for administrators?
5. Evaluate Principal Denko's statements about the differences between dreams and realities in schooling disadvantaged students. Do you agree with him? Why or why not?
6. Amber is surprised that the administrators and faculty have learned to live with pervasive conflict. Specifically, they are on opposite sides in most day-to-day matters but yet have managed to be friends outside of school. Based on your studies and experiences in schools, is such behavior common?
7. Is the principal responsible for the attitudes teachers have about low-performing students? Why or why not?
8. Why is socialization a critical process in schools?
9. Based on what you read in this case, is the culture of Polk Middle School strong or weak?
10. Based on what you have studied and experienced in schools, what must be done to make Polk Middle School more effective?

Suggested Readings

Cantwell, Z. M. (1993). School-based leadership and the professional socialization of the assistant principal. *Urban Education, 28*(1), 49–68.

Derpak, D., & Yarema, J. (2002). Climate control. *Principal Leadership, 3*(4), 42–45.

Glanz, J. (1994). Dilemmas of assistant principals in the supervisory role: Reflections of an assistant principal. *Journal of School Leadership, 4*(5), 577–590.

Glanz, J. (2004). *The assistant principal's handbook: Strategies for success.* Thousand Oaks, CA: Corwin Press.

Golanda, E. L. (1991). Preparing tomorrow's educational leaders: An inquiry regarding the wisdom of utilizing the position of assistant principal as an internship or apprenticeship to prepare future principals. *Journal of School Leadership, 1*(3), 266–283.

Goldring, L. (2002). The power of school culture. *Leadership, 32*(2), 32–35.

Hanna, J. W. (1998). School climate: Changing fear to fun. *Contemporary Education, 69*(2), 83–85.

Hartzell, G. N. (1993). When you're not at the top. *High School Magazine, 1*(2), 16–19.

Hausman, C., Nebeker, A., McCreary, J., & Gordon D. (2002). The worklife of the assistant principal. *Journal of Educational Administration, 40*(2), 136–157.

Keedy, J. L., & Simpson, D. S. (2001). Principal priorities, school norms, and teacher influence: A study of sociocultural leadership in the high school. *Journal of Educational Administration and Foundations, 16*(1), 10–41.

Kohm, B., & Nance, B. (2009). Creating collaborative cultures. *Educational Leadership, 67*(2), 67–72.

Koru, J. M. (1993). The assistant principal: Crisis manager, custodian, or visionary? *NASSP Bulletin, 77*(556), 67–71.

Linn, G. B., Sherman, R., & Gill, P. B. (2007). Making meaning of educational leadership: The principalship in metaphor. *NASSP Bulletin, 91*(2), 161–171.

Marshall, C. (1985). Professional shock: The enculturation of the assistant principal. *Education and Urban Society, 18*(1), 28–58.

Marshall, C., & Greenfield, W. D. (1985). The socialization of the assistant principal: Implications for school leadership. *Education and Urban Society, 18*(1), 3–6.

Marshall, C., & Hooley, R. M. (2006). *The assistant principal: Leadership choices and challenges.* Thousand Oaks, CA: Corwin Press.

Michel, G. J. (1996). *Socialization and career orientation of the assistant principal.* (ERIC Document Reproduction Service No. ED 395 381)

Peterson, K. D. (2002). Positive or negative. *Journal of Staff Development, 23*(3), 10–15.

Picucci, A. C., Brownson, A., & Kahlert, R. (2002). Shaping school culture. *Principal Leadership (Middle School Ed.), 3*(4), 38–41.

Toth, C., & Siemaszko, E. (1996). Restructuring the assistant principalship: A practitioner's guide. *NASSP Bulletin, 80*(578), 87–98.

Weller, L. D., & Weller, S. J. (2002). *The assistant principal: Essentials for effective school leadership.* Thousand Oaks, CA: Corwin Press.

References

Aiken, J. A. (2002). The socialization of new principals: Another perspective on principal retention. *Education Leadership Review, 3*(1), 32–40.

Hanson, E. M. (2003). *Educational administration and organizational behavior* (5th ed.). Boston: Allyn and Bacon.

Heck, R. H. (1995). Organizational and professional socialization: Its impact on the performance of new administrators. *Urban Review, 27*(3), 31–49.

Kowalski, T. J. (2003). *Contemporary school administration: An introduction* (2nd ed.). Boston: Allyn and Bacon.

Kowalski, T. J. (2010). *The school principal: Visionary leadership and competent management.* New York: Routledge.

19 WHO NEEDS CAREER-TECHNICAL EDUCATION?

BACKGROUND INFORMATION

Career-technical education (CTE), formerly called vocational education, is provided through various types of schools across the country. Although institutions providing CTE share a common mission, providing career-related and technical curricula, they are funded and governed in dissimilar ways. Three types of governance approaches are used:

1. In some states, CTE is delivered primarily through centers that are part of a statewide network of schools.
2. In some states, CTE is delivered primarily in a center operated by a single school district or a center operating as a part of a single high school.
3. In most states, CTE is provided through special schools operating under a confederation of two or more school districts.

Typically, the approach used is determined by state policies and funding provisions (Kowalski, 2006).

As the school reform movement gained energy during the 1980s, a number of questions were raised about the continued need for and value of traditional vocational high schools. Ernest Boyer (1983), for example, charged that vocational education neither provided a sufficiently broad education nor prepared students adequately for careers. John Goodlad (1984) added that the mission of vocational schools had become essentially irrelevant after America moved from being a manufacturing-based society to being an information-based society. Other critics (e.g., Brewer, Argys, & Rees, 1995; Oakes, 1985) claimed that vocational schools perpetuated student tracking (a concept that separates students into designated groups so that they can receive a curriculum deemed to be based on their ability and interests), a process thought to affect students of color and low-income students negatively.

Clearly, disapprovals of traditional vocational education have resulted in a revised mission and curricular changes. Today, CTE is presented as a distinctively dissimilar education approach. Career centers claim that when compared to former vocational schools, their curricula are more comprehensive and academically challenging. Moreover, three points are commonly stressed regarding the need for and the effectiveness of career-technical schools:

1. If not for CTE, many more students would drop out of school before graduating.
2. Despite popular opinion, the academic skills of students enrolled in these schools are not inferior; CTE student scores on standardized academic tests have been found to be no different from students at the same ability level attending traditional high schools.
3. Area employers strongly support CTE and view career-technical schools as essential, primarily because demands for skilled workers continue to increase.

Moreover, the mission of contemporary CTE is characterized by four cornerstones: increasing student engagement; improving math, science and literacy skills; meeting America's workforce needs; and meeting employer needs for highly skilled workers (Drage, 2009, p. 32).

Despite the fact that CTE is substantially different from its predecessor, vocational education, the future of career-technical schools is being debated in more than a few states. Policymakers have been especially troubled by a lack of national data demonstrating the extent to which CTE effectively provides essential academic skills as well as career training (Lewis, 2009).

This case is about conflict among members of a confederation, superintendents and high school principals who send students to a career-technical school. The conflict intensifies to the point that the future of the confederation and its career-technical school are placed in doubt.

Key Areas for Reflection

1. Collaboration among school districts
2. Ethical, moral, and legal obligations
3. Career-technical education
4. Reform in high schools

THE CASE

Medford Career-Technical Center (MCTC), formerly Medford Vocational High School, has a proud history. Established in the southeast corner of a Midwestern state in the mid-1960s, it was considered a model vocational school. Located in a serene rural setting, the school still serves nearly 600 students coming from 15 school districts and 19 high schools across 6 counties; all students attend the MCTC for a half day, spending the other half day in their home high schools. The school's governing board consists of the 15 superintendents in the districts making up the confederation. The 19 high school principals form the school's curriculum advisory council.

The name of the school was changed in 1990, reflecting a national trend from traditional vocational education to CTE. Since its founding, the school has had only three principals; the current one, Roscoe Downey, was appointed 8 years ago. Prior to his promotion, he had been a teacher and assistant principal at the center. The transition from a vocational curriculum to a CTE curriculum was difficult and protracted. Many faculty, most of whom had been employed at the center for more than 2 decades, resisted change. Principal Downey, the governing board, and the curriculum advisory committee, however, recognized that the program and curricular changes were essential. Two years after becoming principal, Downey identified six problems he claimed were jeopardizing the school's future and presented them to the governing board members in his annual report.

1. Over the previous 6 years, enrollment at MCTC had been declining steadily at a rate of about 1% per year. If the declines were not reversed, reductions in faculty and staff positions would be necessary.
2. The facility, constructed in 1964, had not been renovated or improved; expectedly, the facility was in poor condition. Maintenance and operating costs (e.g., utility costs) were rising, compounding fiscal problems related to a declining student population.

3. Much of the equipment, purchased prior to 1990 when the school was still a vocational high school, was outdated and inappropriate for delivering a modern CTE curriculum.

4. Although the school's espoused curriculum had changed after 1990, the actual curriculum delivered in some courses was still based on traditional vocational education.

5. Some high school principals were reporting increased parental resistance to enrolling their children in the MCTC, primarily because the school had acquired an image as an institution for low-ability, underachieving, or disruptive students.

Principal Downey recommended that the governing board retain a consultant to study these problems. The recommendation was defeated with only two of the 15 members supporting it. Among those voting against the recommendation, two did not believe the problems identified by the principal were valid; three did not believe that funds were available to deal with the problems; eight questioned the long-term viability of the confederation and the MCTC.

Over the next 5 years, nothing was done to deal with the problems, and as a result, their effects became even more debilitating. At the same time, other issues emerged darkening the cloud that already was hanging over the school. The following are the more notable of these concerns:

- Changes in federal legislation had heightened accountability standards for career-technical schools. Greater attention was being given to academic achievement and curricular relevancy.
- The state legislature had cut funding for CTE.
- Enrollment was now below 600 for the first time since the school opened.
- Some aspects of the deteriorating facility had become health and safety issues and the state fire marshal and state department of education were threatening to close the facility.
- Letters critical of the center, most written by parents or small-business owners, had been published on the local newspaper's editorial page.
- Several superintendents on the governing board were experiencing declining enrollments in their school districts. As an alternative to renovating or replacing the MCTC facility, they proposed that several MCTC courses should be taught in their high schools.
- Conflict had emerged between the principals on the curriculum advisory board and MCTC staff members in two areas: student discipline and decisions to offer some CTE in the home high schools.

All of these issues were troubling, but the last two had created political firestorms. Tensions over student discipline resulted from a disagreement between center personnel and the home school principals regarding authority to exclude students from the center. The MCTC principal contended that he had the authority to suspend or expel students for infractions that occurred either at the center or while students were being transported to and from the center. The home school principals contended that exclusion from the center required the approval of a student's home school principal. Until recently, all parties had honored an unwritten agreement giving the MCTC principal such authority; three home school principals sought to change the prevailing practice after they were threatened with lawsuits from the parents of students who had been excluded from the MCTC.

Conflict over offering some CTE courses in home high schools pertained to funding and the future of the MCTC. Proponents of this idea contended that operating costs and the time some students spent moving between schools could be reduced. Opponents, including the entire MCTC staff and three governing board members, argued that offering some CTE courses in home high schools was at best a temporary solution and at worst a decision that would cause the MCTC to be closed. Two of the superintendents objecting to this idea were employed in contiguous districts experiencing substantial enrollment increases. They threatened to withdraw from the confederation if CTE courses were offered in home high schools.

In light of these circumstances and knowing that he would be retiring in 2 years, Principal Downey again suggested to the governing board that a consultant be retained to address the center's problems. Several superintendents who previously voted against this recommendation were now concerned that the confederation might actually dissolve; moreover, six other superintendents were not on the board when the initial recommendation was rejected.

The governing board's current chair, Madeline Watkins, was superintendent of the second-smallest school district in the confederation. She was a staunch MCTC supporter. Although she wanted to improve the facility and update curricula and equipment, she knew that some of the board members disagreed with her. She spoke privately to all board members and concluded that another vote to retain a consultant could go either way. Even so, she placed the matter on the November board meeting agenda. After a lengthy discussion, a motion to approve Principal Downey's recommendation passed by a vote of eight to three with four members abstaining.

A university professor was retained as a planning consultant, and over the next 6 months he interviewed more than 160 people, including parents, students, staff, home school administrators, board members, and advisory council members. In addition, data were collected from approximately 30 local employers regarding their level of satisfaction with MCTC graduates and their future employment needs.

The consultant presented his findings, conclusions, and recommendations to the governing board in late June. A summary of his report follows:

- The center's curriculum needed to be revamped to provide greater emphasis on technology-based courses and programs. Conversely, several existing programs needed to be eliminated due to low enrollment, low demand for graduates, or both.
- After curricular revisions are completed, the facility should be completely renovated and new spaces created to accommodate the new technology-based courses/programs.
- The center's staff should develop a vision statement and it should be approved by the governing board. Once in place, the principal and staff should develop a public relations plan to communicate the vision to stakeholders and to enhance the school's image.
- CTE courses should not be taught in home high schools. Doing so would result in political and economic problems, such as bickering among home school officials and the MCTC having to pay rent to home high schools, that would further jeopardize the confederation.
- A long-term equipment replacement plan should be developed and coordinated with program changes and facility improvements.
- Any disciplinary action involving suspension or expulsion at the MCTC should be approved by both the MCTC and the home-school principals.

All 15 superintendents on the governing board and Principal Downey were present when the consultant presented his report. Several superintendents asked technical questions about data but none challenged the findings, conclusions, and recommendations. Superintendent Watkins, the board chair, urged her colleagues to study the report over the next month and to contact the consultant or Principal Downey if they had questions.

Because it was late June, most center employees were not working. Nevertheless, Principal Downey arranged for the consultant to make a second presentation to them and to the chairs of the program advisory committees. Approximately half of the employees and all but one of the advisory committee chairs attended the session. Principal Downey told the attendees that he supported all the recommendations. The advisory committee chairs, all representatives of local businesses or trades, also expressed support for them. The center staff supported the recommendations except for the one pertaining to discipline authority.

Principal Downey and Superintendent Watkins had hoped that the governing board would make a decision on whether to pursue all or some of the consultant's recommendations at its July meeting. That meeting, however, was canceled because six board members unable to attend the meeting opposed discussion of or action on the recommendations in their absence. Prior to the August board meeting, Superintendent Watkins attempted to speak with the other board members, either face-to-face or via telephone. She learned that they remained divided in their support for investing in the MCTC. The most controversial and expensive issue was renovating the facility. Under state law, all confederation members had to share the fiscal burden of construction based on their percentage of district enrollment in relation to the aggregate district enrollments in the consortium. Hence, higher-enrollment districts would have to assume a greater percentage of the construction cost. State law also required that all the school boards in the consortium had to approve debt-service obligations for school construction.

Prior to the August meeting, six superintendents vowed to oppose the recommendation for facility renovation and possibly all other recommendations. They also indicated that if a majority of the board approved moving forward with construction, they would likely recommend to their respective school boards withdrawal from the confederation. If this occurred, the MCTC could be forced to close; enrollment would likely drop an additional 150 students, and without better facilities, equipment, and courses, the school would find it nearly impossible to meet new accountability standards.

After Superintendent Watkins told Principal Downey about the sentiments of the six superintendents, he was dejected. Moreover, opposition to the consultant's recommendation on discipline authority was being openly criticized by MCTC staff—and their opposition to this recommendation angered many of the home high school principals.

The August board meeting was several weeks away. Although Superintendent Watkins promised to continue to support the recommendations and to urge her colleagues to do likewise, she told Principal Downey that a majority of the governing board was unlikely to support renovating the facility. She suggested that it may be prudent to delay a vote on this matter for 6 to 12 months. Principal Downey was not inclined to agree. If facility and equipment problems were not resolved, he concluded that needed curricular revisions would not occur. He told Superintendent Watkins he would think about her suggestion to table the matter and communicate his decision in a few days.

Problem Framing

1. Assume you are Principal Downey. First determine the main issue (problem) in this case. Then describe the current state and the desired state of this issue. (The section on problem framing in the Introduction section of this book defines the problem framing process.)

2. Based on evidence provided in the case, describe the difficulty associated with eliminating the gap between the present state and desired state.

Questions and Suggested Activities

1. Did Principal Downey act prudently when his recommendation to conduct a study was initially rejected? If you were he, would you have waited 5 years to make the same recommendation? Why or why not?

2. Based on what you have studied and experienced in schools, are the MCTC's problems common for career-technical schools?

3. The chairs of the program advisory committees support the center and the recommendations to improve it. These individuals represent local businesses and trades. Should Principal Downey involve them in trying to persuade the governing board members to support the consultant's recommendations? Why or why not?

4. If you were a principal in one of the confederation high schools, what stance would you take on the discipline authority issue? What is the basis for your position?

5. To what extent has CTE become a controversial issue in your state?

6. Do you agree with the idea of offering CTE courses in regular high schools if space is available? What are the advantages and disadvantages of doing this?

7. Do most career-technical centers or schools have an image problem? If so, what is the nature of the problem?

8. The MCTC enrolls students for a half-day. What are the advantages and disadvantages of changing the current pattern so that students are enrolled at the MCTC all day?

9. Based on what you have studied and experienced in schools, do principals in traditional high schools use career-technical schools as a "dumping ground" for troubled students?

Suggested Readings

Bamford, P. J. (1995). Success by design: The restructuring of a Vo-Tech center. *Tech Directions, 54*(7), 15–17.

Dembicki, M. (2000). He's got the hook. *Techniques: Connecting Education and Careers, 75*(3), 28–31.

Harkins, A. M. (2002). The futures of career and technical education in a continuous innovation society. *Journal of Vocational Education Research. 27*(1), 35–64.

Hoachlander, G. (2007). New rigor for career education. *Educational Leadership, 64*(7), 34–35.

Jenkins, J. M. (2000). Looking backward: Educational reform in the twentieth century. *International Journal of Educational Reform, 9*(1), 74–78.

Lynch, R. L. (2000). High school career and technical education for the first decade of the 21st century. *Journal of Vocational Education Research, 25*(2), 155–198.

MacIver, M. A., & Legters, N. (2001). Partnerships for career-centered high school reform in an urban school system. *Journal of Vocational Education Research, 26*(3), 412–446.

Plank, S. B., DeLuca, S., & Estacion, A. (2008). High school dropout and the role of Career and Technical Education: A survival analysis of surviving high school. *Sociology of Education, 81*(4), 345–370.

Reese, S. (2001). High school career tech at the crossroads. *Techniques: Connecting Education and Careers, 76*(7), 33–35.

Reese, S. (2005). The new career and technical school. *Techniques: Connecting Education and Careers, 80*(7), 16–17.

Ries, E. (1999). Packed by popular demand. *Techniques: Making Education and Career Connections, 74*(3), 22–25.

Seccurro, W. B., & Thomas, D. W. (1998). School improvement through tech prep: How one vocational school changed its program and image. *Tech Directions, 57*(8), 22–23.

Shibley, I. A. (2005). One school's approach to No Child Left Behind. *Techniques: Connecting Education and Careers, 80*(4), 50–53.

Shumer, R. (2001). A new, old vision of learning, working, and living: Vocational education in the 21st century. *Journal of Vocational Education Research, 26*(3), 447–461.

Stasz, C., & Bodilly, S. (2004). *Efforts to improve the quality of vocational education in secondary schools: Impact of federal and state policies.* Arlington, VA: RAND Corporation.

References

Boyer, E. L. (1983). *High school.* New York: Harper.

Brewer, D. J., Argys, L. M., & Rees, D. I. (1995). Detracking America's schools: The reform without cost? *Phi Delta Kappan, 77*, 210–212.

Drage, K. (2009). Modernizing career and technical education programs. *Techniques, 84*(5), 32–34.

Goodlad, J. I. (1984). *A place called school.* New York: McGraw-Hill.

Kowalski, T. J. (2006). *The school superintendent: Theory, practice, and cases* (2nd ed.). Thousand Oaks, CA: Sage.

Lewis, A. C. (2009). State-level accountability concerns. *Tech Directions, 69*(2), 7–8.

Oakes, J. (1985). *Keeping track: How schools structure inequality.* New Haven, CT: Yale University.

20 | ILLEGAL DRUGS, IN-SCHOOL SUSPENSION, AND THE NOVICE PRINCIPAL

BACKGROUND INFORMATION

Experts often disagree about the causes of substance abuse problems and how they should be handled. Some see this problem largely as a criminal matter; these individuals typically advocate zero-tolerance policies that call for offenders to be excluded from the traditional school environment. Others view the problem as a physical, emotional, or psychological matter; these individuals are more prone to allowing offenders to remain in school provided they receive counseling and other prescribed therapies. Disagreement over the issue of illegal drug use is evidenced by the fact that zero-tolerance policies established by school boards have been the subject of litigation (Henault, 2001; Zirkel, 1999).

Suspension from school is commonly used as a disciplinary measure in high schools for a variety of violations of student conduct rules. Such punishment can occur in several ways:

- The student is not allowed to attend school for a specified period of time.
- The student is not allowed to attend his or her regular school for a specified period of time but is permitted to attend an alternative program while suspended.
- The student is placed in an in-school suspension program—a program that isolates him or her from the main population while requiring continued attendance in school.

Involuntary placement in an alternative school or in-school suspension programs, though punitive, allows a student to continue his or her academic studies. Moreover, some alternative schools (Kowalski & Reynolds, 2003) and in-school suspension programs (Sheets, 1996) require students to receive behavioral remediation therapy as well as academic instruction. Alternative schools are not a feasible option for most suspensions because the exclusion period is almost always 10 days or less. Critics contend that students often view in-school suspension as a slap on the wrist; by allowing them to remain in the school, the behavior being punished may continue to jeopardize the welfare of the general student population.

This case is about a relatively inexperienced principal who establishes an in-school suspension program in a large high school in an effort to reduce high expulsion and dropout rates. Detractors become outraged after two students placed in the program are arrested selling crack cocaine in the school's parking lot. The ensuing conflict causes this second-year principal to question her judgment and her desire to continue as the school's principal.

Key Areas for Reflection

1. Inexperienced principals
2. Job satisfaction
3. Pupil conduct and discipline
4. Job-related stress
5. Principal and staff relationships
6. Zero-tolerance policy

THE CASE

Setting the Stage

"Are you serious?" Lowell Tatum asked his wife as the two were having dinner at their favorite San Francisco restaurant. "Now let me get this straight. You want to leave your job as a curriculum coordinator to become a high school principal? You ought to think about this."

Patricia Tatum has met challenges successfully throughout her life. Reared in a low income family, she is the oldest of six children. Although neither of her parents graduated from high school, they provided a warm, caring family environment where high expectations were the norm. As early as elementary school, her parents and teachers recognized that Patricia was an atypical student. She loved school and she was always at the top or near the top of her class academically. In high school, she earned mostly "A's" even though she was a member of the girls' track team, a cheerleader, and president of the student council. When she graduated, her class rank was 6 out of 389, and she received an academic scholarship to attend a private liberal arts college. She finished her degree in 4 years graduating with honors.

While a college student, Patricia worked part-time as a teacher's aide in a parochial elementary school. That experience prompted her to change her major from pre-law to English; she had decided to become a high school English teacher. After graduating, she married Lowell Tatum, an executive with a San Francisco–based brokerage firm, and worked as a copy editor for a small publishing firm for 2 years. During this time, she managed to complete a master's degree in English Literature and then accepted a position teaching English in an urban high school. Over the next 6 years, she gave birth to a baby girl and began studies to complete a doctoral degree in administration and supervision.

After receiving her doctoral degree and with her daughter now in school, Patricia began applying for administrative vacancies. One day in early July, she received a phone call from the personnel director in a neighboring school district where she had applied for a middle school assistant principal position.

"Dr. Tatum," he said, "I was looking at your application for an assistant principal vacancy. Actually, the reason I'm calling is to talk to you about a different position. Just a few days ago our secondary school curriculum coordinator resigned. We're just 6 weeks away from starting the school term and the superintendent wants to fill this vacancy as soon as possible. I know you applied for a different position but I'm inquiring about your possible interest in the curriculum job."

The personnel director explained that the elementary and secondary curriculum coordinators facilitated the work of principals and teachers. As such, they were staff administrators who did not have line authority for supervising principals.

Two weeks after being contacted about the curriculum position, Patricia was interviewed by a selection committee and offered the job. Although she would have preferred to be an assistant principal or principal, she decided that the opportunity presented to her also could be highly rewarding.

At first, Dr. Tatum felt good about her new job. She was spending about 35% of her time in schools working with administrators and teachers. Yet, she still had a strong desire to be a principal and she shared this information with Dr. Ernesto Javier, the associate superintendent for instruction and her immediate supervisor.

"I don't want you to think I'm unhappy, because I'm not," she said. "It's just that I really like being close to students and teachers."

Dr. Javier previously had been a high school principal for 14 years and he understood Patricia's feelings. When he had been given an opportunity to move to his current position, he was ambivalent about becoming a district-level administrator.

"Patricia, I don't think there will be any assistant principal vacancies in the near future. We just filled two such positions last summer. You are doing a terrific job as a curriculum coordinator. If you are certain that you would rather be a school-level administrator, I will try to help you move in that direction."

The school term was nearly over and Patricia considered applying for vacancies in other districts in the metropolitan area. Based on Dr. Javier's comments, she concluded that the prospects of moving to a school-level position in this district were remote—at least for the next school year. But just a few days later, Dr. Javier walked into Patricia's office and said he had a possible job opportunity.

"Principal Malovidge at Western Valley High School just resigned because he has taken another job in the Seattle area. I met with the superintendent and personnel director this morning. We decided that given the timing of this resignation, we would rather appoint an interim principal and conduct a full search when we have more time. Given your sentiments about being a school-level administrator, would you be interested in this position? Being the interim principal at Western Valley would give you a chance to experience the job. A retired principal is willing to take your position on an interim basis if you move to Western Valley for a year. However, you may opt to apply for the principal's position when a search is conducted, probably around December or January. If you decide that you do not want to seek the position permanently, you can return to your current job. Regardless of your choice, I'm pleased to have you working in this district."

"I must admit, Dr. Javier, I'm surprised. There are three assistant principals at Western Valley and two of them are highly experienced. Why not appoint one of them interim principal?"

"Without going into all the details, the superintendent and I already have discussed that possibility. We believe that promoting one of them is not a good option. Hank Malovidge was not fired, nor was he encouraged to resign. Nevertheless, he knew that the superintendent was displeased with conditions at the school. Hank felt that the superintendent did not appreciate the difficult nature of his job. Both of the male assistant principals have expressed interest in serving as the interim principal, but picking one over the other would almost certainly divide the faculty and support staff. Further, we do not believe either of them would be much different than Hank. And that's a concern, because the superintendent wants to see improvements at the school."

Although she wanted to say yes immediately, Dr. Tatum requested and was granted several days to make a decision. Before she left Dr. Javier's office, she asked him to clarify her status regarding staying in the position for more than 1 year.

"Certainly, you could apply to be the permanent principal. And if you perform as I think you will, you have an excellent chance of remaining the principal. By the time we commence the search, you should know whether you want to stay in the job and we will know how well you are doing."

The next morning, Patricia told Dr. Javier she wanted to be the interim principal.

Dr. Tatum, Interim Principal

Western Valley High School serves about 2,300 students in Grades 9 through 12. The student population is diverse, both economically and racially. Most students live in middle-class homes and about 55% of the graduates enroll in 4-year institutions of higher education.

As secondary school curriculum coordinator, Dr. Tatum had been to Western Valley High School about a dozen times the previous year. She had met many of the teachers and was acquainted with Joe Baldwin and Bill Fine, the two more experienced assistant principals who expressed interest in the job she now had. She also knew the third assistant principal, Sally Farmer.

When the superintendent announced publicly that Dr. Tatum would be the interim principal, the school's employees were stunned that the job was given to the young and inexperienced curriculum coordinator. Most had expected either Joe Baldwin or Bill Fine to be appointed. At least one school employee, Sally Farmer, was especially pleased with the appointment because she did not want to deal with the political tensions that would have occurred had either Baldwin or Fine been selected.

In the first meetings with the school's administrative group, Dr. Tatum outlined three objectives for the forthcoming school term:

1. Reduce the school's dropout rate.
2. Find more effective ways to deal with student discipline.
3. Increase school effectiveness by elevating student achievement test scores.

She pointed out to the assistants that the goals were known to and supported by the superintendent and associate superintendent for instruction.

Principal Tatum then said that the four of them would function as an administrative team, each administrator having designated responsibilities. Specific assignments, however, would be determined collectively. After considerable discussion, the four agreed that Dr. Tatum and Ms. Farmer would have primary responsibility for the instructional programs; Dr. Tatum would be responsible for Grades 11 and 12 and Ms. Farmer would be responsible for Grades 9 and 10. Mr. Baldwin would be responsible for most management functions, such as food services, course scheduling, the school budget, and building maintenance. Mr. Fine would be responsible for supervising extracurricular programs, including athletics. Student discipline, the assignment none of them wanted, would be shared by all four. Each was assigned to oversee discipline for a given grade level, with Principal Tatum being responsible for Grade 12.

After school started in late August, Dr. Tatum realized that spending considerable time with instructional programs was going to be more difficult than she imagined. No matter how meticulously she planned, her intention to spend time working with teachers was thwarted by unanticipated day-to-day problems, especially student behavior issues. Despite the agreement regarding the management of student discipline, she quickly discovered that all serious matters, regardless of grade level, made their way to her office.

The former principal had taken a hard line toward student discipline, especially matters involving illegal drugs. If a student was caught possessing marijuana and it was a first offense, he or she would likely be suspended from school for 10 days. If a student was caught possessing marijuana a second time, possessing "harder" drugs (e.g., cocaine, heroin) or using or selling any illegal drug, he or she were recommended for expulsion. Western Valley had the highest expulsion rate among the district's four high schools.

In the past, none of the assistant principals had opposed the principal's rules regarding illegal drugs. Dr. Tatum, however, considered them inflexible. She preferred to judge infractions individually. As an example, she believed that a second offense for possessing marijuana should not be treated the same as a student selling heroin in the restroom.

After becoming interim principal, Dr. Tatum revealed her intention to revise the school's rule on illegal drugs. The assistant principals, however, did not respond favorably to her plan. Not wanting to be autocratic, she appointed an ad hoc committee to examine the issue; members included two parents, one a social worker and the other a clinical psychologist; a counselor at Western Valley; Mr. Fine; and three Western Valley teachers. The committee was given several months to make a recommendation.

The committee examined school board policy, rules set by the district's other schools and policy and rules enforced in neighboring districts. The members also heard testimony from experts, including narcotics officers, substance-abuse specialists, and a local juvenile judge. The committee members unanimously agreed that the district's zero-tolerance policy concerning sell-ing illegal drugs should not be changed; students found guilty of this offense are expelled. They were deeply divided, however, over disciplinary action for students found guilty of possessing or using illegal drugs. A majority of four members (the two parents, the school counselor, and one of the teachers) voted to support the following two recommendations:

1. An in-school suspension program should be established. Students found guilty of possess-ing or using illegal drugs (all types) for the first time would be placed in this program. The length of suspension would depend on the nature of the drug and the student's overall dis-cipline record. Students placed in the in-school suspension program for possessing or using illegal drugs would be required to see a counselor who would determine whether the students had to enroll in a drug education program.
2. Students found guilty of possessing or using illegal drugs a second time should either receive an out-of-school suspension or be expelled. Students excluded from school would be required to enroll in and complete a drug education program as a condition for re-entering the school.

Mr. Fine openly opposed the recommendations and told Dr. Tatum that she would be mak-ing a big mistake if she accepted them. The other two assistant principals said they were dubious but would not oppose the recommendations openly.

Dr. Tatum discussed the committee's recommendations with Dr. Javier. District policy did not stipulate a specific penalty for first-time possession or use violations; it did, however, require that second-time offenders be expelled. Members of the ad hoc committee recognized that their second recommendation conflicted with existing policy. They presented it anyway, hoping that the superintendent and school board would either grant a waiver to Western Valley for this provision or change the current policy. Dr. Javier immediately indicated that the superintendent was unwilling to recommend changing the existing district policy on ille-gal drugs but noted that permission would be granted to establish the in-school suspension program.

School was opening in 2 weeks and Principal Tatum could wait no longer; she told the school's administrative team and subsequently the faculty that the in-school suspension program would be implemented. She modified the school's rule on illegal drugs and revised the student handbook; the revision was approved by the school board a week before school started. Her plan for establishing an in-school suspension program was approved by the superintendent and school board approximately 1 month later.

During the first semester of operation, the in-school suspension program ran smoothly. Eight students received in-school suspensions, three for possessing marijuana.

Dr. Tatum, Permanent Principal

Dr. Tatum applied to become the permanent principal in early December and was selected for the job. Her status was changed from interim to permanent principal immediately after the school board approved her selection. At the closing faculty meeting in late May, she announced that the in-school suspension program had been highly successful. A total of 17 students had been placed in the program, only 7 for drug-related offenses. All suspensions were completed without inci-dent. Even more noteworthy, she told the faculty, the school's dropout rate had declined 13%, and compared to the previous school year, expulsions dropped by 22%.

During the first 2 months of the next school year, 12 students were disciplined for drug-related offenses—a notable increase over the previous school term. Three were expelled, two received out-of-school suspensions, and the remaining seven received in-school suspensions. At the November faculty meeting, several teachers expressed concern about a rising level of drug use at the school and suggested that the in-school suspension program was a contributing factor. Dr. Tatum also received the following letter from a parent expressing the same conviction:

Dear Dr. Tatum:

This letter is written to object to your policy of allowing students found guilty of possessing drugs to stay in school. As parents, my wife and I think the in-school suspension program sends the wrong message to students. We urge you to discontinue it and to re-adopt the rules that were in place before you were named principal.

Moreover, the school's faculty and staff knew that the assistant principals were not highly supportive of the in-school suspension program. And in the event that they forgot, Bill Fine reminded them. He even told parents that he opposed the program and felt that the previous rules should never have been altered. The other assistant principals kept their promise; they did not make their feelings known publicly.

In late November, two students serving in-school suspensions for possessing marijuana were arrested by an undercover policeman for selling crack cocaine in the school's parking lot. The next day, several reporters received anonymous voice mail messages contending that the use of illegal drugs at the school was out of control and that Dr. Tatum and her liberal discipline policies were responsible. Within 48 hours of the arrests, the incident and rumors of widespread drug use at Western Valley moved to the front page of local newspapers. Parents and several Western Valley teachers opposed to the in-school suspension program stepped forward and were interviewed by reporters.

One of the local television stations aired a 5-minute report on illegal drugs at the school. The commentator began the segment by saying:

In-school suspension at Western Valley. A solution to drug use or an idea making the problem worse? Parents and teachers at Western Valley are up in arms because two students serving in-school suspensions for possessing drugs were arrested selling crack cocaine on school property. Under the school's previous principal, these students would either have been excluded from school for 10 days or the remainder of the school term. But, current principal, Patricia Tatum, placed the students in an in-school suspension program, a decision that allowed them to remain among the school's student population. Critics are charging that the recent arrests are symptomatic of growing drug problems at the school—one that is being fueled by the in-school suspension program. Only 5 days after being placed in this program, the two students were allegedly selling cocaine to other students. School district officials would not comment on the matter beyond saying that they were investigating it.

Given the mounting publicity, Dr. Tatum was asked several questions by the superintendent. The first was whether the students who had been arrested had received counseling as prescribed by the school's new rule. She answered that each had a one-hour session with a school counselor. At the point of their arrest, however, the counselor had not prescribed a drug education program for either of them.

The superintendent also asked Dr. Tatum if she had considered possible alternatives to in-school suspension. The district operated both an alternative high school and an adult evening school; students excluded from regular programs were usually permitted to enroll in these programs.

"Do you think in-school suspension is better than having these students at an alternative school?" he asked.

"Our records show that many students over age 16 quit school instead of enrolling in an alternative school. This option was examined by the committee that recommended the in-school suspension program," Dr. Tatum explained.

As the meeting ended, the superintendent said that the in-school suspension program could continue provided students suspended for drug-related offenses were required to enroll in a drug education program in addition to receiving counseling at school.

Two days later, Dr. Tatum received an anonymous letter blaming her for not controlling the use of illegal drugs at the school and accusing the superintendent and Dr. Javier of conducting a "cover-up." The letter was written on Western Valley High School stationery.

For the first time, Dr. Tatum doubted her ability to be an effective principal. She telephoned Dr. Javier and shared her lack of self-confidence. He offered her encouragement but also provided an escape option. He told her she could return to her curriculum coordinator position at the end of the current school term.

Problem Framing

1. Assume you are Dr. Tatum. First determine the main issue (problem) in this case. Then describe the current state and the desired state of this issue. (The section on problem framing in the Introduction section of this book defines the problem framing process.)

2. Based on evidence provided in the case, describe the difficulty associated with eliminating the gap between the present state and desired state.

Questions and Suggested Activities

1. Did the superintendent and Dr. Javier act prudently in naming Dr. Tatum the interim principal? Why or why not?
2. Evaluate the behavior of the three assistant principals. If you were the principal, would you have tolerated their opposition to the in-school suspension program?
3. What are the advantages and disadvantages of in-school suspensions?
4. What are the arguments for and against zero-tolerance policies?
5. In the school district in which you are employed or reside, how are drug possession, use, and sale offenses handled? Do laws in your state address these issues? If so, in what manner?

6. Based on what you have studied and experienced as an educator, what do you believe should be done to prevent students from using illegal drugs?
7. If you had been the principal, would you have appointed an ad hoc committee to examine the illegal drug rules? Why or why not?
8. To what extent were Dr. Tatum's age, gender, race, and experience relevant to the situation described in this case?
9. The superintendent has decided to allow the in-school suspension program to continue. If you were the principal, would you sustain the program? If yes, why? If no, what would you do to replace it?

Suggested Readings

Barnhart, M. K., Franklin, N. J., & Alleman, J. R. (2008). Lessons learned and strategies used in reducing the frequency of out-of-school suspensions. *Journal of Special Education Leadership, 21*(2), 75–83.

Blair, F. E. (1999). Does zero tolerance work? *Principal, 79*(1), 36–37.

Bunch, E. A. (1998). School discipline under the Individuals with Disabilities Education Act: How the stay-put provision limits schools in providing a safe learning environment. *Journal of Law and Education, 27*(2), 315–321.

Casella, R. (2003). Zero tolerance policy in schools: Rationale, consequences, and alternatives. *Teachers College Record, 105*(5), 872–892.

Costenbader, V., & Markson, S. (1998). School suspension: A study with secondary school students. *Journal of School Psychology, 36*(1), 59–82.

Eckman, E. W. (2002). Women high school principals: Perspectives on role conflict, role commitment, and job satisfaction. *Journal of School Leadership, 12*(1), 57–77.

Henault, C. (2001). Zero tolerance in schools. *Journal of Law and Education, 30*(3), 547–553.

Holtkamp, L. A. (2002). Crossing borders: An analysis of the characteristics and attributes of female public school principals. *Advancing Women in Leadership Journal, 10*(1), 2–6.

Johnston, J. (1989). High school completion of in-school suspension students. *NASSP Bulletin, 73*(521), 89–95.

Jones, R. (1997). Absolute zero. *American School Board Journal, 184*(10), 29–31.

Lohrmann, D., & Fors, S. (1988). Can school-based educational programs really be expected to solve the adolescent drug abuse problem? *Journal of Drug Education, 16*(4), 327–339

Mirsky, L. (2007). SaferSanerSchools: Transforming school cultures with restorative practices. *Reclaiming Children & Youth, 16*(2), 5–12.

Morris, R. C., & Howard, A. C. (2003). Designing an effective in-school suspension program. *Clearing House, 76*(3), 156–159.

Sheets, J. (1996). Designing an effective in-school suspension program to change student behavior. *NASSP Bulletin, 80*(579), 86–90.

Skiba, R., & Peterson, R. (1999). The dark side of zero tolerance: Can punishment lead to safe schools? *Phi Delta Kappan, 80*(5), 372–376, 381–382.

Stader, D. L. (2004). Zero tolerance as public policy: The good, the bad, and the ugly. *Clearing House, 78*(2), 62–66.

Sullivan, J. (1989). Elements of a successful in-school suspension program. *NASSP Bulletin, 73*(516), 32–38.

Watson, D., & Bright, A. (1988). So you caught them using drugs: Now what? *Thrust, 17*(3), 34–36.

Whitfield, D., & Bulach, C. (1996). *A study of the effectiveness of in-school suspension.* (ERIC Document Reproduction Service No. ED 396 372)

Zirkel, P. A. (1996). Discipline and the law. *Executive Educator, 18*(7), 21–23.

Zorn, R. (1988). New alternatives to student suspensions for substance abuse. *American Secondary Education, 17*(2), 30–32.

References

Henault, C. (2001). Zero tolerance in schools. *Journal of Law and Education, 30*(3), 547–553.

Kowalski, T. J., & Reynolds, S. (2003). Knowledge, dispositions, and career orientations of alternative school principals. *Connections: Journal of Principal Preparation and Development, 5*, 22–31.

Sheets, J. (1996). Designing an effective in-school suspension program to change student behavior. *NASSP Bulletin, 80*(579), 86–90.

Zirkel, P. A. (1999). Zero tolerance expulsions. *NASSP Bulletin, 83*(605), 101–105.

21 LET'S NOT RAP

BACKGROUND INFORMATION

The demographic profile of the United States has become increasingly diverse. As a result, most districts and schools are more heterogeneous racially and ethnically than they were 25 years ago. As a result, scholars have paid increased attention to effects of diversity on public institutions (Pitts, 2005); in the case of schools, authors (e.g., Miron, St. John, & Davidson, 1998) point out that resolving racial discord and improving education have become interrelated objectives.

Initiatives intended to reduce tensions spawned by diversity have not been uniformly supported. Multicultural education and bilingual education, for example, have been divisive concepts in more than a few communities. Opponents of such programs claim they foster social values (e.g., equality and social justice) and political philosophy (e.g., liberalism) that they find objectionable (Reich, 2002). In some schools, the courts have had to intervene to address diversity-related conflict (Zirkel, 2001).

This case describes a situation in which school officials have scheduled a "rap" group to perform at a student assembly. The program's intent is to dissuade students from using illegal drugs; however, the performers prove to be controversial, accused of promoting anti-Semitism. Once the accusation is made public, a small but politically influential group of Jewish residents demands that the principal cancel the assembly. This demand is countered by a much larger but supposedly less influential group of African American residents. As you read this case, pay particular attention to how race, ethnicity, and power intertwine.

Key Areas for Reflection

1. Community diversity
2. School and community relationships
3. Race, politics, and public education
4. Conflict resolution
5. Student assemblies
6. Free speech and public schools

THE CASE

Principal Doran

Barb Doran is principal of Roosevelt High School, a highly respected institution enrolling 2,340 students and in a suburb of a major mid-Atlantic city. She has held this position for less than

2 years, but she already is perceived to be an effective administrator by the faculty and many parents. After teaching biology for 12 years, she has had three progressively challenging administrative positions: assistant principal of a 350-student middle school, principal of a 500-student rural high school, and now principal at Roosevelt High School.

A Controversial Assembly

Principal Doran had just returned from a conference in Orlando, Florida, and was driving from the airport to her office at approximately 7:30 in the evening. As she drove, she listened to a local radio program, anticipating that the topic might be Roosevelt High School. She was correct.

"I think the principal should have the courage to cancel this program," a caller proclaimed. "What good is an anti-drug message if the people delivering it are anti-Semites? There are more acceptable ways to tell students not to use drugs. There is no justification for inviting persons who preach hatred toward others to our schools."

The next caller took an opposite position. "We all know that there are racial tensions at the school. Mostly because African American students are not treated the same as white students. Let me give you an example. Someone told me that a white kid who got caught smoking in the restroom received only one hour of detention. The very next day, a black kid who got caught smoking was given a 3-day suspension. Is that fair and equal treatment? My guess is that the principal will bow to political pressure and cancel the assembly. If she does, there will be a lot of angry students and parents."

Rather than responding, the show's host transitioned to a commercial break: "For those of you just joining us, tonight's topic deals with controversy at Roosevelt High. Should the school principal cancel an assembly to be conducted by a rap group that is supposedly anti-Semitic? Clearly, the impending assembly has divided students, parents, and maybe even teachers. Our last caller claims there are deep racial tensions at the school. What do you think? Let us know which side you support. Call me at 555-1500. I'll be back in a moment to answer your calls."

Barb Doran stared at the road ahead as she continued toward her office. Mentally, she asked herself why problems always seemed to erupt when she was out of town. She was gone just 3 days and was returning to a firestorm. Although she knew that the assembly had been scheduled, she did not learn of the group's alleged anti-Semitism until the day before. As she turned into the school's parking lot, she whispered to herself, "Why me, Lord?"

Roosevelt High School

Most Roosevelt students come from middle- or upper-middle class families; however, the student population is diverse racially, ethnically, and religiously. Official school records reveal the following profile:

- Caucasian (non-Hispanic): 61%
- African American: 31%
- Asian: 4%
- Hispanic: 3%
- Other: 1%

Although the school does not maintain religious affiliation data, the superintendent and school board have been sensitive to the fact that a considerable portion of the students is non-Christian. The school's counseling staff estimated that approximately 10% of the students are practicing Jews, approximately 5% are practicing Muslims, and another 2% are practicing Buddhists.

In the past, Roosevelt High School has been considered an excellent institution, both academically and socially. The school has consistently ranked among the top five high schools in the state. In 2005, for example, 81% of the seniors entered either a 4-year or 2-year institution of higher education. In addition, Roosevelt consistently has had the lowest dropout rate in the state among high schools with more than 700 students.

PARA

In a recent interview conducted by a newspaper reporter, Principal Doran said that her greatest concern about Roosevelt High was the perception among some African American students that they were not treated fairly by teachers and administrators. Although she vigorously denied the accusation, leading figures in the African American community were skeptical. A year ago and long before the current controversy evolved, 28 parents of African American students formed an organization they called PARA (Parents Advocating Racial Awareness). In a press release issued by the group's leader, PARA identified its mission as "making sure that all Roosevelt High School students are treated equally and fairly and making sure that unresolved concerns related to the treatment of students of color would be addressed." Three such concerns were identified in the document:

1. The curriculum did not offer African American students ample opportunity to study their cultural heritage.
2. Teachers and administrators often disciplined African American students more frequently and harshly than other students.
3. School officials had done little to give the African American community a representative voice in critical decisions affecting the school and students.

Principal Doran believed the claims of unfair treatment were false; however, she was sensitive to PARA's concerns and wanted to cooperate with its members in order to improve race relations. She attended several PARA meetings in the hope of building constructive dialogue. She also appointed a PARA member to the principal's advisory council, a group consisting of six teachers, six parents, and six students. After the appointment of the PARA representative, 6 of the 18 members were persons of color.

Scheduling the Assembly

Reggie Colter, a senior, was the person who recommended a rap group to conduct a student assembly. The only African American member of Roosevelt's Student Council, he had become a spokesperson for students of color. His father, an attorney, is a PARA member.

Initiating the effort to schedule the rap group for an appearance at the school, Reggie told Principal Doran, "I have a great idea for a school assembly. My cousin is a sound technician for a group called the Inner City. They're going to be in town giving a concert 2 months from now. The group occasionally agrees to do school assemblies while on a concert tour. Their assembly program has an anti-drug theme. My cousin said he might be able to arrange for the group to do an assembly at Roosevelt. If you approve, I can contact my cousin and see if we can work everything out."

Principal Doran knew nothing about the performers or about the messages they delivered to students; so, she was understandably hesitant. "Could you be more specific about what they do during a school assembly?"

"They are rap music artists. The program is usually one hour. The group performs several of its hit songs and in between, members speak to the students discouraging them from using illegal drugs. My cousin said students react very positively to their message. The group carefully selects songs to avoid foul language or other offensive content. Here's a promotional brochure about the group. Students would have to pay at least $35 to attend their concert. By having an assembly, we would be allowing many students who could not afford a ticket to see the group."

Principal Doran was attracted to the idea, in part because she thought PARA might see the assembly as a goodwill gesture. She told Reggie to talk to Wallace Slater, the assistant principal in charge of extracurricular activities. She said she would brief Mr. Slater and ask him to determine whether the assembly should be held. Mr. Wallace was the school's only African American administrator and Reggie was pleased that he would be making the decision.

After being briefed, Assistant Principal Slater asked Reggie to get a list of the schools that had hosted the group. After receiving a list of five large urban high schools, all in other states, Assistant Principal Slater selected two of them randomly and contacted their principals via telephone. Both principals he contacted were African American and the schools in which they were employed enrolled predominately African American students. The feedback about the rap group was positive, both principals saying that the assemblies were successful. Based on this feedback, Assistant Principal Slater told Reggie he was now prepared to talk to the person who had authority to commit the group to doing an assembly.

At that point, Assistant Principal Slater sent the following email message to Principal Doran.

Barb,

After getting a list of five schools that hosted the Inner City for an assembly, I contacted principals of two of them. The feedback from both was very positive. I am anticipating a phone call from the group's agent so we can discuss details. Based on what I have learned, I think we should approve the assembly. Let me know if you do want me to move forward with this matter.

Wallace

Principal Doran sent the following email reply:

Wallace,

Good work. Move forward but make sure that student attendance is voluntary. I don't want parents or students accusing us of promoting rap music. Those who opt not to attend will be required to go to study rooms. Thanks.

Barb

Within a week, arrangements for the assembly were completed. Two days after the program was announced in the student paper, Principal Doran left to attend a conference in Orlando. On the day she departed, several parents called the school about the assembly. Since Principal Doran was gone, they spoke with Assistant Principal Slater. Several callers accused the rap group of being anti-Semitic. Specifically, they contended that some of their songs disparaged Jews and that several group members made anti-Semitic comments in an interview appearing in a national tabloid story. Unaware of these concerns prior to the phone calls, Assistant Principal Slater told the callers he would look into the matter and brief Principal Doran. He added that attendance at the assembly was voluntary.

By the end of the day, Assistant Principal Slater had received nine similar calls; he said the same things to every caller. The following day, the rabbi from the local synagogue and several other Jewish community leaders held a press conference expressing outrage about the student assembly. They distributed copies of the lyrics from a song they found objectionable and comments defending the song that appeared in the tabloid story. The next morning, the controversy was detailed in a front page newspaper story; late that afternoon, PARA officials held their own press conference demanding that the assembly not be canceled and promising to stage a protest if it were.

Recognizing the seriousness of the conflict, Assistant Principal Slater met with the two other assistant principals to discuss what they should do. They agreed that Principal Doran needed to be briefed about the situation immediately. They contacted her via telephone. Principal Doran said that no decision should be made until she returned from Florida. She also instructed Mr. Slater to brief the superintendent and ensure him that she would handle the matter as quickly as possible. Lastly, she told him to inform the media that the accusations would be fully investigated as soon as possible.

Reaching a Decision

After Principal Doran was at her office, she found a folder containing information about the assembly controversy on her desk. It included a copy of a newspaper article published that morning:

Controversy "Rocks" Roosevelt High

Some parents of Roosevelt High School students are objecting to a scheduled student assembly that will be conducted by a rap group called "The Inner City." Persons demanding that the assembly be canceled claim that the group has a history of anti-Semitism. They argue that by allowing the group to appear at Roosevelt High School the administrative staff would be condoning a message of hate and intolerance. Principal Barb Doran is out of town and was not available for comment. Assistant Principal Wallace Slater said the assembly is intended to discourage students from using illegal drugs. He added that principals who have hosted the same assembly uniformly praised the group. Principal Doran is scheduled to return this evening and is meeting with other school officials tomorrow morning. Superintendent Paul Tolliver said that student assemblies are part of the high school's co-curricular activities, and he preferred not to comment on the matter until he has had an opportunity to speak with Principal Doran and to review the facts.

Over two dozen phone messages, most from people opposing the assembly, were also in the folder.

Before going home, Principal Doran placed a telephone call to Dr. Tolliver.

"Barb, isn't it great to be back?" the superintendent asked facetiously. "How did you get tangled up with a rap group?"

"Neither Wallace nor I knew about the anti-Semitism charges until the assembly was approved. Wallace had checked out the group and everything he learned was positive. Quite frankly, I had no evidence at that time suggesting that the assembly would be controversial. Had I known about the anti-Semitism charges, I probably would have not given my approval."

"You have to make a decision about canceling the assembly as soon as possible. The Jewish community is upset, and two of the school board members who are part of that community have made their feelings known to me already. At the same time, PARA is threatening to protest if the assembly is canceled. This situation is only going to get worse with time. Therefore, the sooner we make a decision, the better."

"As you know, I've been working with PARA to improve relationships and maybe I was too anxious to score positive points with this assembly. I'm meeting with my assistants in the morning before school starts. I'll call you before 10 A.M., and my intent is to make my decision at that point."

"Barb, let's say this situation were reversed. Would we allow a Jewish group that made derogatory comments about African Americans to appear at school—regardless of the intended purpose of the assembly?"

"Are you implying that the assembly should be canceled?"

"No. I have confidence that you will make the correct decision."

Principal Doran sat at her desk and considered her options. How would she react to this situation if she were African American? How would she react if she were Jewish? She believed that public schools should encourage the exchange of ideas, even controversial ones, provided that the exchanges did not violate community standards.

During the meeting the following morning, the four administrators reviewed the limited evidence they possessed. Arguably the most pertinent item was a copy of the tabloid interview. It contained comments defending lyrics that blamed Jews for oppressing African Americans in a New York ghetto. The administrators, however, had dissimilar views about whether the comments and lyrics constituted proof of anti-Semitism. They also disagreed about canceling the assembly.

- Assistant Principal Slater opposed canceling the assembly, arguing that allowing a community group to censor school programs sets a bad precedent. He added that students who objected to the group did not have to attend the assembly.
- The second assistant principal disagreed and recommended that the assembly should be canceled. He contended that the anti-drug message would be superseded by the anti-Semitism charges.
- The third assistant principal proposed a compromise. She suggested that two assemblies be held concurrently. The second one would focus on racial and religious tolerance. Students could elect which one they would attend.

Principal Doran tried to achieve consensus, but Mr. Slater would not agree to support a decision to cancel the assembly. The first bell had just sounded and the meeting adjourned without a decision being announced. Principal Doran closed her office door and considered her options once again.

Problem Framing

1. Assume you are Principal Doran. First determine the main issue (problem) in this case. Then describe the current state and the desired state of this issue. (The section on problem framing in the Introduction section of this book defines the problem framing process.)

2. Based on evidence provided in the case, describe the difficulty associated with eliminating the gap between the present state and desired state.

Questions and Suggested Activities

1. Share and critique the problem statements prepared by students in your class.
2. Did Assistant Principal Slater evaluate the credentials of the rap group properly? Why or why not?
3. Three different recommendations were made by the assistant principals. Which one do you favor?
4. Are there other alternatives not identified by the assistant principals? If so, what are they?
5. The principal and Mr. Slater seem to believe that voluntary attendance is a relevant factor. Do you agree with them? Why or why not?
6. If you were the principal, would you be comfortable with the manner in which the superintendent is addressing this matter?
7. Principal Doran believes that public schools should provide a forum for exchanging ideas provided the dialogue conforms to community standards. Do you agree with this belief? Why or why not?
8. What ethical and political considerations are relevant to making a decision about canceling the assembly?
9. To what extent is Principal Doran responsible for the conflict described in the case?
10. What purposes should be served by student assemblies?
11. Is it possible to use the conflict sparked by the assembly as a catalyst for improving racial and ethnic relations at the high school? If so, how might the administrators do this?

Suggested Readings

Banister, J., & Maher, M. (1998). Recentering multiculturalism: Moving toward community. *Urban Education, 33*(2), 182–217.

Harrington-Lueker, D. (1993). Practicing tolerance. *Executive Educator, 15*(5), 14–19.

Margolis, H., & Tewel, K. (1988). Resolving conflict with parents: A guide for administrators. *NASSP Bulletin, 72*(506), 26–28.

Martinson, D. L. (1998). Vulgar, indecent, and offensive student speech: How should public school administrators respond? *Clearing House, 71*(6), 345–349.

Newsome, Y. D. (2001). Transnationalism in Black-Jewish conflict: A study of global identification among established Americans. *Race and Society, 4*(1), 89–107.

Noguera, P. A. (1999). Confronting the challenge of diversity. *School Administrator, 56*(5), 16–19.

Ogbonna, E., & Harris, L. C. (2006). The dynamics of employee relationships in an ethnically diverse workforce. *Human Relations, 59*(3), 379–407.

Sherman, R. (1990). Intergroup conflict on high school campuses. *Journal of Multicultural Counseling and Development, 18*(1), 11–18.

Stover, D. (1990). The new racism. *American School Board Journal, 177*(6), 14–18.

Stover, D. (1991). Racism redux. *Executive Educator, 13*(12), 35–36.

Tam, M. S., & Bassett, G. W. (2004). Does diversity matter? Measuring the impact of high school diversity on freshman GPA. *Policy Studies Journal, 32*(1), 129–143.

Zirkel, P. (1998). Boring or bunkum? *Phi Delta Kappan, 79*(10), 791–792.

Zirkel, P., & Gluckman, I. (1983). Stop, don't raise that curtain. *Principal, 62*, 45–46.

References

Miron, L. F., St. John, E. P., & Davidson, B. (1998). Implementing school restructuring in the inner city. *Urban Review, 30*(2), 137–166.

Pitts, D. W. (2005). Diversity, representation, and performance: Evidence about race and ethnicity in public organizations. *Journal of Public Administration Research and Theory, 15*(4), 615–631.

Reich, R. (2002). *Bridging liberalism and multiculturalism in American education.* Chicago: University of Chicago Press.

Zirkel, P. A. (2001). A gross over-order? *Phi Delta Kappan, 83*(3), 273–274.

22 | IS THE DEVIL TEACHING SPELLING?

BACKGROUND INFORMATION

Educational reform efforts have highlighted perennial tensions between teacher professionalism and citizen control of public schools. Both teacher empowerment and community involvement have been widely touted as effective strategies even though the two concepts are difficult to implement simultaneously. The primary intention of empowerment is giving teachers authority to make decisions based on the real needs of their students. In schools, this means teachers are granted discretion over curricular and instructional decisions (Barth, 2001). Community involvement, on the other hand, is nested in an intricate mix of philosophical, political, and economic objectives. The concept of local control, for example, is an expression of liberty; most citizens believe they have a right to pursue their interests in the realm of public policy. Proponents of stakeholder inclusion argue that the process nurtures community economic support and provides a mechanism for accountability (Kowalski, 2003).

Teachers and parents, though, do not always agree on fundamental issues such as educational priorities and the nature of effective teaching (Davis, 1997). Disparate views can be problematic because many important decisions are made at a point where individual and societal interests intersect (Levin, 1999). When professional discretion conflicts with the will of the people, principals need to intervene and manage the situation adroitly, often by sharing authority without losing control (Kowalski, 2010).

As Fullan (1994) advises, neither top-down nor bottom-up strategies for school reform work well. Centralization tends to err on the side of too much hierarchical control and decentralization tends to err on the side of chaos. Aimlessly or purposefully employing a mix of the two strategies, however, is not a foolproof solution. Dispersing authority in social systems with a hierarchal structure (such as school districts) almost always generates tensions related to accountability. Addressing this point, Corwin and Borman (1988) noted that superintendents are often held responsible for poor decisions, even if they had little control or influence over them.

In practice, school administrators must cope concurrently with political norms, such as being sensitive to individual and group preferences, and professional norms, such as making informed decisions in curriculum and instruction (Shedd & Bacharach, 1991). The extent to which superintendents and principals do this, the manner in which they attempt to do this, and their success rates vary markedly (Kowalski, 2010). Several authors (e.g., Bauch & Goldring, 1998; Darling-Hammond, 1987; Strike, 1993) have explained the dynamics associated with inherent conflict between participatory democracy and pedagogic professionalism, including the relevance of these tensions to modern-day reforms (e.g., Sykes, 1991; Zeichner, 1991). Examining power and authority in the education profession, Sykes (1991) wrote:

> Democracy institutionalizes distrust. Professionalism relies on trust. Because we distrust our rulers, we have instituted a system of checks and balances to prevent any interest of office from amassing too much power. Because certain practices rest on

expertise and knowledge not widely distributed in the populace, we trust professionals on their pledge to use such knowledge in the best interests of their clients. These two systems of preference formation, service delivery, and authority allocation appear fundamentally at odds with one another, and the great historical puzzle is how a strong form of professionalism flourished just in the world's greatest democracy. (p. 137)

Democratic administration certainly is not a new idea; it emerged as a major philosophical movement as far back as 1930. Detractors argued that the concept was overly idealistic and insufficiently attentive to realities of practice (Kowalski, 2006). When confronted with conflicting values, however, the American public, legally and politically, has exhibited a proclivity to forge compromises instead of choosing one value over the other (Kowalski, Petersen, & Fusarelli, 2007). In the case of professionalism versus democracy, neither the quest for citizen involvement nor the expectation of administrative control has been eradicated. Scholars (e.g., Wirt & Kirst, 2001) have concluded that public sector administrators, unlike their counterparts in the private sector, are consistently required to apply their professional knowledge in highly political contexts.

In this case, parents object to the use of instructional materials selected by teachers for a gifted education enrichment program. In addition to demonstrating the tensions between professionalism and parental power, the case reveals the difficulty inherent in empowering teachers and promoting parental involvement simultaneously.

Key Areas for Reflection

1. Democratic school administration
2. Parental rights and power to censor instructional materials
3. Teacher professionalism and empowerment
4. Delegation of authority and corresponding accountability

THE CASE

"I really like this software program. It fits nicely with what we are trying to accomplish with enrichment activities. And besides, students like these types of computer programs."

The evaluation came from Sandy Oberfeld, a second-grade teacher and coordinator of the district's gifted and talented student program. The enrichment program serves eligible students across the district's three elementary schools. The 12 teachers involved with the program meet every other month to discuss curriculum and instructional materials.

"I agree with Sandy," said Beatrice Sachs. "My students like computer games. They have so many toys and gadgets at home, it's become increasingly difficult to motivate them. I think Sorcerer will attract their attention, and the program appears well suited for independent spelling exercises. Most students have learned to process information visually as a result of watching television and playing video games. Thus, I believe they will like Sorcerer."

After several other positive comments about Sorcerer, Lucy McNeil suggested that some parents might object to this software. Cautioning her colleagues, she said, "Today parental standards for determining what is offensive are neither clear nor consistent. Similar games have been intensely criticized by parents who find them objectionable, primarily because they are constructed around a magic or a witchcraft theme."

Mrs. Oberfeld responded, "We can never predict precisely how parents will react to instructional materials. Our responsibility is to make professional judgments. The essential question is whether we believe Sorcerer is an appropriate and effective instructional tool." Several teachers immediately agreed with the comment. Mrs. McNeil pointed out that she did not object personally, but was only describing a possible concern. At that point, the group decided to purchase 15 copies of the software.

Teachers in the district were accustomed to having considerable autonomy with respect to purchasing supplemental instructional materials. They would fill out a purchase order, obtain the principal's signature, and forward the document to the district's business office. The elementary school's gifted and talented program, however, operated differently because it was a district-wide program. Therefore, it had its own budget for supplies, equipment, and materials. Expenditures were approved by the assistant superintendent for instruction because he had supervisory responsibility for the program. Because they had no fiscal responsibility for the gifted and talented program, principals were unsure as to whether they had any level of responsibility for this program. Although one or two principals occasionally attended the bi-monthly teacher meetings, principals generally did not get directly involved in this supplemental program.

Following established practice, Mrs. Oberfeld filled out a purchase order for 15 copies of Sorcerer, signed it, and sent it to Dr. Wilbur Youngman, the assistant superintendent for instruction. After receiving it, he simply determined that adequate funds were available and approved the request.

After five copies of Sorcerer were delivered to each participating school, teachers made them available to students. Students were permitted to take a copy home for up to 7 days.

When using Sorcerer, students spell words and receive either a reward or punishment based on whether they completed the task successfully. As the teachers predicted, students liked the software program, and soon, there was a waiting list to obtain a copy for home use.

The first parental complaint about Sorcerer was expressed about 5 weeks after the product was purchased. Elizabeth Baker, the mother of a second-grade student at Lakeside Elementary School, called Principal Nancy Tannin.

"Miss Tannin, I'm concerned about a computer game a teacher gave to my daughter, Sally. She is in the gifted and talented enrichment program, and as you know, students involved regularly bring home books and other supplementary materials. I became inquisitive about Sorcerer because Sally seemed obsessed with this particular product. I had never heard of Sorcerer until Sally brought it home. Are you familiar with this product?"

The principal admitted that she had never heard of Sorcerer. She then explained to Mrs. Baker that the gifted and talented enrichment program was a district-wide initiative supervised by the assistant superintendent for instruction. Therefore, principals were not directly involved in approving materials for this program. She added, however, that she had confidence in the teachers who recommended the supplemental materials and in the assistant superintendent who approved the request.

"As principal, are you not responsible for all instructional materials used in the school?" the mother asked.

"Normally, I am. But not for the gifted and talented program. Why are you concerned about this particular product? Do you think your daughter is spending too much time with it? Or do you think it is ineffective?"

"My concern is about the witchcraft and black magic aspects of this software," Mrs. Baker responded. "Surely there are less offensive materials available. Today, parents have to be especially sensitive to their children's exposure to destructive materials, especially those that undermine family values and beliefs."

Miss Tannin said she would look into the matter and respond more completely to the concern at a later time. In fact, however, she thought the parent was overreacting and did not treat her complaint as an urgent matter. Two days passed before Principal Tannin discussed Mrs. Baker's complaint with the teacher who allowed Sally Baker to take the software home. The teacher indicated that she was not aware of parental concerns and pointed out the purchase of Sorcerer was approved by all 12 teachers working with the enrichment program and by the assistant superintendent.

Based soley on her conversation with the teacher, Miss Tannin telephoned Mrs. Baker and told her that the product had been approved in accordance with policy.

Mrs. Baker then asked, "Did you look at the product? Did you actually sit at a computer and play the game?"

"Well, no. I didn't think that was necessary," Miss Tannin answered. "Our teachers are competent professionals. I trust them to make effective decisions about instructional materials."

At this point, Mrs. Baker became angry. "Maybe the teachers are wrong. Are you not responsible for what they do? If you are not accountable for instructional materials and teacher supervision in your school, who is? Telling me that the teachers think Sorcerer is suitable for young children does not lessen my concerns. I'm going to pursue this matter further."

After the conversation, Miss Tannin telephoned the principals of the other two elementary schools involved in the enrichment program and asked if they had received any negative feedback about Sorcerer. She learned that they had. They, too, however, treated the complaints as isolated overreactions. Collectively, the three principals had received four complaints. After sharing the nature of the complaints, the principals agreed that the controversy could evolve into a major problem. They met the next day and decided on the following course of action:

- They would co-sign a memorandum to Dr. Youngman informing him that they had received complaints about the software program.
- Copies of this memorandum would be sent to the 12 teachers participating in the enrichment program.
- They would contact the parents who had voiced concerns and inform them that they should contact Dr. Youngman, the administrator responsible for supervising the program.

Less than 2 weeks later, the following letter to the editor, signed by 16 parents, appeared in the local newspaper:

We are parents of elementary school children who participate in the gifted and talented program in the Maple Creek School District. Recently, our children have been exposed to an unacceptable computer game called Sorcerer. Intended to provide enrichment activity for spelling skills, it exposes children to witchcraft and black magic, and we object to this characteristic.

Too often, public schools have become a pawn for those seeking to lower moral standards. Stakeholders providing financial support for local schools have every right to protect children from poor decisions, even those made under the guise of professionalism.

The principals have basically ignored parental complaints about this instructional program. Instead, they claim teachers are competent professionals and express confidence that teachers make good decisions. We urge other stakeholders to join us in our effort to rid our schools of objectionable materials that promote witchcraft, devil worship, and other evil ideas. Call the school board members and superintendent and let them know how you feel.

The district's superintendent, Dr. Montgomery, first learned about the objections to Sorcerer reading the letter to the editor. He was never pleased when he learned about a school-related problem by reading the newspaper; he asked Dr. Youngman why he had not been briefed on this matter. Dr. Youngman responded that the teachers and principals involved had underestimated the depth of parental concerns. Until the letter appeared in the newspaper, they assumed that the controversy would subside with time.

Dr. Montgomery told Dr. Youngman to arrange a meeting with the three principals and Mrs. Oberfeld as soon as possible. The meeting was held in the superintendent's conference room late that same afternoon. Dr. Montgomery attended and began by informing the others that he already had received more than a dozen telephone calls and twice as many emails about the letter that had appeared in that morning's newspaper. Three of the messages were from school board members expressing concerns that the issue may not have been managed effectively. The superintendent then said he wanted answers to four questions:

1. What are the parents' specific objections?
2. Why was Sorcerer still being used after it was clear that some parents found the product to be objectionable?
3. Who purchased the software?
4. Why was software with a potentially controversial theme selected?

Mrs. Oberfeld responded. "At the time we decided to purchase the product, we did not anticipate parental objections because students are not required to use this software. Parents have the option of not allowing their children to have access. I and the other teachers involved in the supplemental program believe that the software is an effective tool for improving spelling skills. As we consider the complaints, I hope we answer a fundamental question: Are we going to allow narrow-minded parents to censor instructional materials?"

Dr. Montgomery asked the principals to share their thoughts on the complaints and question posed by Mrs. Oberfeld. Miss Tannin spoke first.

"We have confidence in Mrs. Oberfeld and the other teachers. They all agreed to purchase Sorcerer. When I first received a complaint, I shared it with the teacher identified by the parent and asked her to comment. She told me that students were not required to use the program and disagreed with the negative assessment of the product."

"But did any of you actually test the material to determine if it was appropriate for students at this age level?" the superintendent asked.

The three principals and assistant superintendent responded that they had not done so. Mrs. Oberfeld, however, said that she and the other 11 teachers involved either had tested the product or observed other teachers using the product.

"Who authorized this purchase?" the superintendent asked.

Miss Tannin answered, "After the teachers agreed to request 15 copies of Sorcerer, I completed a purchase order, signed it, and sent it to Dr. Youngman."

"Yes, I approved the purchase," Dr. Youngman said. "But I did so based on my faith in Mrs. Oberfeld and the other teachers. Therefore, my approval merely ensured that funds were available. I don't think my responsibility is to second-guess teacher decisions."

Mrs. Oberfeld thought Dr. Youngman was being defensive. She said, "Before we start pointing the finger of blame at each other, let's step back and consider what is at stake. As I asked earlier, are we going to allow a small group of parents to control instructional materials? If they win on this matter, they'll be back with more ridiculous demands. Their goal is to control what we read and how we think."

Miss Tannin spoke next. "Assume that Dr. Youngman refused to approve the purchase order. Wouldn't his refusal have created a more serious problem? How would teachers respond if they learned that instructional materials they requisitioned were rejected simply because they might be considered controversial by some parents?"

Mr. Sancheck, one of the other principals, then spoke. "We trust and believe in our teachers. Quite frankly, I prefer to have them rather than radical parents deciding what we use in the schools."

Dr. Montgomery said that he was uncomfortable with the fact that instructional materials could be purchased without principal approval. "When I was a principal," he said, "policy required me to sign every purchase order originated in my building. Apparently, we have no such policy and that too is a problem. Consequently, we must decide how to handle the present situation and decide if policy pertaining to purchasing instructional materials needs to be changed."

Miss Tannin commented, "You may be in a better position than we are to answer both questions."

After hearing that suggestion, Dr. Montgomery got up from his chair and said, "Having me make the decisions is one option, but I'm not an autocrat. I have a meeting at the high school and will be back in about an hour. When I return, I want your recommendations for answering the two questions I posed."

Problem Framing

1. Assume you are the superintendent. First determine the main issue (problem) in this case. Then describe the current state and the desired state of this issue. (The section on problem framing in the Introduction section of this book defines the problem framing process.)

2. Based on evidence provided in the case, describe the difficulty associated with eliminating the gap between the present state and desired state.

Questions and Suggested Activities

1. Share and critique the problem statements prepared by students in your class.

2. To what extent are the teachers responsible for the conflict that has emerged?

3. To what extent are administrators responsible for the conflict that has emerged?

4. What are the advantages and disadvantages of removing Sorcerer as demanded by the complaining parents?

5. Are liberty (expressed through democratic control of schools) and teacher professionalism (expressed through teacher/administrator control of instructional decisions) compatible concepts? Why or why not?

6. Is it possible for principals to maintain control while allowing both teachers and parents to make decisions about instructional materials?

7. To what extent do administrators have a responsibility to exercise authority over teacher decisions?

8. The contention is made that parents could prevent their children from having access to Sorcerer because usage is voluntary. Is this a valid point in responding to the parental complaints? Why or why not?

9. In a democratic society, parents have a right to pursue their interests in public education. Did the complaining parents in this case exercise this right effectively? Why or why not?

10. Should the superintendent and assistant superintendent for instruction be held accountable for the decision to purchase Sorcerer? Why or why not?

Suggested Readings

Browder, L. H. (1998). The religious right, the secular left, and their shared dilemma: The public school. *International Journal of Educational Reform, 7*(4), 309–318.

Donelson, K. (1987a). Censorship: Heading off the attack. *Educational Horizons, 65*(4), 167–170.

Donelson, K. (1987b). Six statements/questions from the censors. *Phi Delta Kappan, 69*(3), 208–214.

Fege, A. F. (1993). The tug of war over tolerance. *Educational Leadership, 51*(4), 22–24.

Georgiady, N., & Romano, L. (1987). Censorship–Back to the front burner. *Middle School Journal, 18,* 12–13.

Jones, J. L. (1993). Targets of the right. *American School Board Journal, 180*(4), 22–29.

Kowalski, T. J. (2003). *Contemporary school administration: An introduction* (2nd ed.). Boston: Allyn and Bacon. (see Chapter 10).

Leahy, M. (1998). The religious right: Would-be censors of the state school curriculum. *Educational Philosophy & Theory, 30*(1), 18, 51.

Meadows, B. J. (1990). The rewards and risks of shared leadership. *Phi Delta Kappan, 71*(7), 545–548.

Perry, L. B. (2009). Conceptualizing education policy in democratic societies. *Educational Policy, 23*(3), 423–450.

Petress, K. (2005). The role of censorship in school. *Journal of Instructional Psychology, 32*(3), 248–252.

Pierard, R. (1987). The new religious right and censorship. *Contemporary Education, 58*(3), 131–137.

Rowell, C. (1986). Allowing parents to screen textbooks would lead to anarchy in the schools. *Chronicle of Higher Education, 33*(26), 34.

Smith, S. (1998). School by school. *American School Board Journal, 185*(6), 22–25.

Sullivan, P. (1998). Parent involvement. *Our Children, 24*(1), 23.

Tveit, A. D. (2009). A parental voice: Parents as equal and dependent — rhetoric about parents, teachers, and their conversations. *Educational Review, 61*(3), 289–300.

Weil, J. (1988). Dealing with censorship: Policy and procedures. *Education Digest, 53*(5), 23–25.

Zirkel, P., & Gluckman, I. (1986). Objections to curricular material on religious grounds. *NASSP Bulletin, 70*(488), 99–100.

References

Barth, R. S. (2001). Teacher leader. *Phi Delta Kappan, 82*(6), 443–449.

Bauch, P., & Goldring, E. B. (1998). Parent-teacher participation in the context of school governance. *Peabody Journal of Education, 73*(1), 15–35.

Corwin, R. G., & Borman, K. M. (1988). School as workplace: Structural constraints on administration. In N. J. Boyan (Ed.), *Handbook of research on educational administration* (pp. 209–238). New York: Longman.

Darling-Hammond, L. (1987). The over-regulated curriculum and the press for teacher professionalism. *NASSP Bulletin, 71*(498), 22, 24–26, 28–29.

Davis, O. L. (1997). Notes on the nature of power. *Journal of Curriculum and Supervision, 12*(3), 189–192.

Fullan, M. (1994). *Systemic reform: Perspectives on personalizing education.* Retrieved from http://www2.ed.gov/pubs/EdReformStudies/SysReforms/fullan1.html

Kowalski, T. J. (2003). *Contemporary school administration: An introduction.* Boston: Allyn and Bacon.

Kowalski, T. J. (2006). *The school superintendent: Theory, practice, and cases* (2nd ed.). Thousand Oaks, CA: Sage.

Kowalski, T. J. (2010). *The school principal: Visionary leadership and competent management.* New York: Routledge.

Kowalski, T. J., Petersen, G. J., & Fusarelli, L. D. (2007). *Effective communication for school administrators: An imperative in an information age.* Lanham, MD: Rowman & Littlefield Education.

Levin, H. M. (1999). The public-private nexus in education. *American Behavioral Scientist, 43*(1), 124–137.

Shedd, J. B., & Bacharach, S. B. (1991). *Tangled hierarchies: Teachers as professionals and the management of schools.* San Francisco: Jossey-Bass.

Strike, K. A. (1993). Professionalism, democracy, and discursive communities: Normative reflections on restructuring. *American Educational Research Journal, 30*(2), 255–275.

Sykes, G. (1991). In defense of teacher professionalism as a policy of choice. *Educational Policy, 5*(2), 137–149.

Wirt, F. M., & Kirst, M. W. (2001). *The political dynamics of American education* (2nd ed.). Berkeley, CA: McCutchan.

Zeichner, K. M. (1991). Contradictions and tensions in the professionalization of teaching and the democratization of schools. *Teachers College Record, 92*(3), 363–379.

23 | THE DARK SIDE OF DECENTRALIZATION

BACKGROUND INFORMATION

During the first half of the 20th century, the governance structure for public education in the United States gradually moved away from being highly decentralized—that is, from allowing local schools to have considerable leeway to determine policy and operating procedures. Although many forces contributed to the transition, the following factors were especially influential.

- *Quest for efficiency.* Efficiency is a value determined by a favorable relationship between inputs and outputs. As early as 1910, officials in some states concluded that very small school districts were inefficient and should be eliminated by merging them with larger districts (King, Swanson, & Sweetland, 2003).
- *Defining education adequacy.* Adequacy is a value that addresses the challenging question: How much education is enough? If local communities were allowed to decide this matter autonomously (i.e., without federal or state oversight), minimum education standards, such as attendance days and graduation requirements, would almost certainly be dissimilar among school districts. This is because local communities value and support public schools at different levels (Kowalski, 2003).
- *Pursuit of equity.* Equity has been defined as providing students across a given state reasonably equal educational opportunities. Achieving this goal was difficult for at least three reasons. First, no universal definition of reasonably equal existed; thus, the concept was open to interpretation. Second, local school districts differed in fiscal ability—that is, taxable wealth determined by dividing the total assessed valuation of taxable property by the number of students served producing a statistic called *assessed valuation per pupil.* Third, local districts differed in fiscal effort—that is, tax rates that were applied to assessed valuations to determine tax levies. As a result, citizens argued over what were or were not reasonably equal opportunities, and districts raised and spent varying levels of resources to support their schools. Having fewer but larger districts became one way to reduce discrepancies that thwarted statewide equity (King et al., 2003).
- *Increased role of state government in elementary and secondary education.* States are ultimately responsible for public education in the United States. In meeting this responsibility, states developed a common curriculum for public schools (Spring, 2001). Incrementally, state policymakers also set other uniform standards that districts and schools had to follow. The result was a more centralized system of governance, meaning that many important policy decisions were made at the state level rather than at the local level (Kowalski, 2006).
- *Legislation and litigation.* Legislation and subsequent litigation also contributed to the centralization of authority. Lawsuits in areas such as civil rights, school finance, and special education made local school systems vulnerable to prolonged legal battles and unfavorable judgments. This exposure played a part in developing a compliance mentality among school board members and administrators—a state of mind that operating procedures needed to be institutionally uniform and controlled (Tyack, 1990).

After 1950, many states enacted consolidation laws requiring small districts and schools to merge. In 1937, for example, there were approximately 119,000 school districts in this country; by 1963, that number dropped to 35,676; today, there are just over 14,000 districts remaining (Kowalski, McCord, Petersen, Young, & Ellerson, 2011).

Critics argue that centralization de facto diminishes liberty and limits democratic decision making. In most school districts today, democratic localism (i.e., direct citizen participation in policy decisions) has given way to representative democracy—a governance concept in which state officials, school board members, and superintendents make decisions on behalf of the community (Kowalski, 2006). In addition to being philosophically objectionable to some, representative democracy arguably diminished opportunities for educators to tailor school reforms to the idiosyncratic needs of districts and schools. By the late 1980s, for example, some scholars (e.g., Hawley, 1988; Kirst, 1988) warned that highly centralized federal and state policies were unresponsive to issues that influenced school effectiveness in many institutions (Kowalski, 2006).

Circa 1990, efforts were made to shift the locus of school-improvement planning to the local level (Kowalski, Petersen, & Fusarelli, 2007). Both deregulation (easing or even eliminating state standards) and decentralization (reducing district control over individual schools) became more popular strategies. These strategic changes were nested in two widely accepted hypotheses: local reforms would be more relevant than state reforms and citizen involvement would spawn essential political and economic support for needed changes (Bauman, 1996). Time has proven, however, that decentralization is not a problem-free strategy. Merely involving teachers and citizens in decision making and forcing administrators to share power do not ensure school effectiveness (Walberg & Niemiec, 1994). In addition, decentralization that extends to funding and spending authority can exacerbate inequities among schools, even those in the same local school system (Nir & Miran, 2006).

Recognizing that both centralization and decentralization have serious limitations, Fullan (2001) advises that the challenge for administrators is not determining which is superior; rather, it is to determine how to meld the two strategies—that is, to determine which functions are best centralized and which functions are best decentralized.

In this case study, a superintendent decentralizes budgets and requires schools to establish governance councils. In less than 2 years, charges of resource disparities among the district's elementary schools emerge. Specifically, a parent who is an attorney questions the legality of the district's approach to decentralization, claiming that the process has resulted in unequal educational opportunities among elementary schools. His accusation raises philosophical and legal questions, and school officials must determine whether they will modify the decentralization program or defend it.

Key Areas for Reflection

1. Centralized and decentralized governance
2. Conflict between liberty and equality
3. Shared decision making
4. Relationship between district and school administration under school-based management
5. Managing change in school districts
6. Role and responsibilities of school councils
7. Possible effects of decentralized budgets on fiscal equity

THE CASE

Haver Ridge

Haver Ridge is the seat of government for Marvin County, in central Illinois. With a population of just over 16,000, the community has grown about 15% since the mid-1950s. Much of the population increase occurred after a new industrial park was developed on the edge of town in 1973. The four new businesses that located there generated slightly more than 400 new jobs.

Marvin County is predominately rural, with grain farms accounting for about 80% of all the acreage. Haver Ridge and Fellington (population, 10,350) are the only two cities in the county with more than 1,000 residents. About 15 years ago, a new hospital and a municipal airport were built midway between Haver Ridge and Fellington, and the corridor connecting the two towns now is dotted with commercial developments.

River Valley Community College and the East Marvin Community School District are two of the largest employers in Haver Ridge. Collectively, they have 958 employees. The college's primary service area is Marvin and two adjoining counties.

School District

In 1962, six public school districts in Marvin County were consolidated into two districts. Their boundaries were established essentially by a north-to-south state road that divides the county almost evenly in terms of acreage. Although the two districts, East Marvin County School District and West Marvin County School District, are equal in terms of land, the former serves a population about 20% greater than the latter. The administrative office, high school, middle school, and three of five elementary schools in the East Marvin district are in Haver Ridge.

The three elementary schools in Haver Ridge are Adams, Clark, and Lincoln. Clark is the oldest facility, having been constructed originally in 1937 and totally renovated in 1981. Located in the downtown business district, the site and classroom sizes measured by today's standards are inadequate; however, referenda to replace the building, held in 1999 and 2005, were soundly defeated. Voters opposed to the referenda were divided into three groups: those who did not want the current school destroyed; those who were against building a new school in the downtown area; those who were opposed to the proposed tax increase.

The other two elementary schools in Haver Ridge, Adams and Lincoln, are situated in residential neighborhoods. Both are relatively modern and spacious buildings. Adams was first occupied in 1983 and Lincoln in 1996. Despite its facility deficiencies, Clark Elementary had the oldest and most experienced faculty; the average age among the teachers is 8 years higher than the average age at any of the district's other elementary schools. Among the five elementary schools in the district, it also has the highest percentage of students qualifying for free and reduced-price lunches—47%.

School Board

Until approximately 1980, farmers made up a majority on the seven-member school board in the East Marvin County School District. After that point, the composition of the board became diverse. Current board members are a loan officer at a local bank, a restaurant owner, a housewife, a community college English instructor, the plant manager of a local factory, a retired school principal, and a farmer.

Although the board members do not always agree on policy issues, the board is not divided into political factions. Members are mutually respectful and work well with one another and with the superintendent. Their relationship with the teachers' union has also been positive.

Administration

When a long-term superintendent retired 3 years ago, the board employed Burton Packard to re-place him. Dr. Packard had been an assistant superintendent for instruction in a suburban dis-trict west of Chicago. A mid-career administrator recognized as an effective instructional leader, he has promoted decentralization, shared decision making, and teacher involvement in school governance. During his employment interview, he defended these convictions telling the school board members, "I think teachers and parents should be our partners, and that includes collabo-rating with us when we make important decisions about how we organize our school and how we spend our resources. I'm not a dictatorial administrator."

Ryan Fulton, the district's assistant superintendent for instruction, moved to his present position 6 years ago after having been the principal of Haver Ridge High School for 8 years. Jane Westerman, the assistant for business, moved to her present position 4 years ago after having been principal at Lincoln Elementary for 5 years. Only two of the district's seven principals have been employed by Dr. Packard: Dr. Elaine Byers at the middle school and Mrs. Norene Vidduci at Adams Elementary School.

Implementing SBM

Shortly after becoming superintendent in East Marvin County, Dr. Packard presented a plan to decentralize authority in the school district. After gaining support for the initiative from the school board, he announced that the changes would begin in the elementary schools and later would be applied in the secondary schools. The plan had three objectives:

1. *Increasing flexibility and accountability at each school.* School personnel would be responsi-ble for identifying instructional needs and priorities. Variance in curriculum and instruc-tional materials, provided that they did not violate state laws and policies, would be allowed to pursue specific school objectives.
2. *Involving teachers and parents in school governance.* Every school would have to establish a governance council that included administrators, teachers, and parents. Council authority would include approving instructional priorities, school budgets, and implementation strategies.
3. *Giving schools greater fiscal autonomy.* The district's budgeting and fiscal management prac-tices would be changed to allow individual schools discretion in expending funds ear-marked for supplies and equipment. Under the decentralization plan, these funds were re-ferred to as "school discretionary allocations."

The board members publicly praised Dr. Packard's plan and voted unanimously to approve it. Reactions among the district's principals, however, were less enthusiastic. Among the five ele-mentary school principals, those assigned to the district's rural elementary schools, Milltown and Wild Creek, were moderately supportive. Both were apprehensive about the implications of having discretion to expend supplies and equipment allocations. The principals at Adams and Lincoln were highly supportive and openly expressed their feelings to stakeholders. Mrs. Simpson, principal at Clark Elementary School, openly opposed the plan opining that a governance council would not be beneficial. Moreover, she feared that school budgets would be determined by enrollment rather than student needs—a decision that would be detrimental to Clark, the school with the highest percentage of children from low income families.

The superintendent's decentralization plan was officially approved by the school board in January, giving the elementary principals about 6 months to determine how they would comply with the three objectives. Each elementary school principal had to submit a school implementation document to Dr. Packard by August 1. The documents had to include specific information about the following:

- The composition of the school's council
- Methods for selecting council members
- A school budget

Between August 1 and the beginning of the first semester (on August 23), Dr. Packard met with each principal to discuss implementation documents. Although he asked the principals many questions and voiced several concerns, he did not require any of them to make modifications.

SBM—The First 2 Years

Differences in the implementation plans for the three elementary schools located in Haver Ridge, especially dissimilarities related to expending discretionary funds, eventually became known to school personnel and parents. As examples, cooperative learning was an instructional priority at Adams Elementary School, and most of this school's discretionary funds were used to support the paradigm (e.g., staff development and putting more computers in classrooms). At Lincoln, computer-assisted instruction was a priority, and most discretionary funds were used to purchase computer hardware and software. At Clark, improving learning outcomes for students scoring below state achievement test benchmarks was a priority, and most of this school's discretionary funds were used to purchase remedial instructional materials.

Notable differences also existed with respect to the governance councils at these three elementary schools. The Adams council had 13 members and was chaired by a fourth-grade teacher; the Lincoln council had 11 members and was chaired by a parent. The Clark council was the smallest with only nine members and it was chaired by the principal.

After the first few months, the Clark council meetings became highly predictable. Principal Simpson would construct an agenda, do most of the talking during the meeting, and members supported all her recommendations. The four teachers on the Clark council, all loyal to the principal, viewed the group and its meetings as perfunctory mandates. The four parents on the council were intimidated by the educators and never questioned or voted against Principal Simpson's recommendations. After the first 2 months, only two of the four parents attended the next three meetings.

Problem

Each year, students in Grades 2, 4, and 6 are required by the state to take standardized achievement tests. Students receive individual results and schools receive an average score for each grade level. For the last 7 years, Lincoln has had the highest average test scores in the district; Clark has had the lowest. Listed below are the results for sixth-grade students for the past 3 years. Results in years 2 and 3 occurred under the decentralization plan.

School	Average test scores	Rank in district
Adams	57.3, 58.2, 58.3	2, 2, 2
Clark	48.7, 48.3, 48.1	5, 5, 5
Lincoln	59.2, 60.1, 61.2	1, 1, 1
Milltown	55.2, 55.3, 55.3	3, 4, 4
Wild Creek	54.6, 55.4, 55.7	4, 3, 3

Previous to decentralization, the local newspaper did not compare school performance on the state achievement tests. Dr. Packard, however, convinced Janice Bell, the reporter covering schools, that doing this would be beneficial. After scores were made public for the current school year, she wrote a series of articles that attempted to connect test scores with instructional priorities and discretionary spending. Her analysis implied that Lincoln and Adams had used their resources productively whereas investments in remedial instruction at Clark appeared to have made no difference in student learning. At the least, the articles gave many readers the impression that there was a nexus between the use of discretionary funds and student learning.

Although Dr. Packard had encouraged the media coverage of student test scores, he was not pleased with the reporter's conclusions. He told her privately that it was premature to judge that the use of discretionary funds at Clark had been ineffective. Expressing confidence in Principal Simpson and the Clark council, he pointed out that many factors affected student performance on standardized tests, including some beyond the school's control.

After receiving the word of caution from Superintendent Packard, Ms. Bell had telephone conversations with three board members. She learned that Dr. Packard had already expressed the same concerns about the articles with them and that the board members agreed with his cautious attitude.

Several parents of Clark students, however, agreed with Ms. Bell's suggestions. The most vocal was Anthony Bacon, an attorney and director of employee relations at the local community college. As an example, he wrote a letter to the editor of the newspaper refuting the notion that Dr. Packard's decentralization plan already had benefited some schools. He also voiced misgivings about decentralized governance at school board meetings. At a recent meeting, he read the following prepared statement:

> Ladies and gentlemen, Dr. Packard, and members of the school staff, I appear here today as the parent of two Clark Elementary School students. When we moved to Haver Ridge 4 years ago, my wife and I bought an older house near downtown. Friends initially attempted to dissuade us from making this decision, pointing out that Clark was the worst elementary school in Haver Ridge if not the entire district. Before purchasing the property, I talked with the former superintendent and he assured me that programmatically, all elementary schools in this district offer the same curriculum and equal instructional opportunities. His assurance influenced our decision to buy the house and send our children to Clark.
>
> I realize that conditions change. When Dr. Packard arrived 3 years ago, he stated publicly that he was dedicated to improving our schools. My wife and I were among the many who applauded him. The recently published articles on student test scores and discretionary spending under decentralization, however, enlightened us; as a result, we are now having second thoughts. Working in public education, I understand that the concept of decentralization has merit, but as an attorney, I am suspicious that its application in the East Marvin County School District has been counterproductive.
>
> I share with you several specific concerns. First, the school councils do not operate uniformly nor are they functioning at the same level of effectiveness. A parent on the Clark council told me that her role is simply to rubber stamp the principal's decisions. But at Lincoln, parents and teachers assume leadership roles, introduce new ideas, and work collaboratively.
>
> Second and more importantly, I believe the superintendent's decentralization plan has produced inequities among the elementary schools. The size of school

budgets is based on per-pupil allocations with no consideration given to differences in student needs. This decision is indefensible in light of the fact that student needs are dissimilar across the five elementary schools. Principal Simpson told me that the Clark council had used most of its discretionary funds for remedial materials. Though I do not question the need for such support services, I believe that they should be provided through supplemental funding. If not, students other than those receiving remedial services are being denied programs and resources provided in the district's other elementary schools.

Given what has occurred over the last 2 years, I ask you: At what point do board members intervene to ensure that educational opportunities remain reasonably equal across our elementary schools? I respectfully request that you reexamine the superintendent's decentralization plan and take necessary measures to restore and maintain equal educational opportunities for all of our students.

Copies of his statement were distributed to attendees. The board president thanked Mr. Bacon for his comments and then asked Dr. Packard if he wanted to respond. The superintendent indicated that he would look into the matter and reply at or prior to the next school board meeting.

Mr. Bacon knew only two of the school board members personally, the English instructor at the community college and the owner of a local business. Prior to attending the school board meeting, he had never met Dr. Packard.

In the days following the board meeting, three of the board members telephoned Dr. Packard suggesting that he not take Mr. Bacon lightly. He was highly respected by his colleagues at the community college, and those who knew him personally said he was not a malcontent.

A week after Mr. Bacon made his statement to the school board, the board president, at the urging of Superintendent Packard, convened an executive session. The purpose was to discuss the concerns and to prepare a formal response to them. The board's attorney also attended the executive meeting, which was not open to the public. Dr. Packard made the following points:

- Mr. Bacon's claims about the behavior of school council members were only partially correct. While it was true that the councils did not function uniformly, differences were not by design, and they certainly were not the fault of school administrators. Mrs. Simpson, he said, had tried repeatedly to have parents become more active on the Clark Elementary School council.
- Members of the Clark Elementary School council were appointed—a decision made by the school's PTA and not by the principal. When the council was formed, Mrs. Simpson asked Mr. Bacon to be a council member; he declined, stating that his position at the community college and his commitment to remodeling his residence did not allow him to devote the time necessary for this assignment.
- Budget allocations to the schools were made on a per-pupil basis as claimed by Mr. Bacon. No exceptions, such as providing additional funding for special needs students, were made because doing so would have been difficult and controversial. For example, had additional funds been given to Clark Elementary, the Lincoln Elementary principal could have requested additional funds to support a gifted and talented program.
- While it was true that the decision to invest heavily in remedial materials at Clark was recommended by the principal, it was approved by the school's council and supported by most faculty members.

- The number of students from low-income families enrolled at Clark was much larger than at any other elementary school. Moreover, the number was still increasing. For example, the percentage of students qualifying for free and reduced-price lunches increased from 50 to 67% in just the last 3 years. The need for remedial education services at the school is obvious and Principal Simpson should be praised for her efforts to help students.
- Programs at all the district's schools, including Clark, meet or exceed state standards. If Mr. Bacon's argument about inequities were taken at face value, virtually every school district with more than one elementary school could be found not to provide equal educational opportunities.

In the summary section of his report, Dr. Packard recommended that the board not alter its decentralization policy, including provisions regarding discretionary budget allocations. He added, however, that Mrs. Simpson would have to allocate at least 25% of the discretionary funds given to Clark Elementary School to purchase additional computer hardware or software.

After reading Dr. Packard's report, the board's attorney said that it was an appropriate and sufficient response to Mr. Bacon's concerns. He urged the board to have Dr. Packard send his report, as written, to Mr. Bacon. The board unanimously agreed.

After receiving the superintendent's report, Mr. Bacon called the board member who was a fellow employee at the community college. He told her, "I don't think the superintendent's perception of equal opportunity is legally correct. Providing the prescribed state curriculum is a matter of adequacy and not equity."

The board member informed Mr. Bacon that the superintendent's response was approved by the board's attorney and subsequently endorsed by the board. She also pointed out that a first step was being taken to ensure that discretionary funds at Clark would be used for computers or software. She then urged Mr. Bacon to meet privately with Superintendent Packard to discuss other possible changes that could diminish his concerns. He said he would follow her advice.

Two days later as suggested, Mr. Bacon met with Dr. Packard, but instead of suggesting ways to modify the decentralization program, he argued that the superintendent's perception of reasonably equal educational opportunities was invalid.

Dr. Packard responded by telling Mr. Bacon, "Differences among our schools are not great. For example, both Milltown and Clark have the same number of computers. There are many ways to define educational opportunities and different perspectives on equality. Computers are not the only instructional tool that matter. I believe schools are most effective when they respond to the real needs of their clients."

The conversation lasted about an hour and at the end, Mr. Bacon remained convinced that the superintendent's decentralization program had exacerbated inequities among the elementary schools. By mid-May, six Clark families joined Mr. Bacon's protest. Collectively, they retained an attorney and informed the school board that they intended to file a lawsuit unless the current approach to allocating funds to elementary schools was rescinded.

The board members did not take the threat lightly and they held another executive session to discuss the matter. The board's attorney was asked to comment about the merits of the lawsuit.

"As I told you previously, Dr. Packard's response to Mr. Bacon's concerns is reasonable. I cannot predict the outcome of a lawsuit, especially prior to reading the legal issues on which it is filed. Litigation is expensive, time consuming, and there is never a guaranteed outcome. At the same time, however, the families pressing this matter will incur legal costs—and they could be substantial. They have retained a competent attorney, and his fees tend to be above average."

The board members were hoping for more specific direction from their attorney. At least three of them appeared to be changing their position on supporting the decentralization plan. They urged Dr. Packard to eliminate the discretionary funding portion of the plan, indicating that Mr. Bacon might drop the matter if this were done.

Before adjourning the meeting, the board president again asked Dr. Packard if he had changed his position on decentralization. The superintendent responded, "In light of concerns now being expressed, I would like to think about this matter and confer with staff members. Let's meet again in one week and I'll give you my recommendation at that time."

Problem Framing

1. Assume you are Superintendent Packard. First determine the main issue (problem) in this case. Then describe the current state and the desired state of this issue. (The section on problem framing in the Introduction section of this book defines the problem framing process.)

2. Based on evidence provided in the case, describe the difficulty associated with eliminating the gap between the present state and desired state.

Questions and Suggested Activities

1. What are the advantages and disadvantages of Dr. Packard's deciding not to eliminate the discretionary funding portion of the decentralization program?
2. Discuss the guiding values of adequacy, equity, and liberty. How does each relate to decentralization of authority?
3. In small groups, identify the intended purposes, strengths, and weaknesses associated with decentralizing authority.
4. Evaluate the manner in which Superintendent Packard introduced and then pursued decentralization.
5. Why have efforts to improve schools at the local level increased interest in concepts such as decentralization and site-based management?
6. Based on what you read, do you think the administrative staff was prepared adequately to implement the changes required by the superintendent's decentralization plan? Why or why not?

7. Do you agree with the superintendent's contention that making associations between average student test scores and discretionary spending is premature? Provide a rationale for your answer.
8. Ideally, what should the superintendent have done to build political support in the community for decentralization?
9. Do you believe that Mrs. Simpson, principal at Clark Elementary School, is responsible for the manner in which the council at that school has operated? Explain your answer.
10. What constitutes reasonably equal educational opportunities?
11. If the discretionary spending portion of the decentralization plan is eliminated, would the remainder of the plan suffer? Why or why not?

Suggested Readings

Björk, L., & Blase, J. (2009). The micropolitics of school district decentralization. *Educational Assessment, Evaluation & Accountability, 21*(3), 195–208.

Brick, B. H. (1993). Changing concepts of equal educational opportunity: A comparison of the views of Thomas Jefferson, Horace Mann, and John Dewey. *Thresholds in Education, 19*(1–2), 2–8.

Candoli, I. C. (1995). *School-based management in education: How to make it work in your school.* Lancaster, PA: Technomic (see Chapter 3).

Dempster, N. (2000). Guilty or not: The impact and effects of site-based management on schools. *Journal of Educational Administration, 38*(1), 47–63.

Florestal, K., & Cooper, R. (1997). *Decentralization of education: Legal issues.* (ERIC Document Reproduction Service No. ED 412 616)

Henkin, A. B., Cistone, P. J., & Dee, J. R. (2000). Conflict management strategies of principals in site-based managed schools. *Journal of Educational Administration, 38*(2), 142–158.

Holloway, J. H. (2000). The promise and pitfalls of site-based management. *Educational Leadership, 57*(7), 81–82.

Hughes, L. W. (1993). School-based management, decentralization, and citizen control—A perspective. *Journal of School Leadership, 3*(1), 40–44.

Kowalski, T. J. (2003). *Contemporary school administration: An introduction* (2nd ed.). Boston: Allyn and Bacon (see Chapter 8).

Kowalski, T. J., Petersen, G. J., & Fusarelli, L. D. (2007). *Effective communication for school administrators: An imperative in an information age.* Lanham, MD: Rowman and Littlefield Education (see Chapter 11).

Leithwood, K., Jantzi, D., & Steinbach, R. (1998). *Do school councils matter?* (ERIC Document Reproduction Service No. ED 424 644)

Leonard, L. J. (1998). Site based management and organizational learning: Conceptualizing their combined potential for meaningful reform. *Planning and Changing, 29*(1), 24–46.

Lifton, F. B. (1992). The legal tangle of shared governance. *School Administrator, 49*(1), 16–19.

Mitchell, J. K., & Poston, W. K. (1992). The equity audit in school reform: Three case studies of educational disparity and incongruity. *International Journal of Educational Reform, 1*(3), 242–247.

Myers, J. A. (1997). Schools make the decisions: The impact of school-based management. *School Business Affairs, 63*(10), 3–9.

Nir, A. E., & Miran, M. (2006). The equity consequences of school-based management. *International Journal of Educational Management, 20*(2), 116–126.

Ortiz, F. I., & Ogawa, R. T. (2000). Site-based decision-making leadership in American public schools. *Journal of Educational Administration, 38*(5), 486–500.

Peternick, L., & Sherman, J. (1998). School-based budgeting in Fort Worth, Texas. *Journal of Education Finance, 23*(4), 532–556.

Polansky, H. B. (1998). Equity and SBM: It can be done. *School Business Affairs, 64*(4), 36–37.

Reyes, A. H. (1994). *The legal implication of school-based budgeting.* (ERIC Document Reproduction Service No. ED 379 753)

Sorenson, L. D., & Evans, R. D. (2001). Superintendent use of site-based councils: Role ambiguity and accountability. *Planning & Changing, 32*(3/4), 184–198.

Walberg, H. J., & Niemiec, R. P. (1994). Is Chicago school reform working? *Phi Delta Kappan, 75,* 713–715.

Wilson, S. M., Iverson, R., & Chrastil, J. (2001). School reform that integrates public education and democratic principles. *Equity and Excellence in Education, 34*(1), 64–70.

References

Bauman, P. C. (1996). *Governing education: Public sector reform or privatization.* Boston: Allyn and Bacon.

Fullan, M. (2001). *Leading in a culture of change.* San Francisco: Jossey-Bass.

Hawley, W. D. (1988). Missing pieces of the educational reform agenda: Or, why the first and second waves may miss the boat. *Educational Administration Quarterly, 24*(4), 416–437.

King, R. A., Swanson, A. D., & Sweetland, S. R. (2003). *School finance: Achieving high standards with equity and efficiency* (3rd ed.). Boston: Allyn and Bacon.

Kirst, M. W. (1988). Recent state education reform in the United States: Looking backward and forward. *Educational Administration Quarterly, 24*(3), 319–328.

Kowalski, T. J. (2003). *Contemporary school administration: An introduction* (2nd ed.). Boston: Allyn and Bacon.

Kowalski, T. J. (2006). *The school superintendent: Theory, practice, and cases* (2nd ed.). Thousand Oaks, CA: Sage.

Kowalski, T. J., McCord, R., Petersen, G. J., Young, I. P., & Ellerson, N. (2011). *The state of the superintendency, 2010.* Lanham, MD: Rowman and Littlefield Education.

Kowalski, T. J., Petersen, G. J., & Fusarelli, L. D. (2007). *Effective communication for school administrators: An imperative in an information age.* Lanham, MD: Rowman and Littlefield Education.

Nir, A. E., & Miran, M. (2006). The equity consequences of school-based management. *International Journal of Educational Management, 20*(2), 116–126.

Spring, J. (2001). *American education* (10th ed.). New York: McGraw-Hill.

Tyack, D. (1990). Restructuring in historical perspective: Tinkering towards utopia. *Teachers College Record, 92*(2), 170–191.

Walberg, H. J., & Niemiec, R. P. (1994). Is Chicago school reform working? *Phi Delta Kappan, 75,* 713–715.

24 | THE MAVERICK SCHOOL BOARD MEMBER

BACKGROUND INFORMATION

Relationships between administrators and stakeholders are an element of institutional climate—that is, they influence the way people feel about districts and schools (Hanson, 2003). For example, the associations often determine if and how school officials respond to political pressures or threats. Because power is typically distributed broadly among internal and external pressure groups embracing different values, every important policy or administrative decision is likely to be criticized or even overtly opposed by one or more factions (Wirt & Kirst, 2009).

Relationships among administrators in a district and between administrators and the school board are especially consequential. Harmony within and between these groups usually discourages counterproductive political behavior and strengthens the institution's ability to manage such behavior when it cannot be avoided (Carr, 2003). This is because positive relationships are an asset that helps administrators to weather political attacks, especially those stemming from philosophical dissonance and other forms of conflict inevitable in all organizations (Hanson, 2003).

When administrators have poor relationships, especially with each other and with school board members, they end up expending a great deal of their time and energy on interpersonal conflict (Vail, 2001). As a result, important responsibilities, such as instructional leadership, are neglected and employees and other stakeholders are more likely to believe that the district's leadership team is in disarray. Interpreting dissonance as a symptom of political vulnerability, pressure groups typically intensify their efforts to influence policy decisions through a show of force (Kowalski, Petersen, & Fusarelli, 2007).

Given the political nature of public education, principals and other administrators are affected by the rapport their superintendent has with the school board. This association, however, is usually complex and dynamic; a superintendent-board relationship is actually a composite of multiple relationships between the superintendent and individual board members. Moreover, school boards are more likely to be factional rather than pluralistic (Shibles, Rallis, & Deck, 2001), and factionalism fosters political behavior. As an example, superintendents working with politically-divided school boards almost always are pressured to align with a faction (Kowalski, 2006), making it difficult for them to establish credibility and trust with all board members (Blumberg, 1985).

This case is about a school board member angered by a high school football coach's decision concerning a star athlete—a decision perceived to be detrimental to the board member's grandson. Seeking revenge, the board member, acting alone and surreptitiously, takes his grievance to the state high school athletic association hoping that the organization will sanction the coach and high school. Although other board members disapprove of his behavior and view it as being unethical, they are unwilling to chastise him. Instead, they urge the superintendent to issue an informal reprimand on their behalf. In summary, the case study raises questions about the relationship between a superintendent and school board members.

Key Areas for Reflection

1. Superintendent and school board member relationships
2. School board member ethical behavior
3. Conflict resolution
4. Scope of superintendent's legitimate authority
5. Superintendent's responsibility to adjudicate intrusions into administration

---

THE CASE

The School District and The School Board

The Richmond County School District, covering 420 square miles of predominantly rural land and including two high schools, five middle schools, and 11 elementary schools, enrolls approximately 8,000 students. The seven school board members are elected to office, each from a designated geographic area in the county. By occupation, the board members include an accountant, an attorney, a farmer, a nurse, a pharmacist, a real estate broker, and a retired business executive. Elmer Hobson, the farmer, is the longest-serving board member, having been in office for 11 years.

In the last 2 years, the superintendent has made about 75 major recommendations to the school board, many of them policy-related. Although 74 were approved by the school board, Mr. Hobson voted against 41; in 39 instances, he cast the only negative vote. Representing two rural townships, he has been fiercely independent and outspoken, yet he describes his personal relationships with other board members and the superintendent as being "congenial."

The Superintendent

Matthew Karman replaced Elton Simcox as superintendent 3 years ago. His predecessor had served for 5 years but support among board members was never unanimous. The school board was divided into two factions—one with four members supporting Superintendent Simcox and one with three members committed to dismissing him. During his fourth year in office, Simcox lost two of his supporters as a result of a school board election. Their replacements aligned with the faction not supporting the superintendent; shortly after they took office, the board voted five to two to dismiss Superintendent Simcox.

Since Superintendent Karman's arrival, another board member who previously supported Simcox left office (he chose not to seek re-election). In the wake of his departure, Mr. Hobson became a maverick without board-member allies. Faced with this reality, he became more congenial but no less compromising—and, he continuously reminded Superintendent Karman that he still felt that Superintendent Simcox should have remained superintendent.

Knowing the history of the relationships between his predecessor and the school board, Superintendent Karman purposefully sought to maintain good relationships will all seven board members. He especially tried to reach out to Mr. Hobson, occasionally inviting him to lunch and visiting him at his farm. Based on the superintendent's last performance evaluation, one could conclude that he succeeded; all seven board members rated their relationship with the superintendent as "excellent."

After receiving his second annual performance evaluation, the board voted unanimously to renew Karman's employment contract for another 3 years. Surprising many observers, Hobson, who had voted against employing Karman initially, voted in favor of the motion to renew the superintendent's contract. Responding to a reporter's question regarding his apparent change of mind, Hobson commented, "He's not been as bad as I thought he would be. But I'm keeping an eye on him".

Trouble Emerges

Superintendent Karman was driving down a lonely country road as the winds swirled across barren cornfields partially covered by snow. He was delivering school board packets for an upcoming meeting. Although it was only mid-November, the chilling temperatures made it feel more like January. The fields were dotted with corn stalks cut about 2 inches above the ground; they looked like wooden spikes someone had arranged to discourage trespassers.

When Karman pulled into the driveway beside a large three-story house, a German shepherd barking alongside his car greeted him. The noise summoned John Mosure from the house. John, a retired vice president of a marketing research firm, had lived in Richmond County until the time that he graduated from high school. Having returned 4 years ago, he purchased a 12-acre property on which he and his wife pursued their hobby, gardening. In Superintendent Karman's mind, John was an ideal school board member. After being elected to the board 2 years earlier, he quickly won the respect of the other board members and was elected president after having been on the board for just 1 year.

The superintendent and board president worked well together and most everyone knew that they had become friends. They and their wives were often seen together publicly.

As the two men sat at the kitchen table, Superintendent Karmen handed the board packet to Mr. Mosure and then said, "John, I hope you've got some time to talk to me today. I want to discuss a potentially messy issue, and it may take a while to go through the details."

John told him to proceed.

"Two days ago, Bob Daily [principal of North Richmond County High School] received a telephone call from Joe Sutton, the associate commissioner of the state high school athletic association. Joe also happens to be Bob's friend; the two were principals in the same school district about 15 years ago. Joe asked Bob if he knew Elmer Hobson."

There was a moment of silence and then John said, "Oh, no!"

John and other board members rarely agreed with Elmer, and they considered him to be a ticking time bomb. When John was first elected to the school board, Elmer attempted to forge a political alliance with him since both represented rural townships. The two men quickly discovered that their philosophies and priorities were dissimilar as exhibited by the opposing votes they cast on many major issues.

The superintendent continued with his story. "Bob acknowledges that he knows Elmer and informs Joe Sutton that Elmer is a school board member. Joe then tells Bob that Elmer is sitting in his outer office waiting to see him. Hobson appeared at the association's offices without an appointment and told the secretary that he wanted to talk to someone in authority. When asked why he wanted to meet with an official, he told the secretary that he was filing a complaint against Coach Yates [the head football coach at North Richmond County High School]."

"A complaint about what?" John asked.

"Joe Sutton didn't know at the time he called Bob because he had not yet talked to Elmer. After discovering that Elmer was a school board member, Joe told Bob he felt obliged to at least listen to what he had to say. So he met with Elmer and called Bob again an hour later. Elmer alleges that Coach Yates violated state high school athletic association rules by allowing his team's starting quarterback to remain enrolled at the school even though his parents and siblings have moved to another state. This student is Jeb Boswell, and he is now living with the Yates family. Elmer demanded that the athletic association declare Boswell ineligible, and sanction Coach Yates and Principal Daily."

"Are Elmer's accusations true?" John asked.

"The Boswell family moved out of the school district last June. However, Jeb's parents agreed to let him live with Coach Yates until he graduated from North Richmond High and they are paying Coach Yates $200 a month for room and board. The parents believe this arrangement is in their son's best interest since it is likely he will receive an athletic scholarship to play college football. Therefore, it is true that Jeb has been living with the Yates family since last June."

"Is such an arrangement permissible by the athletic association rules? Is it in compliance with our district's policies?"

"Coach Yates had asked the athletic director at North Richmond to get a ruling from officials at the athletic association before agreeing to this arrangement. The athletic director has a letter from the state commissioner stating that the arrangement was acceptable, provided it was approved by the student's family and by the school principal. Principal Dailey and the parents assured Coach Yates in writing that they had no objections. As to school district policy, I could find nothing that addresses this issue. I don't believe there is precedent."

"So from the association's perspective, Elmer's complaint is invalid?" John asked.

"Yes, but there is more. We are a few weeks away from the state football tournament. North Richmond has a 7 and 1 record and is one of the favorites to win the championship in their division. Jeb Boswell is the quarterback and star of the team. Any guess who is the backup quarterback?"

John said he had no idea. "You have to remember, Matt, I don't live in the North Richmond area. I'm a South Richmond High booster [the other high school in the district]."

"The second-string quarterback is another senior, Ron Hobson, Elmer Hobson's grandson. Get the picture? Elmer has always felt that his grandson had not been given a fair chance to be the team's starting quarterback. Now that the team is having a successful season, Elmer may do almost anything to have his grandson assume the starting role in the state tournament. As a sidebar, Bob Dailey told me the grandson is a good student and probably is unaware of his grandfather's shenanigans."

John then commented, "I just remembered something. Last summer when we were approving contracts for driver education teachers, Elmer opposed your recommendation to extend a contract to Coach Yates. Elmer claimed that he had received complaints about Coach Yates being a poor instructor. Do you think that matter was connected to all of this?"

"Who knows," the superintendent answered. "With Elmer, everything is potentially connected. He votes against a lot of things. Going to the athletic association without informing the board or the administration, however, is an ethical matter. As a board member, he should have informed either you or me that he would be filing a complaint to the state athletic association. Had he done so, we would have had an opportunity to explain to him why his accusation is invalid. Besides, board members should not be dealing directly with the athletic association; that is an administrative responsibility."

"What did Joe Sutton from the athletic association do with Elmer's complaint?"

"Elmer demanded to know what would be done to adjudicate the matter. Joe Sutton explained that there was no violation, and he then showed him a copy of the letter the commissioner had written to North Richmond's athletic director last May. Elmer then stormed out of the office indicating that keeping this letter from the school board was additional evidence of a conspiracy involving several administrators and coaches."

"Matt, I have a suggestion. Let's forget about this. Elmer is never going to behave as we would like him to behave and I can assure you, we aren't going to change his behavior. On the bright side, few people take him seriously. Sure they are amused by his outrageous statements and actions, but basically, he's a harmless pain in the neck. I believe voters keep electing him because he is amusing."

The superintendent had a different opinion. "At the very least, we need to inform the other board members, and I believe that the board should reprimand him for what he did. That can be done privately and tactfully, but at least there will be a record indicating that his behavior was unacceptable."

John replied, "I don't know. A reprimand is likely to make him act out even more. He's a pretty stubborn person. He loves getting his name in the paper and relishes conflict. Matt, how about if you talk to him privately? You're experienced in dealing with these matters and you have a pretty good relationship with him. Maybe the best way to handle this is to tell him he made a mistake and to advise him that in the future, he should talk to you before he does this sort of thing. The other board members will support this course of action, I'm sure. In fact, I'll call them today if you wish. That way, you can tell Elmer that you are speaking for all of us."

Problem Framing

1. Assume you are the superintendent. First determine the main issue (problem) in this case. Then describe the current state and the desired state of this issue. (The section on problem framing in the Introduction section of this book defines the problem framing process.)

2. Based on evidence provided in the case, describe the difficulty associated with eliminating the gap between the present state and desired state.

Questions and Suggested Activities

1. Do you agree that Elmer Hobson's behavior was unethical? Why or why not?
2. John Mosure, the board president, first suggested that nothing should be done. What are the advantages and disadvantages of this course of action?
3. Mr. Mosure subsequently suggests that the superintendent talk to Hobson on behalf of the other board members. What are the advantages and disadvantages of this course of action?
4. Who is responsible for ensuring that board members act ethically?
5. In response to a question from the board president, Superintendent Karman indicated that there was no school district policy or precedent addressing the situa-

tion in question. Does the absence of district policy affect the decision made by the principal, athletic director, and coach? Why or why not?
6. Obtain a copy of the code of ethics for your state's association of school boards. Determine whether the code addresses behavior pertinent to this case.
7. Do school board members have authority to act independently? What is the basis of your answer?
8. Do you agree with the superintendent that it is important to reprimand Hobson? Why or why not?
9. Does a superintendent have authority to regulate the behavior of school board members? What evidence do you have to support your answer?

Suggested Readings

Adamson, M. T. (2009). The rogue member in the boardroom. *School Administrator, 66*(8), 6.

Bolman, L., & Deal, T. (1992). Images of leadership. *American School Board Journal, 179*(4), 36–39.

Bryant, M., & Grady, M. (1990). Where boards cross the line. *American School Board Journal, 177*(10), 20–21.

Caruso, N. D. (2004). Managing board members with personal agendas. *School Administrator, 61*(10), 6.

Castallo, R. (1992). Clear signals. *American School Board Journal, 179*(2), 32–34.

Dawson, L. J., & Quinn, R. (2004). Why board culture matters. *American School Board Journal, 191*(9), 28–31.

Duffy, F. M. (2002). Courage, passion, and vision: Leading systemic school improvement. *International Journal of Educational Reform, 11*(1), 63–76.

Hamilton, D. (1987). Healing power: How your board can overcome the heartbreak of disharmony. *American School Board Journal, 174*(9), 36–37.

Harrison, P. (2002). Can this marriage be saved? *American School Board Journal, 189*(6), 36–37.

Hayden, J. (1987). Superintendent-board conflict: Working it out. *Education Digest, 52*(8), 11–13.

Herman, J. (1991). Coping with conflict. *American School Board Journal, 178*(8), 39–41.

Irvine, J. (1998). Welcome to the board. *American School Board Journal, 185*(7), 38–40.

Kowalski, T. J. (2006). *The school superintendent: Theory, practice, and cases* (2nd ed.). Thousand Oaks, CA: Sage (see Chapters 5 and 6).

Lister, B. (2006). A pocket guide to board service. *American School Board Journal, 193*(5), 48–49.

Marlowe, J. (1997). Good board, bad board. *American School Board Journal, 184*(6), 22–24.

Meredith, T. C. (2009). Developing rules of engagement for boards. *Trusteeship, 17*(4), 6.

Myer, R. (1983). How to handle a board member who wants to play his own game. *American School Board Journal, 170*(11), 27–29.

Natale, J. (1990). School board ethics: On thin ice? *American School Board Journal, 177*(10), 16–19.

Ondrovich, P. (1997). Hold them, fold them, or walk away: Twelve cardinal rules for dealing with school board conflict. *School Administrator, 5*(2), 12–15.

Petersen, G., & Williams, B. M. (2005). The board president and superintendent: An examination of influence through the eyes of the decision makers. In G. Petersen & L. Fusarelli (Eds.), *The politics of leadership: Superintendents and school boards in changing times* (pp. 21–36). Greenwich, CT: Information Age Publishing.

Riede, P. (2004). Board ethics: In states and communities, the ongoing struggle to codify appropriate behavior of school board members. *School Administrator, 61*(8), 20.

Rickabaugh, J. R., & Kremer, M. L. (1997). Six habits to make you a hit with your school board. *The School Administrator, 54*(6), 30–32.

Stover, D. (2009). Out of control. *American School Board Journal, 196*(3), 14–18.

Trainor, C. K. (2008). Conflicted interests. *The American School Board Journal, 195*(12), 46–47.

References

Blumberg, A. (1985). *The school superintendent: Living with conflict.* New York: Teachers College Press.

Carr, N. (2003). Leadership: The toughest job in America. *Education Vital Signs: A Supplement to the American School Board Journal, 14*, 15, 18–20.

Hanson, E. M. (2003). *Educational administration and organizational behavior* (5th ed.). Boston: Allyn and Bacon.

Kowalski, T. J. (2006). *The school superintendent: Theory, practice, and cases* (2nd ed.). Thousand Oaks, CA: Sage.

Kowalski, T. J., Petersen, G. J., & Fusarelli, L. D. (2007). *Effective communication for school administrators: An imperative in an information age.* Lanham, MD: Rowman and Littlefield Education.

Shibles, M. R., Rallis, R. F., & Deck, L. L. (2001). A new political balance between superintendent and board: Clarifying purpose and generating knowledge. In C. C. Brunner & L. G. Björk (Eds.), *The new superintendency* (pp. 169–181). New York: JAI.

Vail, K. (2001). Teamwork at the top. *American School Board Journal, 188*(11), 23–25.

Wirt, F. M., & Kirst, M. W. (2009). The political dynamics of American education (4th ed.). Berkeley, CA: McCutchan.